THE
INDUSTRIAL PUNJAB

THE INDUSTRIAL PUNJAB:

A Survey of Facts, Conditions and Possibilities

BY

A. LATIFI

Of

of the Indian Civil Service.

PUBLISHED FOR THE PUNJAB GOVERNMENT

ISBN: 978-93-5128-453-6(HB)

First Published in 1911
Indian Reprint in 2017

Published by

Kalpaz Publications
C-30, Satyawati Nagar,
Delhi – 110052
E-mail: kalpaz@hotmail.com
Website: kalpazpublications.com
Ph.: +91-9212142040

AGENTS FOR THE SALE OF PUNJAB GOVERNMENT PUBLICATIONS.

IN LONDON

E. A. ARNOLD, 41 and 43, Maddox Street, Bond Street, W.

CONSTABLE AND CO., 10, Orange Street, Leicester Square, W.C.

GRINDLAY AND CO., 54, Parliament Street, S.W.

HENRY S. KING AND CO., 65, Cornhill, E.C.

P. S. KING AND SON, 2 and 4, Great Smith Street, Westminster, S.W.

KEGAN PAUL, TRENCH, TRÜBNER AND CO., 43, Gerrard Street, Soho, W.

B. QUARITCH, 11, Grafton Street, New Bond Street, W.

T. FISHER UNWIN, 1, Adelphi Terrace, W.C.

W. THACKER AND CO., 2, Creed Lane, London, E.C.

LUZAC AND CO., 46, Great Russell Street, London, W.C.

ON THE CONTINENT.

FRIEDLANDER AND SOHN, 11, Carlstrasse, Berlin.

OTTO HARRASSOWITZ, Leipzig.

CARL W. HIERSEMANN, Leipzig.

ERNEST LEROUX, 28, Rue Bonaparte, Paris.

MARTINUS NIJHOFF, The Hague.

IN INDIA.

THACKER, SPINK AND CO., Calcutta and Simla.

NEWMAN AND CO., Calcutta.

R. CAMBRAY AND CO., Calcutta.

THACKER AND CO., Bombay.

HIGGINBOTHAM AND CO., Madras.

V. KALYANARAM IYER AND CO., 189, Esplanade Row, Madras.

G A. NATESAN AND CO., Madras.

SUPERINTENDENT, American Baptist Mission Press, Rangoon.

A. CHAND AND CO., Imperial Book Depôt Office, Delhi.

GULAB SINGH AND SONS, Mufid-i-'Am Press, Lahore.

MANAGER, Punjab Law Book Depôt, Anàrkali Bazaar, Lahore.

S. MUMTAZ ALI AND SON, Rafah-i-'Am Press, Lahore [for Vernacular Publications, only].

MANAGER, The Aryan Printing, Publishing and General Trading Co., Limited, Lahore.

N. B. MATHUR, Superintendent and Proprietor, Nazáir Kánún Hind Press, Allahabad.

D. B. TARAPOREVALA, SONS AND CO., Bombay.

TABLE OF CONTENTS.

INTRODUCTION-PREFATORY.

The advantages of an industrial survey have generally been recognised, but they are apt to be exaggerated on the one hand, and undervalued on the other. By some, the inquiry is expected to mark an epoch, if not to usher in a millennium, while others, with a less optimistic bent of mind, consider it to be of necessity superficial, and useless for practical purposes unless supplemented by a complete economic survey.

Neither attitude is altogether correct. A review of the present state of Punjab manufactures can effect no miracle; it cannot even obviate the need for the detailed investigation which should be made by technical experts before any new enterprise is set on foot. At the same time its result need not be a mere anthology of barren platitudes, strung together for the delectation of the carpet knights of industry. A survey, if properly made, may bring to light much useful information that has so far lain hidden in Government offices, and may supplement such information with the facts and the figures which can often be collected satisfactorily only through the agency of public servants. It may go a little further, and set in correct perspective the actual and possible industries of the Province in accordance with their local importance.

The work now presented to the reader does not travel beyond the British Punjab, and it deals only with its manufacturing industries, that is to say, with those industries in which the raw material is appreciably altered by means of human skill or labour. Mineral, agricultural and forest products, with the exception of such as constitute the basis of a manufacture, lie, therefore, outside its scope. On the other hand, though most of the industries included in its range are already in existence, or are capable of being started at once, it treats of several that are mere possibilities, destined to await a higher standard of general and technical education, and a greater familiarity with methods of industrial combination than yet exist in the Punjab.

Even with these limitations, the task before the writer is of wide extent ; and there would seem to be no end to the multitude or complexity of the questions he is called upon to answer. He will congratulate himself if these pages do nothing more than help to form a sound public opinion on the resources and possibilities of this Province, and the extent to which they could be developed by the people with the support of the Government.

The procedure followed in making the survey was as follows : The writer studied, in the first place, all the available literature, published or otherwise, on the arts and crafts of the Province, and then visited the principal centres of trade and industry in order to inquire personally into the state of the markets, and the local resources in labour, capital, communications and raw products. He interviewed the workers in every industry, and heard and considered all they had to say about their difficulties and requirements. He also put himself in touch everywhere with officials and others likely to supply him with reliable information on industrial matters. At the same time he discussed with selected capitalists (not necessarily the richest or best known), the kind of information which they would like to see collected on various heads.

Exhaustive interrogatories on the points that remained for further inquiry were then sent to correspondents all over the Province, and, pending the receipt of their replies, the writer toured through some of the important seats of commerce and manufacture in other parts of India. He had the good fortune to meet not a few industrial and business experts, and he visited many factories and trading establishments of interest to an inquirer from the Punjab. He takes this opportunity of acknowledging the courtesy with which he was everywhere received.

The second stage of his labours was reached when he commenced the draft of this work. Copies of each chapter as first written were sent for criticism both to scientists and practical experts, and on receipt of their observations further information was requisitioned from the local reporters. The chapter in question was then revised or re-written, the whole process being repeated several times in some cases.

It is hardly necessary to mention that the statements in this work are to be taken on the sole responsibility of the writer.

He must place on record his deep sense of obligation to the many distinguished gentlemen who helped him at every turn. Without their co-operation, indeed, he would have failed to obtain results of any value. In the first place he thanks Mr. W. S. Hamilton, I.C.S.,

Director of Industries, under whose departmental control the survey was made, for constant support and sympathetic advice and criticism, which, in a work of this kind, were invaluable. Professor Wyndham R. Dunstan, LL.D., F.R.S., Director of the Imperial Institute, London, looked through several chapters of the book, and sent much original information on drugs and animal products, as well as the valuable note on loofahs (Appendix II.). The Hon'ble Mr A. Chatterton, Director of Industries, Madras, contributed useful information on cotton, wool, silk, tanning and glass. Sardar Puran Singh, Imperial Forest Chemist, was good enough to write exhaustive notes for the writer's use on essential oils, turpentine, wood distillation, etc. The Hon'ble Mr. B. Robertson, I.C.S., C.S.I., C.I.E., lately Member, and Mr. W. Maxwell, I.C S., lately Secretary, Department of Commerce and Industry, enabled him to consult some confidential papers of the Government of India, which proved of great use. H. H. the Maharaja of Gwalior afforded him every facility for inspecting the pioneer factories set up by him in his model state. Much assistance was received in various directions from Mr. W. C. Renouf, I.C.S., Director of Agriculture, as well as from the staff of his Department ; from Mr. F. Noel-Paton, Director-General of Commercial Intelligence, Mr. C. W. E. Cotton, I.C.S., Offg. Director of Industries, Madras, Mr. I. H. Burkill, Reporter on Economic Products, Professor F. W. Sedgwick, Thomason College, Roorkee, the Hon'ble Rao Bahadur N. R. N. Madholkar, Akola (Berar), Dr. Rash Bihari Ghosh, C.I.E., Calcutta, the Hon'ble Mr. Justice Sankaran Nair, Madras, Mr. James S. Cotton, lately Editor, *Imperial Gazetteer of India*, and Mr. E. Burdon, I.C.S. Useful items of information were supplied by Messrs. A. Shakespear, Cawnpore, D. W. Aikman, Sanitary Engineer, Punjab, D. Souter Robertson, Thomason College, Roorkee, A. J. Gibson, I.F.S., M. L. Darling, I.C.S., and W. Mayes, I.F.S., by the Secretaries of the Chambers of Commerce, Karachi and Bombay, and the Collectors of Customs of those ports and of Calcutta. Messrs. Bergmann, Hoffmann & Co., of Bombay, and Messrs. Martin & Co., of Calcutta, supplied a number of estimates of plants and machinery.

Coming now to particular subjects, the writer must tender his cordial thanks to the Hon'ble Mr. J. McC. Douie, I.C.S., C.S.I., Col. C. J. Bamber, I.M.S., Mr. D. Hooper, Indian Museum, Calcutta, Professor C. C. Caleb, Lahore Medical College, and Mr. A. C. Hartless, Superintendent, Botanical Gardens, Saharanpur (Botanical subjects) ; the Hon'ble Mr. Fazalbhoy C. Ibrahim, President, Bombay Millowners' Association, Seth Narotamdas Morarji Goculdas, Millowner, Bombay; Khan Bahadur Bezonjee D. Mehta, Manager, Empress Mills, Nagpur, and Mr. G. K. Tipnis, Manager, Hanooman Mahadeo Mills, Delhi (Cotton Industries) ; the Manager, New Egerton Woollen Mills, Dhariwal, and Mr. A. H. Silver, Manager, Cawnpore Woollen Mills (Wool) ; Mr. G. C. Sen, M.A., F.C.S., Dyeing Expert, Bengal Technical Institute, Calcutta, and Dr. Suter, Consulting Chemist to the Badische Anilin-und Soda-Fabrik agency, Bombay, both of whom contributed able and exhaustive notes (Dyeing and Calico Printing) ; Mr. A. Fraustadt, Skin Merchant, Amritsar, Sir Adamjee Peerbhoy, Proprietor, Sion Tannery, Bombay, and the Manager, N.-W. Tannery, Co. Ld.,

Cawnpore (Tanning and Leather-work) ; The Rev. Professors of Science, St. Xavier's College, Bombay, and Professor B. Mouat Jones, Government College, Lahore (Chemical Industries) ; Dr. Hoffman, Manager, Cotton-oil Mill, Akola (Oils) ; Mr. W. H. Harrison, Madras Agricultural Chemist, Coimbatore (Sugar, etc.); Mr. P. H. Swinchatt, Headmaster, Government Industrial School, Lucknow (Woodwork) ; Mr. R. Pearson, Imperial Forest Economist, and Mr. C. P. Fisher, Conservator of Forests, Punjab (Forest Products) ; Mr. T. H. D. LaTouche, Officiating Director of the Geological Survey of India, Dr. L. L. Fermor of the same Department, and the Bikaner State Department of Mineralogy (Mineralogical subjects) ; Mr. W. S. Hadaway, Principal, School of Arts, Madras (Enamelling on Metals, etc.) ; Mr. E. J. Hawkins, Manager, Indian Aluminium Co., Madras, and Sir Thomas Holland, F.R.S., Director of the Geological Survey of India (Aluminium) ; Mr. E. R. Fern, Pottery Expert, J. J. School of Arts, Bombay (Pottery) ; Professor B. M. Mukerji, Thomason College, Roorkee, and Lala Alakh Dhari, Secretary, Ambala Glass Works (Glass) ; Mr. D. Thomson, Mining Engineer, Dandot (Dandot Colliery).

Finally, the thanks of the writer are due to all the Deputy Commissioners and Settlement Officers in the Province, the Engineers of the Punjab Irrigation Department, and the Settlement Commissioner, Kashmir, for the information which they have courteously sent him from time to time.

Excellent reports on the industries of their respective districts were received from the following members of the Provincial Service : Khwaja Tasadduk

Husain, B.A., Delhi; Munshi Nasir-ud-din, Gurdaspur; Pir Kamar-ud-din, Ludhiana; and Sheikh Din Mohammad, M.A., Jullundur. Also from Lala Shankar Das, Tahsildar, Amritsar; K. B. Sheikh Ghulám Sádik, Hon. Magistrate, Amritsar; Sheikh Ghulam Yasin, Pleader, Jhang; Lala Niamat Rai, Inspector of Sanitation, Multan; Lala Kundan Lal, B.A., LL.B., Munsiff, Hoshiarpur; and Munshi Barkat Ali Khan, M.A.,LL.B., Munsiff, Hoshiarpur. A useful account of the industries of Lahore City was compiled by Partab Singh, Octroi Superintendent, Lahore.

GENERAL INTRODUCTION.

The Punjab lies between 27°39′ and 34°2′ N., and between 69°23′ and 79°2′ E., and, including the Feudatory States (36,532 sq. miles), covers 133,741 square miles, or about a fifth of the area of Japan. It is for the most part a vast alluvial plain, but is naturally divided into (1) The Himalayan region, (2) The submontane region from the Jumna to the Indus, (3) The Salt Range plateau, (4) The south-western plains, and (5) The western portion of the Indo-Gangetic Plain West.

Of these divisions the submontane, including the districts of Hoshiarpur, Jullundur, Gurdaspur and Sialkot, is the most fertile, and may also be considered to be the heart of the industrial Punjab. The Canal Colonies in the centre of the Province, however, are among the most flourishing agricultural communities in the Indian Empire. The Salt Range is barren in places, while the last two divisions become so towards the south, where they merge into the limitless wastes of Sind and Rajasthán.

The climate of the plains is subject to great extremes in both winter and summer. In January and February the temperature commonly falls below freezing point at night, while it seldom rises above 75° F. in the daytime: and nothing can surpass the bright sunshine and the keen invigorating air of the four cold weather months. In summer, on the other hand, the fierce dry heat, which is at its worst in the south-west, is only exceeded on the sun-baked plains of Sind. The thermometer then records from 115° to 121° F. in the shade by day, and seldom less than 79° by night.

There are two rainy seasons, the first between the end of December and the end of February, and the second from the latter part of June to the middle of September. The rainfall is heavy on the Himalayas and ranges between 30 and 40 inches in the sub-montane zone; but it decreases rapidly the further one travels away from the hills, until it sinks to a low and variable figure in the west and the south-west.

The population of the province amounts to 20 millions in 1911, besides the 4¼ millions in the Feudatory States. The average density in British territory is 205 persons per square mile, but the figure rises to 305 in the submontane, and to 294 in the Indo-Gangetic Plain, while it is as low as 124 in the south-west dry area. Of the several districts, the most thickly populated are Jullundur, with an average of 560 per square mile, Amritsar with 550, and Delhi with 510. The Mohammadans form the most numerous community, being 55 per cent. of the whole. They predominate in the west and in the submontane tract, while the Hindus are in the majority in the Indo-Gangetic plain and in the Himalayan hills. The Sikhs constitute about 10½ per cent. of the population.

Nowhere in India is the caste system looser than in the villages of the Punjab, and even in the towns, where its bonds are more rigid, Hindus of the higher castes will eat with each other. It is only within the

Delhi division that the strict Brahmanism of the Gangetic Valley comes into evidence. Occupations, however, still continue to be hereditary, even among the Mohammadans, and the action of the new economic forces has not yet materially disturbed a system evolved by the necessities of an immemorial past.

The typical Panjabi is tall, spare and muscular, attaining to a splendid physique in the villages of the Mánjhá and the Málwá.[1] He is an enterprising emigrant, and not only moves freely over the Indian Empire, but has penetrated to the four corners of the earth in search for higher wages. Hongkong and Aden are only the first stages of his peregrinations to the east and to the west. The Californian navvy already fears his competition, while Uganda and West Africa, Singapore and the Treaty Ports of China welcome him for police and other service.

No fewer than 56 per cent. of the total population of the Province are supported by agriculture. The artisans follow long behind with barely 20 per cent., while commerce and the professions afford a livelihood to only 2·8 and 2·2 per cent. respectively. A few facts relating to the dominant industry may therefore be given.

There are two harvests, the *rabi* or spring, sown in October or November and reaped in April or May, and the *kharif* or autumn sown from June to August, and reaped from early September to the end of December. The *kharif* harvest is closely followed by the *rabi* sowings, while to the *rabi* often succeeds an extra harvest, called *záid rabi*, chiefly of tobacco and

[1] The type degenerates, however, in the riverain tracts, while in the south-east it approaches to that of Hindustan.

the like, gathered in June. The total cultivated area is 44,612 square miles, of which 35 per cent. is irrigated by artificial means : 24 per cent. from canals, 10 per cent. from wells and 1 per cent. from tanks and other sources. To this will be added within the next decade the area protected by the vast irrigation scheme sanctioned in 1905, which will cost 1,019 lacs of rupees. At the present time, two tracts are exposed to drought, one to the south-east embracing a part of the Delhi division, and the other extending over the districts of Gujrat and Jhelum, with parts of Attock and Gurdaspur. So far, famines have been severe only in the former region, of which Hissar is the centre.

The unparalleled economic progress of England in the latter half of the eighteenth century was in no small measure due to the simultaneous development of agriculture and manufactures. In the Punjab the two are so intimately allied that permanent improvement in either is impossible unless they grow in close interdependence. Agriculture not only supplies the raw material to all the local industries (the mineral wealth of the Province is small), but also affords a subsidiary occupation to a great many artisans, who flourish with its prosperity and are ruined when the crops fail. Agriculture needs, therefore, to be improved here in the interest of manufacture, while industries should be started in the interest of agriculture.

Efficient means of communication always stimulate the production of commodities, and nature has been generous to the Punjab in providing ample facilities for the construction of railways. The Province is served by the North-Western Railway, which, with its feeders and strategic extensions, commands the whole of the Province, and links it up with Karachi, its natural port. Into Karachi is poured all its agricultural wealth, and through Karachi come the sugar and the piece-goods, the bullion, hardware and copper that are brought in exchange.

In addition to 3,750 miles of railway there are 2,000 miles of metalled and 20,000 of unmetalled roads, which connect town with town and village with village, and lead the produce of the country to the markets. There are, besides, the river Indus and the lower reaches of the Jhelum, the Chenab and the Sutlej, which are all navigable throughout the year. On the Indus a small and diminishing trade with Sind is still carried in rude country craft, but the other waterways are only utilised for the transport of timber. Only 387 miles of the immense canal system of the Punjab are navigable—the Western Jumna Canal from its head to Delhi, and the Sirhind Canal from its head to Rupar, and from Patiala to Ferozepur.

The rise of a nation in the industrial scale may often be measured by the growth of its large towns, where capital and labour come together. As many as 19 per cent., for example, of the people of the United States, and over 32 per cent. of the people of Great Britain and Ireland live in cities, that is to say, in places with more than 100,000 inhabitants. According to the census of 1911 there are only 3 such cities in the Punjab, Delhi (232,837), Lahore (228,687), and Amritsar (152,756), although there are 38 towns with a population of 10,000 to 100,000, amongst which may be mentioned Multan (99,243), Rawalpindi (86,483), Amballa (80,131), Jullundur (69,318), Sialkot (64,869), and Ferozpur (50,836), all of which include large military cantonments. Villages on the other hand number 33,421, of which 11,825 contain 500 persons or more.[1] Except in the hills and in the south-west tract these are compact groups of dwellings constituting self-sufficing organisms, which produce and consume, increase and decrease, flourish and decline independently of each other. Each one of them is provided with an almost complete establishment of trades and occupations, which, in return for a fixed share of the produce of the soil, supply almost all the simple necessities of the inhabitants.

Three of the four essentials of every industry, namely, labour, capital and facilities for the distribution of commodities, must now be considered. The fourth essential—supply of raw material—will be discussed to greater advantage in the body of the work.

Labour, both skilled and unskilled, is scarce and unsatisfactory in the Punjab. The percentage of literate males, according to the census of 1901, was only 6·8, and the number even of skilled artisans able to read and write must be exceedingly small. As for ordinary labour for industrial enterprises, the supply, never very abundant, has been diminished by the ravages of plague and malaria, the spread of cultivation, the growth of the Canal Colonies, and the ever-increasing demands of the Irrigation Department for their new works. The result is that few factories are able to work to their full strength. The social system of the people still further reduces the numbers available,

[1] There are, besides, 59 towns with a population of 5,000 to 10,000, which are usually little more than overgrown villages.

by compelling every wage-earner to support a host of idle but able-bodied relations, who would, if forced to earn their daily bread, add to the resources of the country as a whole. Moreover, not a small proportion of the drones of society is composed of sturdy mendicants, who fatten in half-naked sloth on the mistaken charity of those who work.

If labour is scarce and unsatisfactory, capital is still more hard to procure. The savings of the people, especially of the Mohammadans, who generally consider interest unlawful, are hoarded in the form of massive ornaments, while the cash of the Hindu capitalists is mostly employed in commerce or in usury. The few banks of Delhi, Lahore and Amritsar do not, as a rule, finance industries. Joint-stock enterprise is in its infancy, and has not made an auspicious beginning. The Land Alienation Act of 1901, however, by preventing the money-lending classes from acquiring an interest in land, has unlocked a large amount of capital, which might, by wise and cautious means, be made to flow into the channels of industry.

The idea of co-operative credit has taken firm root in the Punjab, the number of societies having risen from about 300 in 1901 to over 1,000 in 1911 in the twenty-four districts where they have been introduced; but though the movement is fraught with unlimited possibilities of good, it has, so far, touched only the fringe of the artisan classes. Almost all the existing societies are composed of agriculturists.[1]

---

[1] For an account of co-operative societies for the promotion of industries in the Punjab see the note by Mr. A. Langley, I.C.S., on pages 286-287 of the *Indian Trade Journal* of March 2nd, 1911.

It is necessary to explain at this stage that the difficulties as regards labour and capital completely dominate the larger or factory industries, which are as yet in an elementary stage. They affect to rather a less extent the cottage industries, to which category most of those treated of in this work belong, and which, therefore, the writer has studied with special care. The encouragement of cottage industries is not only an economic, but also a social and moral problem of the highest importance to this country. By affording the cultivator and his family a subsidiary occupation during his slack time, they will go far towards helping him over seasons of drought and famine. They will also prove a boon to the large number of *parda* women who now live in want or on the charity of relations.

Both the mill and the cottage depend equally, however, on the third condition indicated above, namely, a suitable organisation for distributing commodities among the people who consume them. An industrial enterprise will not necessarily thrive because it produces articles at a rate which yields a profit on paper. Its success may depend even more on the possibility of placing its manufactures upon the market. The state of this market, the means of distribution, the tastes and prejudices of the customers, must all be studied. The expert organisation required to do this hardly exists yet in the Punjab, for of the small proportion of the population returned as earning a livelihood by commerce, only an infinitesimal number have the business capacity and training necessary for striking out new lines. Except in a few trades even the commercial traveller is unknown. A firm who make metal-ware by machinery complained to the writer that it was impossible to sell their stock simply because they were unable to secure proper agents and travellers to push their goods.

Most people now admit that it is an important function of Government to develop the strength and skill of the people, to induce them to economise their energy by the aid of science and art, and, by the multiplication of industries, to afford them a livelihood from the greatest possible varieties of sources.[1] But there has always been great controversy as to the exact relations that ought to subsist between the State and the industrial interests of the country. The disputants have often argued with the conditions of different countries and different ages before their eyes, forgetting the homely saying that what is one man's food may be another's poison. Nobody denies, however, that where private enterprise is, for any reason, unable to develop a given industry, even a free-trading state may lawfully create a condition of things that will set private enterprise in motion. The statesmen of every country should, therefore, be in a position to adopt the golden mean between the dangers of paternalism on the one hand, and of *laissez-faire* on the other.

The methods by which Government could help particular industries will be suggested in the course of this work, but it will be convenient to collect here a few matters of more general importance under the three heads of labour, capital and distribution, mentioned above.

The most important remedy for the dearth of skilled labour is the spread of industrial education, which should be accompanied, however, by a rise in the

[1] See for example Mr. Valentine Chirol's *Indian Unrest*, p. 259.

standard of general education, and by the introduction of manual training into the curricula of the primary schools of the country. It is impossible for any set of laboratory educationists to draft a scheme that could be guaranteed to hold good for all parts of India. Valuable experimental work has already been done in Europe and America by men of the highest ability, but Indian social and economic conditions are so different that it would be most unwise to apply any of their conclusions here without further examination. Detailed and prolonged experiments will have to be carried out in each province of India under the supervision of the best talent and knowledge that Government and private bodies can command. Take, for example, the scheme under which scholars are sent every year to Europe to learn industries. Though highly successful in other countries, it has, so far as the writer knows, proved a failure here. The factories in Europe are most unwilling to teach possible rivals, and the utmost which even a diligent learner can acquire is a certain amount of theoretical knowledge which is useless by itself, and which could, besides, be taught to him at less expense in his own country. The money now wasted on these scholarships would be far better spent in setting up a well-equipped technical college on the model of those now established at Birmingham, Manchester and Leeds.[1]

The attraction of capital to the growing industries of the Province is a task which must necessarily be

---

1 This is the view taken by Mr. R. N Mukerjee, C.I.E., of Messrs. Martin and Co., Calcutta, in his presidential address to the Indian Industrial Conference at Allahabad in December, 1910 (see the *Report* of the Conference). The opinion of this eminent captain of industry is shared by every employer of skilled labour the writer has consulted.

eft to time and circumstances, but the advisability of more direct inducements in the shape of Government guarantees and subsidies has already been recognised in individual cases. A crying need of the Province, in the writer's opinion, is a drastic amendment of the law relating to joint-stock companies, which in its present shape, is only suitable for countries where the principle of self-government permeates the industrial as well as the political life. If more power is given to the Registrar of Companies to look into the affairs of these bodies, and if a system of voluntary audit by Government auditors[1] is introduced, everybody will be pleased except a few company-promoters. When a strong check is placed on the directors, the people will learn to confide in limited companies, and the hoarded wealth of the country will be forthcoming in abundance.[2]

The distribution of commodities is facilitated by measures such as the promotion of commercial education, the improvement of communications, the dissemination of commercial intelligence, etc., all of them problems too wide to be touched on here.

The question of freights, however, claims at least a passing notice. Few problems of industrial organisa-

---

[1] What is suggested is a system which will empower limited companies to subject themselves, *if they so choose*, to periodical audit by Government auditors. Such companies would be given the right to put the word 'Government audited' after their names. It may be mentioned that the accounts of Municipalities and other local bodies are audited by a very efficient staff of peripatetic Government auditors.

[2] The *Société en Commandite* of France, which stands half-way between the ordinary Partnership and the Joint-stock Company of Anglo-Indian law—with unlimited liability of the Directors and limited liability of the other shareholders—is eminently suited to the special conditions of this Province.

tion loom so large upon the inquirer as those relating to the responsibility of railways in this connection.[1] There is great misunderstanding as to rights and obligations on both sides. It is clear on the one hand, that railway companies cannot be treated entirely as private corporations as they are of the nature of large trusts or monopolies created by the help of the Government, and enjoying, by delegation, considerable powers that are ordinarily the function of the State alone. At the same time, they are primarily commercial undertakings, brought into being with the object of earning good dividends for their shareholders, and not with any philanthropic motives. Hence, though a certain amount of control should be exercised over freight-rates in the interest of local industries, it would be most unfair to compel the railways as such to give up their profits for the benefit of other commercial enterprises. Even where the reduction of the rates on a commodity like manure is likely to result ultimately in the general advantage of the Indian railways, it is not to be expected that an individual company, not expecting to be benefited by the prosperity of agriculture in other parts of the country, will give up its profits merely for the public good.

The writer has found this problem, which appears very easy of solution on the first view, so complicated and difficult at close quarters, that he has, so far as possible, avoided it. He ventures to suggest that a matter of such vast practical importance should be examined by a mixed commission of Government and

---

[1] On the subject generally see S. C. Ghose, *Indian Railways and Indian Trade* (Calcutta, 1911).

railway officials and business men. Such a commission might recommend that the Government should give the railways subsidies for carrying certain classes of commodities, such as manure and sulphuric acid, either free of charge or at reduced rates, as is done in some countries.[1]

Some of the chief methods by which labour could be improved, capital made more mobile, and the distribution of commodities facilitated, have been passed in review. But the adoption of any given line of action is not a simple matter, and it is most important to guard against the dangers which must inevitably follow on hasty or haphazard measures. It is necessary, therefore, to gather all the information available, to take the best advice money can procure, and to lay down a definite and comprehensive scheme of industrial progress. One mode of evolving a programme of this kind would be to hold annual conferences of all the high officials concerned with industries in India, on the lines of the conference of the registrars of co-operative societies.

Such a gathering would also enable provincial departments to derive benefit from each other's experimental work and would possibly prevent a certain amount of reduplication of labour, which, under present conditions, is inevitable. A corollary to this

[1] This does not involve any kind of protection. Since the bulk of the commodities imported into India is less than the bulk of those exported, shipping freights from most European countries to India are usually cheaper than those from India to Europe. Some articles, such as Belgian salt-cellars, are actually brought free of charge as ballast. This means that the imported article is subsidised as compared with the Indian article that has to pay freight from inland centres to the sea-ports.

plan would be the deputation of selected officials from the provinces for training in the Department of Commerce and Industry of the Government of India.

The circumstances of the lives of no two men are ever exactly alike, and yet there is much to learn from the experience of others. It is the same in the case of Governments. The Indian Department of Industry should, therefore, study, as the pioneer statesmen of modern Japan studied, the industrial history and actual conditions of other countries, analyse all the factors in their progress, and see where it is possible for this country to imitate them. The requisite information has never been collected from an Indian point of view. It is available neither in libraries nor in official records. To arrive at the exact data required, a commission, composed of persons fully equipped with a knowledge of local conditions, must be sent to the countries whose economic development bears some analogy to that of India.

There are two in particular which could furnish valuable object-lessons.

The first is the little state of Württemberg in the German Empire, where the initiative of the Government, supported by the hearty co-operation of the people, sufficed, in a single generation, to transform a purely agricultural country into a highly developed industrial state. Fifty years ago Württemberg maintained with difficulty a large rural population. It is now one of the most thriving industrial communities on the continent of Europe. Its industries are carried on by a people who, fifty years ago, were entirely devoid of mechanical knowledge, and who, in taking to these industries, have not abandoned the cultivation of the soil. On the contrary, their agriculture has prospered through the growth of a working class in their towns and villages. The prime cause of this astonishing revolution was the enthusiasm of one man, the illustrious Dr. Von Steinbeiss, who, inspired by the accumulated wonders of the London Exhibition of 1851, persuaded his Government to adopt measures which accomplished little short of a miracle.[1] He was instrumental above all in the organisation of a Board of Industry, which "takes care, while encouraging private enterprise, never to supersede it. It gives advice; it advances money for the establishment of industries; it introduces schools for teaching trades; it sometimes starts industries itself, but always on lines which eventually lead to the absorption of these industries by private enterprise in the form of companies or associations .... It has managed to introduce industries into given localities by sending skilled workmen abroad to acquire a knowledge of new methods in trade and agriculture, who, on their return, go about towns and villages, giving instruction, and by introducing foreign workmen and instructors."[1]

In the earlier period of his labours, Von Steinbeiss was driven almost to despair by the apparent hopelessness of the task before him. "After ten years' exertion," he writes "I was often tempted to doubt if any practical result would ensue." But he persevered and succeeded.

No less suggestive is the example of Japan, where

---

[1] *Report of the Recess Committee on a Department of Agriculture and Industries in Ireland* (Browne and Nolan, Dublin, pp. 60, 112, 255, *et seq.*)

agriculture was almost the only important industry till 1868. That year marks the commencement of a new policy under which the commercial and industrial interests of the country have been aided by lavish expenditure on technical education, by the dissemination of useful intelligence, and by the subsidising of struggling industries. The Government made a beginning in 1872 with the establishment of a silk filature, followed by a woollen factory, two cotton-mills and a mill to utilise waste silk and cocoons. Ten spinning plants, of 2,000 spindles each, were also procured from England and made over to private individuals on the hire-purchase system. It was the Government that pioneered the manufacture of cement, glass, soap, paper, paint, type and machinery.

The setting up of model factories did not exhaust its zeal. Experts were deputed to tour all over the country to encourage industrial enterprise by lectures and practical demonstrations. Technical laboratories were established, and merchants, manufacturers and students were sent to foreign countries to study new arts and trades, and to investigate commercial and industrial problems. Special pains were also taken to arrange frequent exhibitions at home, and to participate officially in all those instituted abroad. The latter course, in particular, has contributed not a little to the development of the export trade. Take the single example of porcelain: "Up to the time of the London Exhibition in 1862, the civilised people of the West were as ignorant of Japanese art as were the artists of the eighteenth century of the Elgin marbles. But since then it has been thoroughly advertised by means of the expositions of Paris, Vienna and Philadelphia,

The 'Japanese court' in which carefully selected specimens were displayed, attracted the attention of all true lovers of art, and a great variety of artistic products have since found their way to the cities of both Europe and America."[1]

Local authorities followed the lead of the Imperial Government with enthusiasm, and vied with one another in the establishment of technical schools and laboratories, the organisation of exhibitions, the hiring out of costly machinery, and the advancing of loans to the promoters of novel enterprises. The Local Office of Kyoto, for example, set up a dyeing factory, a model weaving-mill and a research laboratory for ceramics, dyeing and soap-making, and also sent a number of weavers to Lyons to learn improved methods.[2]

---

[1] Yeijiro Ono, *Industrial Transition in Japan* (1880) p. 48.

[2] For further details see *Japan in the Beginning of the Twentieth Century*, published by the Japanese Government (London, 1904), pp. 404 *et seq.*

TABLES.

WEIGHTS.

80 Tolas = 1 Seer = 2·06 lbs.

40 Seers = 1 Maund = 82·28 lbs.

MONEY.

12 Pies = 1 Anna

16 Annas = 1 Rupee

15 Rupees = 1 Pound Sterling.

NOTE.

Except where the contrary is expressly stated, the population statistics given in this work are those of the Census of 1901.

CHAPTER I.

Cotton—The Hand Industry.

Notwithstanding the great revolution effected by steam in the cotton industry, hand-weaving still holds its place as the premier handicraft of the Punjab, as of the rest of India, and provides no less than five per cent. of the population [1] with their daily bread.

The following table gives the number of the workers in selected districts in 1901 :—

District	Workers	District	Workers
Sialkot	61,715	Gurgaon	18,704
Hoshiarpur	62,082	Shahpur	27,060
Jullundur	47,788	Jhang	24,409
Lahore	40,603	Montgomery	18,752
Amritsar	46,165	Multan	33,506
Ludhiana	19,914	Mianwali	16,382
Delhi	9,543		

The weaver class includes a small proportion of recruits from the lower orders of the population such as Meghs, Mochis, and Barwalas, Churas and Chamars, and in the Delhi Division, Dhanaks, Kolis and others ; but the majority are Mohammadan Julahas or Paolis. Successive waves of Kashmiri immigrants have passed over the Punjab, leaving large colonies in Sialkot, Gujranwalla and Gujrat, but isolated groups of these deft artisans are found much further afield. They do the best work for which Amritsar is noted, and

[1] The total number of cotton spinners, weavers, etc., with their dependants, came to 954,961 in 1901. Of these, 322,944 were workers.

Ludhiana owes not a little of its prosperity to their inherited skill and industry.

In the eastern districts, the Julahas constitute a real caste, but further westwards, distinctions of race tend to disappear. Khokhars and Pathans, Mirasis and Rajputs, and even needy Sayyads are found plying the weaver's shuttle for their livelihood in Jhang and Multan.

The local varieties of hand-made cloth are legion, but only the chief ones need be mentioned. The commonest is *khaddar,* a coarse white cloth with a single warp and weft, which is made in almost every village of the province. The coarse yarn of the Punjab mills is generally used for it, but in many districts, especially in those of the Delhi Division, much home-spun material [1] is also woven for the cultivators' own wear. In the Kangra district, and also in the larger cities, such as Multan and Amritsar, the local production of *khaddar* is not equal to the demand and it has to be imported. The next most important fabrics are *lungis* and *patkas,* or turban cloths. The former have a border on one side only, and have coloured and gold-embroidered ends. The latter have a double border but no ornamental ends. Both are well known as the speciality of Ludhiana, but they are also made in the surrounding country as well as in the Jhang, Shahpur, Multan and Montgomery districts.

Khés is a coarse stuff, plain or checked, with a double warp and double weft, and is generally used for wrappers in the winter, and for bedspreads. *Súsi* is a smooth evenly woven cloth with stripes of all

[1] Hand-spun yarn is used for warp as well as woof or for woof only. The price of 1 to 1½ seer is one rupee.

colours, chiefly made into women's trousers. It is produced in most of the important weaving districts such as Hoshiarpur, Amritsar, Sialkot, Jhang, Shahpur and Multan, but the demand for it is rapidly declining. *Gabroon* is really only a species of *khês* with checks or stripes and with a double warp and weft of different colours. A smooth evenly woven variety of *gabroon* called *gaigum*, suitable for shirtings, with a single warp and weft, is also made in Ludhiana and other places. Both kinds are giving way to Bombay checks.

The principal centres of the industry in the Province will now be surveyed.

Starting with the Sialkot district, in Sialkot City itself there are 600 looms, of which 400 belong to Kashmiris and 200 to Julahas. Gondal Chami has 300 and Hail and Juggo Chak have 150 each. The industry is in a bad way, especially in the first-named place, where a number of weavers have set their children to work as masons or carpenters and even as unskilled day-labourers. They would welcome a school to teach profitable industries to the rising generation.

Batala, with 150 looms, is the only locality of note in this connection in the Gurdaspur district, where the craft is, on the whole, worse off than even in Sialkot. At one time much *khaddar* was exported from this tract to the Kangra Hills, but the trade has long ceased. The Hoshiarpur district, on the other hand, sends large quantities of this stuff not only to the hills, but also to Peshawar and even Afghanistan. The most important centres of its weaving trade and industry are Jaijon, Khanpur and Tanda.

Westward in the Jullundur district, 150 looms each are found in Rahon, Kartarpur and Nakodar, where *lungis* and *gabroons* are turned out for export to various places. The *khaddar* of Nakodar in particular boasts a special reputation for quality, and, until Ahmedabad cloth took the field against it, had a market as far as Sukkur and Shikarpur in Sind. Jullundur is now losing its trade even in *lungis*, so that many weavers from Rahon have emigrated to Ludhiana, where they get better wages. Ludhiana City has 350 workers engaged in the manufacture of *lungis* and *patkas* for the Indian army, but the demand for its manufactures still exceeds the supply. In fact, a good many of the so-called "Ludhiana lungis" are really woven in Hoshiarpur and Jullundur and imported here only to be embroidered and finished. The cloth industry of Ludhiana has, however, declined on the whole, as its drills and *gabroons*, for which also it used to be noted, are retiring before the products of the Bombay mills. Its *súsí* has long disappeared. Though the sepoy still glories in his "Ludhiana lungi," his wife has abandoned the *súsí* she wore as a girl for the more attractive patterns of imported chintz.

Lahore need only be mentioned as having close on 900 weavers, according to the census of 1901. Amritsar City has 300 looms, and Jandiala, 11 miles off, 100.

In the Lahnda tract, Khushab possesses 460 looms, and Girot (Shahpur) 170; in both these places the industry seems to thrive more than in any other locality in the Punjab. Though the number of weavers is increasing, the supply is not yet equal to the demand, and every yard of *khaddar* woven is immediately bought up for export to the frontier districts and Waziristan. Bhera, another centre in the same district, has 250 looms and is noted for its *khés*.

The three tahsil towns of the Jhang district—Jhang-Maghiana, Chiniot and Shorkot, have 600, 325, and 80 looms, respectively. Here the industry is fairly stable in spite of the fact that here as elsewhere the finer imported fabrics are making headway. At one time there was a brisk export of *khaddar* to Afghanistan, Khorasan, etc., but the demand has very much decreased of late years. Still further south, in the Montgomery district, the 200 looms at Pak Pattan and the 100 at Kamalia are by no means as busy as they might be. The only centre of note in the Mianwali district is Mari-Kalabagh on the Indus, with 480 looms in Kalabagh and 300 on the other side of the river. Very durable *khés* and *súsi* of special designs are woven here not only for local consumption, but for export to the frontier districts and beyond. Complaints are, however, frequent that Manchester is cutting into the trade.

The industry may be described as flourishing in the Multan district. Multan City has 1,500 looms and forms with Delhi, which has an equal number, the largest cotton weaving centre in the Province. It exports its *lungis* eastward to the Punjab districts, and its *súsi* to Kohat, Bannu, and other places in the North-West Frontier Province. Chequered saddle-cloths and other fabrics are also made at Thatta Paolian, Jalalpur and Obaona in the same district.

In the opposite corner of the province there are 360 looms in Rewari in the Gurgaon district. About 200 of these belong to "Multani Julahas," descendants of immigrants from the Western Punjab, and the rest to Kabir-bansis, Kolis, Murid-Bagris, and other castes of a more southern origin. The chief local manufacture is that of *péch*, a kind of fine turban 6 inches by 16 feet, used as an under-turban in Rajputana as well as in the Punjab. It is generally sent to Delhi, where it is also produced, to be bleached and fringed with gold tinsel and then exported. Besides this, a turban of somewhat greater width is also woven for export to Indore. English yarn of 40 to 200 counts is used for these fabrics. The looms are very small and the Ludhiana or Kahnuwan *gótă* machines [1] might no doubt take their place with advantage. The local Julahas are intelligent and may be persuaded to adopt co-operative methods.

The hand-loom industry has now been reviewed in the typical districts. The condition of the weaver is in all places, even where there is a flourishing trade in his goods, miserable. He is everywhere ignorant and impoverished, and earns a bare subsistence for himself and his family by a handicraft which is becoming less and less profitable every day. He is almost without exception under the thumb of the capitalist. Even if the yarn he weaves is legally his own, it will be found that he has bought it on credit from a shopkeeper to whom he is bound to sell the finished product. In rare cases, as, for example, in some of the villages of the Sialkot district, he may be found working independently with his own little capital of Rs. 10 or 15, but, as a rule, he is only a labourer working up his customer's materials. In Multan, Mianwali and Ludhiana he is said to earn from four to twelve annas a day, but in Hoshiarpur his profits never go beyond eight annas, while in Gurdaspur and Jullundur they are reported to be as low as from three to four annas.

---

[1] See under *Tinsel* in Chapter XVIII.

It is, however, over half a century since the unequal duel between the hand-weaver and the power-loom began. The former was cheered at the very start with dismal prophecies of speedy ruin ; but, starved and despised, he continues to show a vitality that is little short of marvellous. The causes that tend to keep his ancient craft alive deserve consideration. Some of these causes are to his advantage, while others are his misfortune.

1. There is, in the first place, a general belief that hand-made cloths, though rougher in texture, are more lasting than the products of the mills, and that it pays to use them even if they are more expensive. In fact, their very coarseness is held to be a proof of strength and durability, an opinion which is perhaps not quite justifiable.

It has been shown, however, that in spite of this belief, fashions are changing and the general rise in the standard of comfort amongst the agricultural classes is all in favour of the softer and more attractive imported article.

2. The ordinary pit-loom or *khaddi* can weave successfully any low-grade yarn, mill-made or spun by the cultivator's women-folk in their leisure moments. In this respect it is superior not only to the power-loom but also to the fly-shuttle loom, both of which require good yarns.

3. The third point in the hand-loom weaver's favour is that there is no limit to the designs he can produce. He is in a position to cater for special and limited markets, with which he is familiar, and where it would not pay the power-loom to compete. The demand for Ludhiana *lungis* is greater than the supply. Why ? Because the cost of machinery to weave the various

borders wanted for them would be prohibitive.[1] It is the same with the *péch* of Rewari, the *khés* of Bhera and the fancy cloths of Khusháb. If the checked fabrics of Gujrat and Multan are being driven out, it is because the craftsmen do not weave new designs, and the few old ones they have are being copied on a large scale on the power-looms of Bombay and Manchester.[2]

4. The hand-loom weaver, especially when he lives in a village, enjoys advantages that compensate him, to a certain extent, for the difference between his earnings and those of the factory hand. He lives in his own house, surrounded by his family and relations, who help him in his work, and only those who know the home-loving Punjabi can realise how much the Julaha values the privilege of staying at home. There is a flavour of independence about a craft which permits you to take up your work or leave it when you like. The weaver can pack up his loom to feast at the weddings or to weep at the funerals of his friends. This habit of mind does not lead to efficiency, but then he is not ambitious, and so long as he gets the very little he needs to keep body and soul together, he is content.

---

[1] Not only have dobbie machines been found suitable for hand-weaving in the south of India, but even jacquard harness is now employed to weave the complicated patterns found on solid bordered cloths of the better varieties.

[2] The example of Würtemberg proves that the manufacture of the highest class of goods can be carried on with hand-looms, notwithstanding the competition of machinery, by a rural population engaged part of their time in agriculture. Beautiful table-cloths, and white and coloured linens of superior design for borders, are a speciality of the village of Laichingen, which exports them to America and other foreign lands. (*Recess Committee's Report on a Dept. of Agr. and Ind. in Ireland*, 1896, p. 62.)

It must be noted, however, that the weaver's ability to lay aside his work at any time without loss (his total capital rarely goes beyond Rs. 20) is not without some advantages from an economic point of view. In the rural tracts, where the greater part of the weaving community of the province live, labour is getting very scarce and commands high wages, especially at harvest time. The weaver often turns his hand to agriculture and earns a little spare cash by cutting the crops of his customers.[1]

5. It is his misfortune to be tied to his handicraft by the strong bonds of custom. The sentiment of caste is weaker in this Province than in other parts of India, but the inherited traditions of long ages impel a man to follow on the path of his forefathers. Thus, a weaver will be content with far lower profits in his ancestral calling, than he would in any other. It is true that these traditions are slowly melting away under the influence of changing circumstances, but they are still a force to be reckoned with by the administrator and the reformer.

6. Finally, in addition to the above facts, it must be remembered that the Punjabi weaver is notorious for his stupidity and ignorance. It is seldom he can count beyond twenty. Nothing short of starvation will compel him to use his scanty brains to think whether he cannot take up a more profitable trade than the one in which he was born.

Regeneration of the Weaver.—The movement to improve the lot of the weaver is of recent date and

[1] Hand-weaving is an important subsidiary industry in agricultural Japan, being chiefly practised by the farmer's wife and daughters. 380,000 women and 5,000 men were engaged in it in 1907. (Shimooka *Japanese Agriculture*, Tokyo, 1910, p. 80.)

owes its present force in no small measure to the efforts of Mr. Chatterton in Madras, Mr. Churchill in Bombay, and that unyielding champion of Indian arts and crafts, Mr. Havell of Bengal. Since the beginning of 1907 the Punjab Government has given special attention to the promotion of hand-loom weaving within its jurisdiction. Its sympathy has already taken practical form in various directions and the vein of its goodwill shows no signs of exhaustion.

It has been shown that the weavers form a considerable section of the population. It is also true that as a class they are stupid, ignorant, physically weak and overwhelmed with debt, and therefore amongst the first to fall when famine comes on the land. Even if some of the remedies now proposed may not be wholly consistent with the stern maxims of Malthus or of Adam Smith,[1] they can still be defended on the broad ground of humanity as being precautionary measures of famine relief.

Co-operation. The most important step towards improvement will be the wide diffusion of the co-operative principle, justly called "one of the great industrial discoveries of the last century." The weaver is in the clutches of the money-lender and does not hope to be free of him till death. "His bonds of slavery are huge debts, capable of enforcement if he attempts to transfer his custom elsewhere." He knows that whatever he earns beyond his barest necessities must go to pay off an ever-

[1] "Economic truths and economic principles which are true in England at the present time are not perpetual. They were not true for her a hundred years ago, and they may not be true for her a hundred years hence." (Lees Smith, *Studies in Indian Economics*, p. 21.)

increasing debt,[1] and the natural consequence is that he has no ambition to improve the quality or the output of his cloth. The regeneration of the weaver cannot, therefore, be hoped for until a system of cheap and yet not unlimited credit is substituted for the present arrangement.

Progress must, of course, be along the line of least resistance. Localities such as Rewari and Ludhiana should be selected, where the craftsmen are not all badly off or divided by bitter feuds, and have some intelligent leaders amongst them, whose sole ambition is not "to become slave-drivers themselves." The societies might be on the lines of the Big Conjeeveram Weavers' Union,[2] and, in addition to lending

[1] Much has been said of the benefits conferred by the Swadeshi movement on the weaver of Eastern Bengal. According to Mr. Gupta, however, "we find that although the impetus imparted by the Swadeshi movement has not yet resulted in any marked improvement in the material condition of the weaver, yet enterprising shopkeepers and wholesale dealers in country-made cloth have made quite decent profits out of their business. I think the real explanation is to be found in the fact that only one anna of the weavers of Dacca town are free from the clutches of the Mahajans, and the rest are steeped in debt, and receive artificial wages fixed by their creditors, the Mahajans. They, therefore, do not earn more than two to three annas a day." (Mr. G. N. Gupta's *Report on the Industries and Resources of Eastern Bengal and Assam*, 1907-08, p. 14.)

[2] "In the Agricultural Societies of Germany, which are all on the Raffeisan system, there is practically no share capital. The money with which they conduct their operations consists entirely of deposits. A beginning is made by a few of the more important and well-to-do men of the district placing money on deposit. When once the process has been set in operation, their example is followed throughout the country districts, and the peasant invests his savings in the agricultural societies with as much confidence as if they were Government securities" (Lees Smith, *op. cit.*, p. 112). This was the course followed in the case of the Big Conjeeveram society. In the Bombay Presidency, however, a few deposits made by the members and a corresponding loan from Government form a very usual beginning.

small sums of money in exceptional cases, they might themselves buy yarn for sale at cash or slightly higher credit prices to the members. There might also be a common warehouse where the cloths woven by the members could be purchased and stored for sale on commission. The weavers should not be debarred from selling their work to outsiders if they choose to do so, provided they do not give them more favourable terms than those given to the society. The goods bought by the warehouse could be appraised by a committee who would also be responsible for advertising the stock and sending out books of patterns. At the start the financing would have to be wholly by borrowed capital, and as the weavers themselves would not command credit, a few public-spirited gentlemen of means might be associated as members. The ultimate aim of the society, however, should be to build up by thrift a capital of its own. Every weaver, for example, might be made to take up as many shares of Rs. 10-8 each as he has looms, and pay them up by 84 monthly instalments of two annas. The direction should be in the hands of a *panch* or committee of the members, but if there is a danger of factions of rich and poor springing up, an outsider of weight would have to be appointed president, and in some cases a paid manager, not a weaver, may be desirable. Lastly, as the aim of a co-operative society is not only to improve the economic condition of the members but to raise their moral standard, there should be a strict rule against admitting to membership anyone who does not bear a good character. Government might supply such societies with new looms, etc., for trial, free of charge. A society of this kind, once established on a firm basis, might invest in a warping, sizing and beaming mill, and other improved appliances of its own. It might also arrange for the sizing of warps by specialists if necessary.[1]

Need for a Research Institute.

Before inducing the weaver to invest his very scanty capital in "improved" appliances, it must not only be proved that the improvements are genuine, but it must also be ascertained which of the appliances are best suited to local circumstances. This can only be done after patient and careful trials by experts. There are, for example, a great many looms on the market, all of which have their merits, but what is a merit in one part of the country may be a defect in another. A loom may be discarded by Madras, because the foot-action is too heavy for the puny legs of the Telugu weaver, but it may be appreciated by the sturdier Julaha of the Punjab. Again, a picking arrangement that will work admirably in a moist province like Bengal,[2] might be quite out of place in the drier climate of the Punjab plains. A central research institute and school of weaving is therefore a necessity. The province already possesses an efficient school of weaving in the Sir Louis Dane School at Ludhiana, which could be taken over by Government to form a nucleus for the proposed institution. The teaching department should be run on strictly commercial lines, except

---

[1] There are five weavers' societies in Bengal, four in the Bombay Presidency and three in the Mysore State. Small societies at Bham, Kala Afghanan and one or two other places have already been started in the Punjab.

[2] The importance of climate as a factor in cotton weaving is practically beyond dispute. See the discussion on the subject in the Report of the All-India Weaving Conference at Madras in 1908.

that it should not be allowed to encroach on the markets already exploited by the local weaver. It should be provided with all the better kinds of looms on the market, with complete sets of warping and beaming machinery, etc., and there should be textile experts on its staff to test the comparative merits of these appliances and suggest improvements. The institute might also employ a qualified dyeing expert, who should make experiments with the various vegetable and mineral dyes in the market and teach their use to the pupils of the school. It would also be his business to test the various kinds of "sizes" locally used and to select the best for such of the new looms as might be approved by the textile experts.[1]

Several District Boards have already sent weavers to the Sir Louis Dane Weaving School, Ludhiana, paying their travelling expenses, and it will not be difficult to persuade them to offer scholarships tenable at the institute to intelligent young men. The more successful pupils of the school would be available for employment as weaving-masters, while facilities could be given to others for obtaining improved looms on the hire-purchase system.

Travelling Schools.

The Central Institute should have several peripatetic sections moving over the Province with their looms

---

[1] Institutions of this kind are already in existence at Salem (Madras Presidency), Serampore (Bengal) and Bara Banki (United Provinces). The staff of the Serampore School consists of a European principal, an assistant principal, a drawing master, a jobbing mechanic and four pupil-teachers. There is no dyer nor any laboratory attached to the school. The initial cost was Rs. 75,255, and the annual recurring expenditure is about Rs. 35,000. The initial cost of the Bara Banki School was Rs. 15,500 and the recurring expenditure is about Rs. 10,000.

and other machinery, and stopping in temporary buildings at each favourable centre for a sufficient length of time. The Department of Industries has already sent round travelling exhibitions of looms to some weaving villages, such as Bham in the Gurdaspur district. These have not been very successful so far, but some valuable lessons have been learnt from their failure.

1. Careful inquiries into the local conditions of the villages to be visited should be made in advance, and those should be avoided where the weavers (*a*) do not use machine-made yarn, which alone gives good results on improved looms, (*b*) do not work for the general market, or (*c*) are partially agriculturists.

2. The School should be armed with orders from Government departments, as well as from respectable wholesale cloth-dealers, for such goods as can be made on improved looms by the weavers of the village. This will do more to attract their attention than the most eloquent professions of sympathy with their lot.

3. The School should have funds to engage local weavers as employees to work the looms.

4. After the members of the school have settled down and discovered what they can do with the local fashions, an exhibition, combined with a competition in weaving in the styles of cloth popular in the neighbourhood, might be held to demonstrate the superiority of the new methods.

After remaining abroad for a season, the first batch of sectional instructors should return to headquarters and another go forth. This system will keep the central establishment in living touch with the weaving industry of the Province and put the results of its researches to a constant and thoroughly practical test.[1]

Sale Depôts.

Agencies might be established in connection with the Institute and its branches on the lines of the depôts of the Sir Louis Dane School at Ludhiana, to obtain orders, not only for the school, but for other weavers as well. It would be their function to study the market and keep the weavers informed of its requirements, thus acting as connecting links between the producers and the consumers. The need for such agencies is, however, less urgent than is supposed, since the ordinary weaver, as has already been noticed, is in debt to the village shopkeeper and dare not sell his goods elsewhere.

An alternative proposal is for Government to establish factories in connection with the weaving-schools where weavers, independently or under contractors, might work under supervision, and their work be hall-marked with the approval of the school authorities.

New industries for the weaver caste.

The hand-loom weaver has a good but not an unlimited market; hence he will find it difficult to sell his cloth if the output is increased very much beyond what it is now. If the efficiency of the weaver class is increased, its numbers must proportionately be decreased, and openings in other trades, such as wool-weaving, carpentry, etc., provided for its more energetic and enterprising members, by setting up small industrial schools at weaving centres. There is a great dearth of skilled labour in many trades which the overflow of the hand-loom industry might well help to remove. Manufacturers everywhere say they

[1] It must be mentioned that in the Madras Presidency peripatetic weaving exhibitions have proved a total failure.

could easily produce and sell twice what they do now, if only they could get the labour they want.

Encouragement of private bodies.

Government might also encourage private philanthropic and religious bodies in their efforts to ameliorate the condition of the weaving community.

This has already been done in the case of the Salvation Army, whose weaving school at Ludhiana was started in November 1908 with the object of being "not merely a school of instruction or a factory for the production of cloth, but, so far as possible, a central heart and head for the promotion of the hand-loom weaving industry of the Punjab." In addition to the free occupation of the Ludhiana Fort, the Punjab Government has granted it a donation of Rs. 2,800, a loan of Rs. 5,000 at 6¼ per cent. interest, and a subsidy of Rs. 3,000 for one year.[1] It was, perhaps, the military guise of the instructors combined with the forbidding exterior of the school that frightened away the first batch of district stipend-holders, and still keeps the weavers of Ludhiana itself at an awed distance. The missionary character of the Salvation Army, however, has probably most to do with this attitude on the part of the people, in spite of the fact that proselytism is not an object of the School.

The institution is now fairly flourishing and promises to do good to the hand-loom industry of the Province. Like the one at Bara Banki, however, it must take to weaving finer grades of cloth, with better designs than the weaver can produce untaught, if it is to become really popular.

The Arya Samaj of Sialkot is showing great activity in the improvement of the Megh weavers of the

[1] This subsidy has subsequently been renewed for another year.

district, and some assistance might be given to enable it to introduce improved implements amongst them. Further, the great majority of the weavers of the Punjab are Mohammadans, and when their more enlightened co-religionists awaken to their needs, help of the same kind will have to be given to them also.

Weaving in Jails.

There are about 200 weavers amongst the 15,000 prisoners in the Punjab jails, and they are chiefly made to do their hard labour on improved looms—fly-shuttle, Thakral's and Salvation Army. The jails, in fact, try every promising invention in the ordinary course of business. It would be an advantage to the public if the Department made experiments in the various kinds of "sizes" also, and published an account of all its weaving operations in the annual reports.

Improvements in the worker's methods.

We now come to the question of improvements in the various processes connected with weaving. The subject is one for specialists and little can be done in a work of this kind beyond indicating, as far as one can, the balance of expert opinion on the subject.

At the outset the inquirer must discard the popular belief that the improved loom is the panacea for all the ills of the industry. The loom is a very important implement to the weaver, but it is not everything. There are many questions regarding the processes before and after weaving that are of equal, if not of greater, consequence.

The warp.

It is important that long warps should be used on fast looms of any description, as otherwise the delay caused by connecting the short threads with each other, largely diminishes the advantage. The present system, under which the weaver uses short warps prepared by himself, causes waste of material as well as loss of valuable time, even on the country loom.[1] "The old hand-loom is in the possession of the poorest weaver, and it is capable of weaving anything that human skill can think of. If this loom is supplied with long well-made warps properly wound on a wooden roller[2] and the latter properly mounted on supports and suitably weighted, the weaver will be able to increase his outturn by nearly 20 per cent., doing his work in the usual way. The weaver will thereby be enabled to do the work of weaving continuously, and all the detentions incidental to the use of short stretched warp avoided. To use a warp beam in conjunction with the ordinary primitive pit-loom does not demand any special skill or expense worth mentioning. All that the weaver is required to do, is to dig a small pit about a couple of yards away from the pit he is sitting in, to suitably accommodate the yarn beams on supports so that the warp may be very nearly in a line with the cloth roller of the weaver. The tensioning of the warp is the essential feature of this arrangement."[3] Instead of taking

[1] Apart from the waste of time, each operation of warping causes the loss of a seer of yarn at least. This seems to be well understood in many places. In Multan the warps are made 88 yards, and in Montgomery 200 yards long. They are made very long in Dera Ghazi Khan also.

[2] "The use of the yarn roller beam offers great advantages, because it enables long lengths of warp to be used, besides permitting the yarn to be wound straight and in an untangled condition, thus facilitating the continuous weaving of the cloth and saving much waste of material, loss of time, labour and wages for frequent dressing, drawing in or twisting in of warps and getting the same on the looms." (Mehta, *Report on the Hand-loom Industry of Bombay*, 1910, p. 10.)

[3] *Ibid.*

the yarn in bundles, the weaver should have the opportunity of buying it ready warped for a required pattern, sized and wound on wooden rollers. The Empress Mills at Nagpur provide yarn so prepared, chiefly, however, to the Central Provinces Jails. District Boards might arrange demonstrations to prove the superiority of this system at local fairs.

It would, in fact, pay yarn merchants to set up small hand-power mills for winding, warping and beaming, as has been done in Madras, where the yarn is warped "in a very efficient manner on two different types of apparatus—one horizontal and one vertical. It is the practice of many weavers, and also the Salem weaving factory, to give out the warping to the owners of these mills."[1] An ordinary factory of this kind could be established for Rs. 2,000 and would reduce the cost of the preliminary process to a third of what it is now.[2]

Failing these facilities, the weaver should be taught to adopt the portable warping frames used in the Bara Banki Weaving School, an improvement entirely in harmony with the Julaha's traditions, and one that has now become very popular in the villages of the Bara Banki District. It is, in fact, known in several districts in Bengal. The present practice in the Punjab is for the weaver's wife to take two threads at a time when preparing the warp, whereas the Bara Banki frame has fifty reels that take fifty threads in one operation. It is very light and can be carried about by a boy, while a woman arranges the fifty threads on the warp sticks on the ground. It is a contrivance simple enough for the ordinary village carpenter to copy.

---

[1] Chatterjee, *Industries of the United Provinces*, p. 27.

[2] Mehta's Report cited above, p. 10.

It may be objected that facilities for warping will not really help the weaver, as his wife now does all that work, and if relieved of it, she will do nothing. There is no reason, however, why the Julaha woman should not learn to weave like her sister in the United Provinces. As to the boys, they could go to school or they too could weave.

"Sizing" is a most important process [1] on which the behaviour of the yarn on the loom largely depends. Indeed, one of the reasons why some of the ingenious new looms have not succeeded as well as they were expected to do, is that no suitable "sizing" material has been devised for them. The usual "size" (*máwá*) of the Punjab, consists of boiled flour or a solution of half-cooked *chapátis* (wheaten cakes); but boiled rice is used in Sialkot for finer work. A little sesame, rape or castor oil is generally added to the preparation to facilitate the separation of the threads, tallow with a dash of soap being sometimes employed in place of oil in Gujranwala for the coarser counts. "Size" is occasionally adulterated with chalk or *kharia matti* in order to increase the weight of the fabric. Sizing.

[1] In the Punjab, yarn is "sized" after being warped by the weaver himself, except in Multan City and in the larger centres of the Dera Ghazi Khan District, where it is handed over to a special caste for the purpose. In Multan, the weavers themselves "size" the warps in the case of all coarse counts. The finer counts are "sized" in the hank by a caste called Piláwás, who treat it with a kind of starch they themselves prepare from wheat. A special caste does the work in the Dera Ghazi Khan district also. The wages are 8 annas per 100 yards of warp "sized." Long warps are the rule in both districts (note 1 on p. 19 *supra*). In Bengal, too, the use of long warps has brought it about that weavers never size their own yarn (*Report of the All-India Weaving Conference*, 1908, p. 18).

A "sizing" machine suitable for use by the hand-weaver has yet to be invented. The "slasher" type is said to be quite unsuitable for village conditions.

The Loom. There are a great many improved looms on the market, most of which are better than the Indian pit-loom. Amongst the best known are the "Japanese," the Dhariwal and the Salvation Army frame-looms, and the ordinary fly-shuttle loom. The frame-loom works faster than the fly-shuttle, but is far more expensive,[1] and requires a thick and strong warp, except in the rare cases where the weaver can be trusted to do the beaming very carefully.

The merit of the fly-shuttle loom, on the other hand, is that it is very simple[2] and very cheap. It is possible to get one for about Rs. 15, or to have the fly-shuttle arrangement fitted to a country pit-loom for less than Rs. 8.[3] Further, while doing twice the amount of work possible on a pit-loom, it can weave very fine counts of cotton as well as of Italian silk. For 80's and below, it is universally used in Chandernagore, Chinsura and elsewhere in the Hugli and Howrah Districts of Bengal,[4] while at the Lahore Exhibition there were a couple that wove Madras turbans of 150's quite well.

The ordinary country loom with the fly-shuttle arrangement would seem to be the loom for the village

[1] They cost from about Rs. 75 upwards, a sum entirely beyond the average weaver's means.

[2] The temptation to bring in the very best thing available when you are making a change is great; but implements, like institutions, cannot be improved beyond recognition without danger.

[3] The automatic take-up motion is indispensable for the quick and proper working of the Salvation Army loom. The Salvation Army slay cannot, therefore, be attached to a pit-loom with advantage.

[4] See Mr. Chatterjee's note for the Nainital Industrial Conference on p. 39 of the Report.

weaver. The more expensive frame-loom is for the capitalist and for beginners[1] learning to weave.

A few years back improved hand-looms were quite the rage in some towns in the Punjab. "Baroda," "Dhariwal," and "Japanese" hand-looms were set up at Bhera, Hafizabad, Ferozepur, Kahnuwan (Gurdaspur), Werka (Amritsar), Chakwal and other places, in most cases by persons who knew nothing about weaving themselves and were absolutely ignorant of the conditions of the market. Almost all these factories failed, as the profits of the few looms naturally did not make up for the cost of supervision, and the machinery very soon got out of order. The practical way to set about it would have been for the proprietor of the looms himself to go through a practical course at one of the weaving schools before setting up his factory and then work at a loom with his own hands as a master-weaver, as is now done by a good many men at Bara Banki.

There appears to be an opening in the industry for men of energy and education with some capital, say Rs. 5,000. According to Mr. Chatterton a hundred looms will probably be sufficient to give an adequate return on the capital invested and the cost of management. The Capitalist.

---

[1] The reader is referred to the discussion in the *Report of the All-India Weaving Competition*, pp. 41-50.

It may be noted here for the information of hand-loom manufacturers that there is an opening for a trade in improved hand-looms with Bagdad. According to the *Indian Trade Journal* of June 30th, 1910, a small company, formed to organise a weaving industry in Bagdad, imported a hand-loom from England which proved so successful that others of the same kind, and also a spinning machine, were ordered.

CHAPTER II.

COTTON—THE POWER INDUSTRY.

Ginning.

The Punjab annually raises about 15½ lacs of maunds of cleaned cotton, or 7 per cent. of the produce of all India, and of this 11½ lacs are exported.[1] Most of it is ginned in the numerous factories scattered over the cotton districts. The ginning season ends in March, beginning in Delhi in October and further north in November. The general complaint everywhere, except perhaps in Lyallpur, is that there are too many of these factories in the Province and that competition has reduced profits almost to *nil.*[2] Further, in many centres labour is scarce and dear, as will appear from the following table :—

District.	*Wages of unskilled labour.* Males.	Females.
Karnal	5 to 6 annas	3 to 4 annas.
Lahore	8 to 12 annas	4 to 5 annas.
Gujranwala . . .	6 to 8 annas	4 annas.
Lyallpur	8 to 10 annas	4 to 7 annas.
Ambala	7 to 8 annas	4 to 4½ annas.

Ambala alone does not suffer from scarcity of labour.

The old hand-ginning machine has died out everywhere except in isolated tracts, and so has the *pinjárá* or cotton cleaner. Two thousand maunds of hand-ginned cotton is said, however, to be still exported yearly from Daska in the Sialkot district.

---

[1] These figures represent the average for the 5 years 1904-09. The average acreage of cotton amounts to 11 lacs, *i.e.*, 4·6 of the whole crop area of the province.

[2] For the combination of cotton-oil with ginning factories, see under Cotton-Oil.

The cotton-mill industry of the Province cannot be described as flourishing. It comprises at present the following seven mills, but two more will shortly be added. The All-India Spinning and Weaving Mill, Ld., with an authorised capital of Rs. 25,00,000, is about to be established in the Gurdaspur district. The prospectus states that it will be erected on the most approved and up-to-date lines and will also be fitted up with machinery for the bleaching, dyeing, printing, and finishing of cloths. The Bhiwani Cotton Spinning and Weaving Co., Ld., was registered at Bombay in August 1910 with a Capital of Rs. 7,00,000, and will probably commence working in 1912 with 300 looms and 10,000 spindles. **Spinning and Weaving.**

No.	NAME.	Year of Estabt.	No. of looms.	No. of Spindles.	Capital (paid up).	Dividend per cent.		
						'07	'08	'09
1	Delhi Cloth and General Mills, Ld., Delhi . . .	1889	177	20,456	700,000	9	6	5
2	Krishna Mills, Ld., Delhi . . .	1893	*nil*	22,968	700,000	*nil*	3	*nil*
3	Jamna Mills, Delhi.	1896	3 tape looms.	15,000	450,000	12	9	*nil*
4	Hanooman and Mahadeva Mills, Delhi . . .	—	200	15,936	650,000	—	—	—
5	The Lahore Spinning and Weaving Mills, Ld. . .	1898	150	21,208	701,998	7	6	*nil*
6	Mela Ram Cotton Mills, Lahore .	1897	*nil*	13,248	—	—	—	—
7	Amritsar Cotton Mills Company, Ld., Amritsar .	1896	*nil*	16,500	700,000	6	5¼	6

4

These employ on an average 3,600 men, women and children, and produce annually about 160,000 maunds of yarn, 99 per cent. of which is of 20 counts and below. On the other hand, the province yearly imports, in round figures, 50,000 maunds of yarn, mostly of the higher counts.

The chief markets for Punjab yarn outside the province are Agra, Hathras, Moradabad, Aligarh, and Cawnpore. Ahmedabad yarn of 10's and 16's is said to be better than that of Delhi and is often preferred to it.

Of woven goods the Punjab produced about 5,700 maunds and imported about a million maunds in 1908-09.[1]

The causes that impede the development of the industry are as follows :—

1. The locally grown cotton, known to the trade as Bengals, Low Bengals or Delhi-Bengals, has a very short staple, its maximum length being ⅝ inch, so that it cannot be spun to higher counts than 14's and 16's, *i.e.*, yarn suitable only for coarse cloth, *daris*, tents, ropes, etc. Peshawar is the only district in the Punjab or North-West Frontier Province that produces a staple able to spin up to 20's. Bombay, on the other hand, has good varieties of local cotton, and the Central Provinces are in a position to import better cotton to mix with their own.

2. The Punjab is out of the great cotton market. For such an industry it is absolutely necessary to have the raw material in abundance and variety,

[1] The average of woven goods produced by the Punjab mills in the five years 1904-09 was 4,456 maunds per annum and of net imports for the same period, 879,571 maunds.

for mixing, substitution, etc. All the cotton of the Punjab is sent out of the province as soon as it is ginned and the local mills are compelled to keep large stocks of it for themselves. The Bombay mills, which can draw upon their local market all the year round, are under no such necessity.

3. The province is unfavourably situated as regards its fuel supply.[1] Wood is diminishing and is already too dear to be used by any factory, while a ton of Bengal coal delivered at Delhi Station costs from Rs. 10-8 to Rs. 13, according to quality. Moreover, coal is usually carried from Bengal in open wagons, and it is asserted on all hands that it loses from 5 to 10 per cent. on the way. An obvious remedy would be for the railways to provide iron netting to prevent the coal in the waggons from being stolen or blown away on the journey.

5. The founders of the existing mills in the Punjab left out of account the exceptional shortness of the staple of their cotton, and set up machinery really designed for the mills of Bombay and Nagpur, which use a greater length. The result is that the Punjab yarn is insufficiently twisted and weak, and hence only fit for the hand-loom. It will not stand the rapid movement of the power-loom shuttle.

6. There is a universal complaint of the shortage of skilled labour both in Delhi and Lahore, where no mill can ever be worked to its full capacity. Almost all the operatives in the Delhi mills are natives of

[1] Lahore and Amritsar together use about 1,885 effective H.P. for all their factories. The cost per H. P. hour is 6·6 pies, *i.e.*, 8·8 pies per kilowatt hour. The cotton mills of Delhi use about 1,700 H.P., the cost per H.P. hour being 6 pies or 8 pies per kilowatt hour. For the Jumna electric scheme, which will supply Delhi with power, see the notes in Chapter XVIII.

Cawnpore and other districts of the United Provinces. The Punjabi, at his best inferior even to the Bombay mill-hand,[1] finds more profitable employment in other walks of life.

There seems to be no royal road to the encouragement of the cotton-mill industry in the Punjab. The proposal to prohibit the emigration of free labour to foreign countries in order to remedy the shortage of labour may be dismissed as impracticable. Time and the operation of natural laws alone can cure this evil. As to the inefficiency of the mill-hand, it must be admitted that it is due in some measure to the excessive hours of labour. Another undoubted cause, the lack of mental and moral training, can only be removed gradually, and that by the spread of education amongst the masses.[2]

The Punjab Agricultural Department is already doing what it can to promote the cultivation of cottons of a larger staple. The recognised methods for the improvement of the cotton plant are : (*a*) introduction of suitable exotics; (*b*) selection of indigenous varieties ; (*c*) hybridisation.

As to exotics, experiments have been made with American varieties since 1902, and in 1904 Egyptians and Bombays, as well as acclimatised and newly-imported Americans, were tried. So far the Upland Americans seem to have been the most promising.

---

[1] The Indian Factory Commission reported that a Lancashire mill-hand produces 2½ times as much as the Indian. (*Report of the Factory Commission*, 1908, p. 19).

[2] It is not suggested that the existing system of education in the country is calculated to turn out good mill-hands. On the contrary, it is believed that if universalised without modification it will lead to disaster.

Selection from local varieties is an exceedingly slow operation, but the work is in hand at Lyallpur and the results so far are fairly encouraging. Hybridisation is now being effected by the Economic Botanist. It will, however, take years of patient experiment before the results are worked out and new types fixed.

The difficulty now is to secure a good price for the long-stapled cottons grown under Government patronage, and until it is solved, the improved varieties will not become popular with the cultivator. However, it is hoped that the zeal of the various local firms which have taken part in the auctions of the last two years will increase. The self-interest, if not the public spirit, of the spinning and weaving mills of Delhi, Lahore and Amritsar ought to persuade them to second the efforts of the Director of Agriculture. Considering the benefit they will ultimately derive, it is not too much to expect each one of them to undertake to buy every year a given quantity of the long-stapled cotton at a fair premium. So far, it is sad to record, they have been appealed to in vain : they do nothing to encourage the cultivator.

CHAPTER III.

COTTON—MINOR INDUSTRIES.

Hosiery.

India imports annually over sixty lacs worth of cotton and mixed hosiery,[1] of which 55 per cent. comes from Japan. So vigorously, indeed, have the Japanese exploited the markets of Asia that their exports rose from £33,000 in 1902 to £378,000 in 1907, and this in spite of the fact that they are dependent on raw cotton imported from India for their manufactures. Their success is due to : (*a*) cheap machinery and processes ; (*b*) cheap labour ; (*c*) the skill they have developed in the manufacture ; (*d*) knowledge of their markets.[2]

---

[1] The imports in 1908-09 were valued at Rs. 63,45,113. The imports of woollen hosiery for the same year (which was normal) were valued at Rs. 9,69,955.

The growing consumption of hosiery in the Punjab will be illustrated by the figures for Sirsa, a small and somewhat decayed town of 14,600 inhabitants, which does not possess a single hosiery machine.

	Qty. sold yearly.	*Wholesale prices per doz.*
Socks—		
Amritsar, Ludhiana, Gujrat and Jullundur .	3,000 dozens.	As. 12, Re. 1, 1-4
Japanese . . .	1,000 ,,	Rs. 1-4, Rs. 2, 2-8
Undervests—		
Amritsar, etc.. . .	1,500 ,,	,, 2-8 to 3.
Japanese . . .	1,500 ,,	,, 1 to 5.

[2] In Japan the work is done by hand, mostly by females, the daily wage for skilled labour being about 6½ annas for women and 12½ annas for men. The factories generally consist of 8 to 10 workers and are estimated to give a profit of 10 per cent. to the proprietor.—*Indian Trade Journal*, Aug. 20, 1900, p. 166.

With slow and halting steps, this country, too, is attempting to follow in the footsteps of Japan. The ordinary hand-machine for socks, etc., costs only about Rs. 115. It is not difficult to learn and has consequently become popular everywhere.

Ludhiana is, perhaps, the largest hosiery centre in the Province. It has 150 machines for socks and eight for undervests, all of which are busy throughout the winter. During eight months in the year, however, there is only work enough for fifty. At Wazirabad, there is a hosiery factory with ten sock-making and two vest-making machines. It employs ten trained workers at Rs. 12 to 15 per month and twenty indentured apprentices, besides giving job work to some fifteen females in their own homes. There are also a dyer at Rs. 20 and a mechanic at Rs. 25 per mensem on the staff.

Ludhiana and Wazirabad hosiery finds a market all over Upper India, but has to suffer the keen competition of the imported article, which, though less durable, is better finished, and sells, if anything, cheaper than that made locally.

A steam hosiery factory was set up at Delhi at a cost, it is said, of Rs. 60,000, by a local capitalist, who has now converted it into a limited company with a capital of one lac of rupees. The factory is at a standstill as the share-capital has not yet been fully subscribed.

The chief difficulties of the industry are lack of organisation, and want of finish in the article produced. Except in the two places named above, no attempt appears to have been made to study markets or to follow a definite system of production or distribution.

Of the 30 hand-machines at Bhera, for example, only ten or twelve are at work as a rule ; the rest are at a standstill, because competing machines have been set up in almost every village of the district, and their owners do not care to try any outside markets. Socks at Bhera sell at Rs. 1-8 per dozen for inferior grades made of homespun thread, and from Rs. 2 to Rs. 2-8 for the best kinds. At the Hewett School at Bara Banki, cotton socks are made with mill-spun yarn on similar machines at a cost price of Rs. 1-2 a dozen, and no difficulty is found in selling them at Rs. 3 retail and Rs. 2-4 wholesale per dozen in Oudh. The hosiery makers of Bhera and other out-of-the-way places should get in touch with dealers in the big markets of the Punjab, such as Amritsar and Delhi, and even further afield. Calcutta and Bombay are out of the question, until a finer quality of goods is produced.

Systematic efforts should be made to improve the finish of the articles. It is suggested that hosiery classes for men and also for *pardá nashin* women should be established at centres like Lahore, Amritsar and Delhi, and good work encouraged by local exhibitions.

The system of the Bara Banki School, where instruction is free, but is only given to pupils who buy machines for themselves, appears to be very sound. Hosiery schools might at the start undertake to sell the work of ex-pupils until relieved of the duty by private enterprise.

The industry is eminently suitable for *pardá nashin* women, and is likely to bring them more profit than spinning, *phulkári* making, or *gótá* weaving, provided suitable arrangements exist for the disposal of their work. It is a matter for congratulation that women have taken to sock-making in Ludhiana as well as Wazirabad.

To a certain extent, lace-making has already been introduced into girls' schools all over India, chiefly in those started under missionary auspices. Some of the articles turned out are extremely good, and if the necessary organisation existed for studying and exploiting the European, and especially the London, markets, a very lucrative industry would soon arise behind the *purdá*. The main difficulty of the lace-maker at present is to get in touch with the consumer. This would be solved by the formation of committees of philanthropic ladies in Lahore, Amritsar and Delhi with the object of collecting, grading and pricing women's work, and disposing of it to the dealers in India or in Europe. The committees would also procure the latest patterns, through the fashion journals or otherwise, and give them to the workers. Moreover, they would put them in the way of purchasing simple labour-saving appliances, such as are used in Saxony and France. *Lace.*

The extent to which the industry might be developed is illustrated by the instance of Calais, where the average production of cotton, silk, and miscellaneous laces in 1897 was estimated at £2,500,000 giving employment to many thousands.[1]

The Indian *dari* is specially suitable as a floor covering in a warm country, but its manufacture is of little importance in the Punjab. Small quantities are made in most districts and also in the Multan, Montgomery and Delhi jails. The chief centres of the *Daris.*

[1] *Journal of the Society of Arts*, Oct. 8, 1897, p. 1136.

industry, however, are Ludhiana, Ambala and Sialkot, with 200, 80 and 25 looms, respectively.

Daris are usually woven on a frame over which the warp is stretched. The weft is wound on an iron skewer which is carried across the warp threads from hand to hand, two men at least being required to work this arrangement.[1] Machine-spun yarn, costing from Rs. 43 to 46 per maund, is used for the warp, and hand-made, at Rs. 27 to 32 per maund, for the weft. The best *daris* of Ambala are made with hand-made warp as well as weft. The workers in all these places belong to miscellaneous Mohammadan castes, such as Mochis, Sheikhs and Julahas in Ludhiana and Ambala, and Kashmiris in Sialkot, but the trade is controlled by the shopkeepers, who are mainly Hindus. The artisans work either in their own homes or in factories, of which there are four large ones in Ambala. Wages rarely exceed six annas a day.

Amritsar is the chief market for Ludhiana *daris*, while those of Ambala are exported direct to every part of the Province. An average Ludhiana or Sialkot *dari* costs Re. 1 per seer, while those of Ambala can be had from 10 annas to Re. 1-4 a square yard.

Under present conditions the Punjab *dari* industry is declining from several causes, the chief of which is the rise in the price of cotton yarn without a corresponding increase in the rates allowed by the dealers for the finished article.[2] The establishment of co-operative societies at Ludhiana and Ambala will, doubtless,

[1] For an account of the process see Latimer, *Monograph on Carpet-making in the Punjab*, 1905-06, pp. 1-2. An inferior kind of *dari* is also made on the ordinary hand-loom, modified for the purpose.

[2] Contrast with this the position of the more enterprising brass-workers, *infra*.

strengthen the position of the artisans in this respect. Further, the Punjab *dari*, though a useful article, is at the same time quite unattractive, the only patterns woven in it being plain stripes of blue and red. An attempt ought to be made to improve it from an artistic point of view by the introduction of new and attractive designs from other provinces. The Ludhiana Weaving School might add this industry to its curriculum and so lead the way to a better state of things.

Cotton pile carpets.

A very substantial and useful carpet is made in Multan with a pile of cotton or mixed wool and cotton resembling the genuine article in feel and design. A cotton carpet made of locally spun cotton yarn costs from Rs. 6 to 7, and of imported yarn from Rs. 8 to 12 per square yard.[1]

Tape, etc.

The best *newár*[2] used in the Punjab comes from Meerut and Farrukhabad in the United Provinces, and a Rawalpindi firm finds it cheaper to import it thence than to weave it. A fair quantity of *newár* as well as cotton string is, however, prepared in Ambala and also to a certain extent in other cantonments. In Amritsar there are three factories with six to ten men each, besides some stray artisans. One hundred and fifty tape-makers were enumerated in Lahore in 1901.

One Akbarali of Ludhiana[3] has patented a machine for rapidly weaving *newár*, lamp-wicks and tape, as well as gold-lace. It is a pity he has not been able to find a capitalist to take up his invention, which might

---

[1] For an account of the Multan carpet industry, see Chapter V.

[2] *Newár* is a kind of coarse cotton tape, about 2½ inches wide, used for *chárpáis* or bedsteads.

[3] He is now, it is believed, in Gwalior, but communications may be addressed to him at Mohalla Sofian, Ludhiana.

give rise to several useful domestic industries, especially suitable for *pardá-nashin* women. The quantity of lamp-wicks and tape consumed in the Punjab must be enormous.

Tents. There are five tent factories in Lahore, two in Sialkot, a few in Multan and one in Rawalpindi, all of which depend more or less on the custom of Government departments. A recent notification, which gives a practical monopoly of official patronage to the jails, has dealt a serious blow to the industry.

CHAPTER IV.

THE SILK INDUSTRY.

The silk industry is important and flourishing in the Punjab,[1] notwithstanding the fact that, with the insignificant exception of the Gurdaspur district, the raw material all comes from elsewhere. Most of what is used in the Province is imported from China and Japan *viâ* Bombay ; the remainder consists of either raw silk from Bokhara or yarn from Italy.[2] The silk yarn

[1] The history of sericulture in the Punjab up till 1899, as given in Mr. Hailey's excellent monograph on the subject, is a record of failure ; but a small experiment made in 1907 in the Hoshiarpur District by Mr. Wakefield, Revenue Assistant, gave hopeful results. The experiments carried on under Government auspices since 1908 in the Gurdaspur district and at Changa Manga and Lyallpur, however, show that the rearing of the worm from imported disease-free eggs has a future as a cottage industry in the submontane districts.

The Irrigation Department is planting mulberry trees on the Sirhind and Upper Bari-Doab Canals. *Broussonetia papyrifera* might also be tried. See Chapter VI. *infra*.

Silk-worm rearing has been taken up as a commercial venture by K. B. Sheikh Ghulam Sadik of Amritsar, who distributed 200 oz. of eggs in the Gurdaspur district on the Kashmir system (see Appendix I. to this volume) in 1909, and 300 oz. in 1910. § 34, *Report, Punjab Agricultural Dept.* 1909-1910.

[2] The following table gives, for what they are worth, the figures for the net imports of raw silk, Indian and foreign, by goods train and by land into the Punjab. As much of it comes by passenger train, the figures are in no way accurate.

Years.	*Net Imports in maunds.*	*Value in rupees.*
1904-05	8,141	40,87,262
1905-06	9,346	34,69,173
1906-07	8,752	41,23,604
1907-08	1,308	8,93,814
1908-09	1,964	8,64,337

Imports from Kashmir ceased to be recorded in 1907-08. This explains the falling off in that and subsequent years.

of Kashmir, which is in such demand in France, is not used at all here, since in price as well as in quality the Chinese is held to be better. Very little Bengal silk is used, except for embroidering *phulkáris* and for similar low-grade work, as it is said to be very "dry."

The manufacture of silk includes four operations :—(1) The preparation of the yarn; (2) Dyeing; (3) Weaving; and (4) Embroidering.

The first two are carried on only at the chief centres,[1] but in most districts a few stray weavers are found, who prepare silk or mixed silk and cotton fabrics. The art of embroidering with silk is even more general, —it is, in fact, practically universal.

Amritsar.

Amritsar is the metropolis of both the silk trade and the silk industry in the Punjab, and counts no less than 7,000 men, women and children, mostly Mohammadans, who make their living by handling this material. There are about 1,700 looms whose products [2] find a market all over India from Peshawar to Hyderabad (Deccan). Several factories in the city are owned by

[1] The weight in maunds of the imports of silk of all kinds, raw and manufactured, at the four chief centres in the Punjab is given below. The same remark applies to them as to the provincial figures given in note (2) on page 37 :—

	1906-07	1907-08	1908-09.
Amritsar . . .	5,818	5,227	4,222
Jullundur . . .	717	716	844
Multan . . .	1,026	439	763
Lahore . . .	194	178	57
Delhi . . .	1,762	2,765	1,521

[2] The fabrics chiefly made are *daryāi*, a material made of the finer counts and of one colour, *gulbadan*, striped silk, *kanávéz*, a thick stuff much used for skirts, and *gardá*, a material about 34 inches wide with a border on one side only, specially made for the skirts of Hindu ladies. *Gardá* costs from Re. 1-4 to Rs. 3 a yard; *daryái* and *kanávéz* of good quality, 27 inches wide, about Re. 1-8 a yard.

capitalists, who employ a number of dyers, winders and weavers [1] on a monthly wage. The largest of these establishments is that of Basantamal Keshomal, with over 150 looms.

Multan is another great centre with 300 looms for pure silk and over 1,500 workers in the various branches of the industry. Its fabrics are higher-priced and said to be better than those of Amritsar,[2] and are largely exported to the surrounding districts and to Sind. Multan is also the chief place in the Province for the manufacture of mixed cotton and silk fabrics called *mashru*,[3] meaning "allowed" to Mohammadans, amongst whom men are forbidden to wear pure silk, except on very special occasions. **Multan.**

For the lower grades of all-silk cloth, Italian yarn is used for the warp and Chinese for the weft. In fabrics of a better quality Bokhara silk takes the place of Italian.

Most of the yarn used at Multan is locally prepared and dyed. There are about 400 *pat-phérás* and 50 *tanzis*, who earn from 4 to 5 annas a day.

Jullundur, with its suburbs, has about 250 looms, which mostly turn out *daryáis* at from 5 annas to Rs. 2-8 a yard. The average annual output is estimated at about **Jullundur.**

---

[1] The raw silk is wound by the *pat-phérá*, and prepared for the warp by the *tanzi*. They earn from 5 to 6 annas a day. The silk dyer is called *patrang*, and the weaver, *daryái-báf*.

[2] For example, the local *kanávéz*, 27 inches wide, costs from Rs. 1-10 to Rs. 2-4 a yard, whereas that of Amritsar costs Re. 1-8. (*Daryái* and *kanàvēz* up to Rs. 3 a yard are, however, sometimes made in Amritsar as well.)

[3] The chief *mashru* articles produced are *lungis*, *i.e.*, long pieces of cotton cloth with silk borders or ends, used for turbans; *súfi*, a stuff with a silk warp and cotton woof; and *garbi* which has a cotton warp and silk weft.

two lacs of rupees. Amritsar is becoming more and more the entrepôt for the export of Jullundur silk fabrics to the Canal Colonies.

Other centres.

Lahore has a couple of hundred looms and from 30 to 40 *pat-phérás*. The dyeing is done at Amritsar. At Delhi, less than 700 persons were engaged in the industry in 1901. Silk-weaving, however, is not a speciality of this city, most of the yarn being used for embroidery for which there is a large demand, chiefly amongst Europeans. There are a dozen looms in Ludhiana for the manufacture of pure silk turban-cloths. About 50 looms at Khushab weave plain and bordered *daryáis* and turban-cloths with Bokhara silk imported from Amritsar. The weavers are, however, finding it more profitable to produce the coarse cotton fabrics for which this is a flourishing centre.[1] Batala has about 100 weavers, who form a sort of outpost of the industry at Amritsar, whence they bring silk to weave for a piece-wage. Of the 40 odd looms in the Sialkot district, 20 are at the headquarters station. They chiefly produce *daryáis*.

Kashi (Cossi) Silk.

The material known as Kashi (Cossi) silk, which is now so popular for summer wear in Northern India, was first woven in Benares about twelve years ago. The yarn used is called *schappe* in Europe and is made of waste silk and damaged cocoons. It is imported from Italy, *viâ* Bombay.[2] Kashi silk is a cheap, strong and handsome material, which can stand being washed even by the Indian dhobi. It is not yet produced in the

[1] See p. 4 *supra*.

[2] All the Italian schappe silk yarn companies have combined into a trust, their sole agents for India being Messrs. Bottoni, Gorio and Co., of Bombay and Milan.

Punjab, but might be taken up with profit by the improved hand-loom factories of Amritsar, as the yarn can be satisfactorily woven into various patterns and textures on the Swadeshi, Automatic, and similar looms. It would pay to advertise the goods in the Indian and Anglo-Indian press, and to circulate price lists with patterns as the Benares manufacturers do.

Phulkaris.

Phulkáris, or silk embroidered *chaddars* or veils for women, are made in different styles, chiefly by the Jat women of the Hissar, Gurgaon, Delhi, Karnal and Rohtak Districts, and also by Bhabra women in the Jullundur division and elsewhere. They are going out of fashion as an article of female dress in the Punjab, but they are collected in large numbers for several firms in Amritsar and Ludhiana, who export them to America. Mrs. Flora Annie Steel deplores the degeneration of taste consequent on the introduction of the commercial element in their manufacture. However, the patient needlewomen who make them must suit their market. It is impossible to live on unremunerated art; and everybody, except the art connoisseur, will agree that it is better to be well fed yourself than merely interesting to well-meaning strangers.

The following points suggest themselves for the development of the silk industry in the Punjab :—

1. *Co-operative Production.*—The workers in silk are, if anything, more than other artisans under the thumb of the money-lender. They are poor, and handle a very expensive raw material, and this has been sufficient to overwhelm them with debt. They are, in fact, rarely more than skilled labourers who weave the shopkeepers' yarn for a piece wage. It is believed that societies on the line of the Benares Silk Weavers'

Association will prove successful amongst them, especially at centres like Batala, where they are a compact and orderly community.[1]

2. *Study of Markets.*—The capitalists of Amritsar and Multan should make much greater efforts than they are now doing to study the wants of their consumers and to develop new markets. They should aspire to be real captains of industry and not mere money-lenders, whose only aim is to finance and enslave the craftsmen. Punjab silk fabrics, if properly pushed and advertised, might find a wide sale among the wealthier classes of Bombay and Calcutta. They are also appreciated in Bagdad and might possibly be introduced into Persia, where the shawls of "Ambarsar" still have fame, though no longer a market.

Proper attention should be paid to the dyeing and finishing of the fabrics. A promising connection was once lost in Bombay because coats made of Amritsar silk were found to lose colour at the slightest touch of perspiration.

3. *A School of Artistic Silk-weaving at Amritsar.*—Large numbers of weavers are already abandoning their ancient craft, in which a rude inherited skill no longer suffices. A great desideratum for the Province is, therefore, a school which should develop the hereditary aptitude of these men by teaching them the higher forms of their art, and thus enable them to earn a better wage than the hire of a common labourer. Silk-weaving is a sumptuary industry, which chiefly caters for the well-to-do, who want a thing of beauty and can afford to pay

---

[1] See p. 3 *supra*.

a good price for it. The *daryái-báf* of Amritsar or of Multan has so far been able to satisfy the æsthetic cravings of the people of the Province; but the increasing imports of French as well as Japanese stuffs show that fashions are slowly changing with the times. The Punjabi lady will not always be content with the stiff froufrou of a plain *kanávéz* skirt or the monotonous sheen of a *daryái* jacket. Amritsar must learn to imitate the soft watered silks of Surat and the gold-fringed fabrics of Benares, if she is to retain her much-prized handicraft.

CHAPTER V.

Wool and Hair.

The Punjab is the only province where the indigenous wool industry is of any importance. The Hindus consider the material ceremonially pure, and have been acquainted with it from the remotest times, but its comparatively high cost and the fact that it is unsuited to the climate during the greater part of the year have always stood in the way of its popularity on the plains of India.

The raw material. There are over 4½ million sheep in the province, of which the largest number are found in the Mianwali, Kangra, Shahpur, Lahore, Ferozepur, Multan, Montgomery, Attock, and Dera Ghazi Khan districts in this order.[1] To these must be added 620,000 for the Frontier Province, the greater part of whose fleeces ultimately find their way to Darya Khan or Multan for further export. The best variety of wool grown in the Punjab is that of the Kangra hills and of Hissar. On the whole, the product of the plains is poor, being coarse, dirty and short-stapled.

In addition to these supplies, much wool is imported from the adjacent tracts for local consumption or for

---

[1] See *Season and Crop Report* (1909-10) Statement VII. Sheep are clipped twice every year (March and October), and yield from half to three quarters of a seer of wool each time on the plains, and up to one seer in the hills.

export to Europe. The best is Kirmani wool,[1] brought from the Persian province from which it takes its name by the Nushki-Seistan route. It is beautifully soft and white and has a long staple, which is very easy to work. In Persia it is largely used for fabrics which have superseded the use of Kashmir shawls in that country. In the Punjab it is made by itself, or with Tibetan *pashm*, into a cheaper grade of shawl.

Next, in order of excellence, come the wool of Bikaner, which is the best for woollen manufactures, and the fleeces of Tibet[2] and Kangra, which take the first place for worsteds.[3] Genuine Bikaner wool has the peculiarity of not requiring to be washed before being spun, but it is generally full of burr, which largely detracts from its value.

Tibetan wool, on the other hand, is entirely free from this pest, and has a longer and more uniform staple; but it loses 25 per cent. of its weight in washing, and is marred by the presence of an excess of dead hairs.

Amongst others may be mentioned the wool of Jodhpur and that of Afghanistan, known in Liverpool

---

[1] Kirmani wool is also called "Waháb Sháhi *pashm*" in the Punjab, after one of its first importers, Sheikh Abdul Wahúb, father of Khan Bahadur Sheikh Ghulám Sádik, the well-known carpet manufacturer of Amritsar. The imports into India amounted to 3,806 maunds, valued at Rs. 1,05,530 in 1909-10. The wool is largely exported from Persia to England *viâ* Bagdad.

[2] Tibetan wool is imported into India chiefly *viâ* Almora or rather Tanikpore, which is its mart. Tanikpore will shortly be connected by rail with Pilibhit 40 miles off.

About 2,200 maunds per annum (including 200 or so from Kashgar) are brought into Kulu also. Half of this quantity is sold in the district and the rest goes to Dhariwal and Cawnpore.

[3] In a worsted yarn the fibres are so manipulated as to lie parallel to one another, while in a woollen yarn the fibres cross one another in all directions.

as "Kandahar." The Jodhpur State has half a million sheep, which produce a staple superior to that of the Punjab but coarser than the Bikaner. The most important Afghan variety is that yielded by the *dumbá* or large-tailed sheep common in Kabul and Peshawar and the neighbouring districts. From it are made the finer sorts of cloaks used on the frontier.[1]

The chief wool markets of the province are Fazilka, Lahore, Multan, and Darya Khan.[2] The material is brought to these places by road or rail, to be booked direct to Europe and America after being cleaned, pressed and baled.

Fazilka is the entrepôt chiefly of Bikaner, Jodhpur, Hissar, Patiala and Bahawalpore, but also draws, to a smaller extent, on most districts of the province.[3] The following brief account of its industry may be of interest.

Genuine Bikaner wool needs to be burred, an operation which is now performed by women, who cut off the fibres held by the burr with a pair of scissors.

---

[1] Some wool is also imported from Australia by the Dhariwal mills.

[2] The following table gives the railway traffic in raw wool at the principal wool centres during the three years 1906-09 :—

	1906-07		1907-08		1908-09	
	Imports	Exports	Imports	Exports	Imports	Exports
Fazilka . .	56,450	78,758	43,629	79,772	32,850	73,268
Lahore . .	29,487	41,872	21,040	38,691	19,782	31,037
Multan . .	31,205	31,437	28,875	21,704	59,270	45,511
Darya Khan .	85	12,485	153	14,684	138	28,743
Amritsar . .	6,331	7,109	4,635	7,948	3,978	7,690

[3] Fazilka wool is graded in Liverpool as follows :—

Vikaner best Vikaner ordinary	Genuine Bikaner wool, the difference between the grades being only in their freedom from dirt.
Bikaner =	Mixed varieties which may or may not contain genuine Bikaner wool.

The wages are from Re. 1-4 to 1-8 a maund. The waste fibres are sent to the steam burring-mill to be cleaned at a charge of Rs. 2 for every maund of wool returned to the customer. The whole process involves much waste and a local capitalist is now setting up machinery which will remove the burr without any necessity for cutting and shortening the fibres.

All other varieties of wool are washed and cleaned by hand-labour in the 100 *nohras* or yards belonging to the wool-dealers in the town. The material is first freed from dirt; it is then washed (not perhaps as thoroughly as might be desired), dried, and finally cleared of such foreign substances as still adhere to it, by beating with a stick. It is then sent to the pressing-mill. The wage for sorting is five annas per maund, and the same for the entire operation of washing, carrying and cleaning. An adult labourer will earn as much as from ten to twelve annas a day in the season.

There are three presses in Fazilka, but as there is not enough wool for them all, the firms have agreed to share the profits of the West Patent Press Co., the only one at work. The charge for pressing and baling is Rs. 8 for a bale of three maunds and twenty-five seers.

Multan is the market for the produce of the surrounding districts, and save that it needs practically no burring, the wool is treated here in the same way as at Fazilka. The wage for washing, drying and sorting is three annas and a half, and for cleaning four annas in addition, per maund. There are five pressing factories, of which two only are at work. They charge Rs. 4 per bale of 4 to $4\frac{1}{4}$ maunds.

Two or three of the cotton-presses in Lahore, the chief of which is that of Asmatullah, also handle wool.

The material is first washed and then beaten with a stick, and finally sorted into six grades before baling.[1]

Darya Khan is the mart not only for the wool grown in the locality, but also for that of Dera Ismail Khan and other Frontier Districts. The material is first cleaned by beating with a stick, and then simply put into bags. It is railed chiefly to Karachi, but a large amount also goes to Multan, and some to Lahore, Rawalpindi, and Fazilka. There is no press in Darya Khan and no system of through-booking.

Before passing on to woollen manufactures, a few suggestions may be made for the improvement or better management of the raw material.

1. The most important problem of all is the improvement of the local breed of sheep. The Civil Veterinary Department introduced 25 Merino rams into the Kangra district in 1908, but no one will contend that this measure is in any way adequate. Indeed, the importance of the matter would seem to require that a special officer should be put in charge of sheep-breeding operations. Such an officer may find it possible not only to select good rams of the local breed, but also to import new breeds from a climate approximating to that of the Punjab, *e.g.*, Western Australia. The fine long wool of the Tibetan sheep would, no doubt, be improved by a strain of Lincolns, which can boast a still longer staple, while Bikaner sheep should be crossed with Merinos. District Boards ought to take as much interest in the matter as in the breeding of horses and donkeys.

---

[1] An important firm of wool-brokers in London state that the wool packed in cotton-presses sometimes contains pieces of cotton owing to the press not having been properly cleaned; otherwise the present system appears to be satisfactory.

2. As Bikaner wool would gain at least Rs. 5 per maund in value if it were free of burr, the State might seriously consider the problem of keeping down the pest within its territories. In some parts of Australia this is effected by the levy of a fine from the owner of every estate where burr is allowed to exist.

3. The advantages of grading wool are understood in Lahore but not in Fazilka and elsewhere. If wool is carefully cleaned and graded before export it will realise far better prices on the whole transaction than it does now. The practice of mixing wools of different staples, now so prevalent in the Punjab, is doing great harm to the trade.[1]

4. Neither the wool of the Punjab, nor of Bikaner, has much "yolk"—only from 5 to 7½ per cent.—but that of Kangra and Tibet loses as much as 25 per cent., and of Afghanistan 30 per cent. of its weight in cleaning. It might pay mills dealing with the latter varieties to set up plants for the recovery of the valuable substances now wasted with the wool wash-water.[2]

---

[1] The Bikaner State has about half a million sheep within its borders, most of them within the Suratgarh Tahsil. The Darbar would derive far more profit from its flocks if, instead of driving them away by the levy of heavy taxes, it set up a wool-depôt at Suratgarh, bought up all the wool in the State at a fair price, and sold it under its own guarantee after proper cleaning and grading by an expert.

[2] The "yolk" of wool consists of two impurities—wool-fat and wool-perspiration—which cover and protect the fibre. Wool-perspiration, unlike wool-fat, is soluble in water and consists largely of potash salts, the wash-water when evaporated leaving a residue which yields potassium carbonate on ignition. The utilisation of wool wash-water in France is calculated to yield a million kilos of potassium carbonate yearly.

Wool wash-water may further become a valuable source for obtaining acetic, propionic, benzoic, lactic and caprinic acids, all of which are present in it in good quantities, see Sadtler, *Inorg. Indust. Chem.*, p. 306, and Thorpe, *Dict. Appl. Chem.*, Vol. III., art. *Wool-grease.*

New Egerton Woollen Mills.

The New Egerton Woollen Mills, Ld., of Dhariwal, represent the factory industry of the province. Originally established in 1882, the company went into liquidation seven years later, when it came into the hands of the present management. It now has a capital of six lacs of rupees in ordinary and an equal amount in 7 per cent. preference shares, and its dividends for the three years 1907-1909, viz., 10, 10, and 15 per cent., show that it is flourishing. Its annual output of manufactured goods does not fall short of 11,000 maunds.

The mills are situated on the Bari-Doab Canal and are worked by water-power, supplemented by steam during canal closures. The staff includes fourteen Europeans, *viz.*, a manager, four assistants and nine overseers, in addition to over a thousand hands recruited from the surrounding villages. A co-operative credit society has been started among the latter, and a model village is in course of construction for their accommodation.

The Army, Police and other departments are large purchasers of woollen goods, but the management complain that a smaller proportion is taken from the Indian mills than is justifiable on grounds of economy or efficiency. The enterprise was started with the express object of meeting the demands of Government, and now manufactures every kind of high-class hosiery, worsteds and woollens of a quality admittedly equal, if not superior, to any imported article of the same price; but with the lapse of years it finds official patronage reduced almost to nothing. The orders received for the Indian Army amounted to Rs. 5,74,000 in 1896, but only Rs. 75,715, or about 6 per cent. of its total sales, in 1909.

The hand-industry in wool is chiefly carried on by the lower orders of the weaver class, such as Mazbis, Chamárs and Ramdásias, but more skilled artisans, such as Kashmiris and Julahas, monopolise the manufacture of the better kinds of fabrics. The variety of articles produced is not great: coarse but durable *kammals*[1] or blankets, "garbi lois" or blankets of mixed wool and cotton,[2] *pattús*—long narrow pieces of excellent, if somewhat rough cloth. Flannels and tweeds from imported yarn, and a small quantity of *namdas*, shawls and hosiery, complete the tale of the indigenous woollen manufactures of the Punjab. The Indigenous Industry.

The blanket industry is scattered all over the wool-producing districts. It is nowhere centralised save, oddly enough, in the submontane tract between the Jhelum and the Jumna, which has comparatively fewer sheep than the rest of the province. *Pattús* are a speciality of Kangra, where there is hardly a hamlet without its looms, and almost every pastoral family uses coats and blankets of home-grown wool made by its own members from start to finish. The hill *pattú* is a very suitable material for shooting jackets and similar articles of European wear. Blankets.

The chief centres of blanket-weaving will now be briefly passed in review.

---

1 "There is no essential difference between *loi* and *bhura* and *kammal*. *Lois* seem generally to be made white and *kammals* black (dyed or natural); while *bhuras* are much the same as *lois* and the two words may be taken almost to be synonyms." Johnstone, *Monog. on Woollen Manufactures in the Punjab* (1884-85), p. 8. The names, however, are differently used in different localities to denote the various grades of the same material. The *loi* is everywhere the best.

2 Usually in the proportion of 8 or 9 parts of woollen yarn to 3 of cotton.

The blankets of Kahuta in the Rawalpindi district are noteworthy, but the products of the Chakwal Tahsil, as well as of the Domeli circle of Jhelum, are especially good and in demand with regimental contractors, who export them to Peshawar, Quetta and other large military cantonments. The local weavers, who purchase small quantities at a time, contrive to pick out the best lots of wool, much to the annoyance of the large buyers. The yearly output, however, does not exceed 6,500 pieces in the Chakwal Tahsil and 4,500 in the Domeli Circle. Jalalpur, in the Gujrat district, has five hundred looms, including a good many fly-shuttles, which use three species of yarn for *lois* and *chadars* : (*a*) imported woollen yarn known as *raffal* ; (*b*) home-made yarn of Tibetan wool ; and (*c*) home-made yarn of locally grown wool.[1] The exports are estimated at Rs. 3½ lacs of the first variety, a lac of the second and Rs. 15,000 of the third. The Gurdaspur district has only one centre of note, Sujanpur, where all-wool *lois* are made of hand-spun Kangra wool, but the speciality of the place is the "garbi loi," which will be separately noticed. The places deserving mention in the Hoshiarpur district are Hariána, Hajipur, Bambéli and Hoshiarpur city, but none of these is very important, the largest centre, Hariána, having only 25 weavers. Bilga in the Jullundur district has 50. The products of the dozen odd looms respectively of Dad and Pamal in the Ludhiana district, are largely purchased for horse-cloths by the Indian Army, while the black and white blankets of Jagraon, like those of all other wool-manufacturing centres of the province, find a ready sale amongst the thriving cultivators of the Canal Colonies. The 150

[1] 1,260 yards of this go to the seer, which costs a rupee.

looms of Panipat still command a good market in Lahore, Delhi and Amritsar, but the general rise in the wages of labour has killed the trade in the well-known Sirsa *lois*, which no weaver will now make for less than double the former price. A Sirsa loi $7\frac{1}{2}$ yards by $1\frac{1}{2}$ yard, weighing $4\frac{1}{8}$ seers, which could be had for Rs. 6 ten years ago, is at present worth Rs. 12 in the bazaar, and can no longer compete with the machine-made article.

Of the districts of the Western Punjab, reference need only be made to Dera Ghazi Khan, where rude woollen fabrics for the use of agriculturists, and also more ambitious articles such as rugs, prayer-carpets and camel-trappings, are woven by the Biloch women of the border hill-country. The fabrics are interesting because of their sober colouring and quaint ornamentation with shells and silk rosettes.

The profits of the industry are said not to exceed 4 annas a day in Jhang, 6 annas in Jalalpur, and 8 annas in the Hoshiarpur district. They are everywhere on the decline, as the hand-weaver finds it increasingly difficult to compete with the cheap shoddy articles of Europe, which beguile the simple customer by their excellent feel and finish.[1]

[1] It is impossible for the European *all-wool* blanket to compete with the Indian article, the latter being sold at a price very little above the cost of the raw material, as the following representative prices will show:—

		Weight. Seers.	Price. Rs.	a.
Bilga	black	$4\frac{3}{4}$	4	12
	white	$3\frac{1}{16}$	4	0
Hariana & Gujranwala		2	2	8
Chakwal		$8\frac{1}{2}$	3	0
Panipat	black	Re. 1 per seer.		
	white	Re. 1 to Rs. 2 per seer.		

There are 100 looms in Sialkot which make a speciality of "garbi lois"; their annual output is estimated at 46,000 pairs, valued at a lac of rupees. An equal number are busy at Sujánpur (Gurdaspur district) and a great many are scattered in the villages of the Nurpur Tahsil of the Kangra district.

A "garbi loi" of Sujanpur, 6 yards by 1½ yard, weighing 1½ seer, costs Rs. 2-8, while in Sialkot city, one 6 yards by 1⅝ yard, and weighing 1⅝ seers, can be had for Rs. 2-4. There is a good export of these to Lahore, Delhi and Amritsar for further distribution all over India, but the margin of profit is contracting and the number of looms is consequently on the decline.

Flannels and Tweeds. Much woollen yarn, locally known as *raffal*, is imported into the province from Europe,[1] to be woven into cheap and serviceable flannels and tweeds. The headquarters of the industry is Amritsar, where not only are a very large number of pit-looms engaged in it, but a number of factories with Japanese, Dhariwal and other improved modern looms have been set up by capitalists. Such factories are also found at Jullundur and Batála. *Raffal* yarn is woven, as above mentioned, on ordinary pit-looms in Jalalpur and also at Ludhiana and many other places.

The industry received a great impetus from the "Swadeshi movement," but increasing competition is already reducing profits.

---

[1] Imports of woollen yarn and knitting-wool in India in lbs.:—

Years.	At Karachi.	Total.	From Germany.
1905-06	201,193	599,093	270,168
1906-07	594,513	979,024	635,025
1907-08	347,757	781,854	494,674
1908-09	381,520	757,780	537,488

Some *namdas* or felt rugs are prepared in Ludhiana, and cheap ones with "large barbaric patterns" are also turned out at Bhera and Khushab; but they are made of dirty wool, poorly felted, and too often mixed with goat's hair. Miscellaneous.

A few Kashmiris in Jalalpur (Gujrat), Sujanpur and Dera Nanak (Gurdaspur), Kila Sobha Singh, and a few other places in the Sialkot district, weave shawls of Kirmani wool.

The art of knitting socks and gloves by hand, from worsted and woollen yarn, is practised in many places, as for example in Ludhiana, where 25 men and 100 women and children are said to be engaged in the industry for eight months in the year. The knitting machine is also used.[1]

The necessity for co-operation in the purchase of the raw material, as well as the sale of the finished products, is no less urgent in the case of the wool than of the cotton weaver,[2] for the former is, if anything, more at the mercy of the shopkeeper than the latter.

The middleman levies a heavy tax on the industry. Secondly, the woollen hand-industry, no less than the cotton, stands in need of improved methods and appliances.[3] The importations of machine-made goods have dealt it heavy and frequent blows, but it is not past hope, at all events in the winter fastnesses of the Kangra hills.[4] What can be achieved by well-directed effort

---

[1] See p. 31 *supra*.

[2] " p. 10 "

[3] " p. 18 "

[4] In a country so advanced industrially as Italy, 20,000 hand-looms are still at work in the artisans' own homes as compared with 8,000 power-looms and 3,000 hand-looms in the factories.

is shown by the success of the Irish Industries Association and the Congested District Boards in Donegal, where these agencies introduced the wool-industry. Besides popularising an improved foot-driven spinning-wheel, they have taught the peasant to size yarn and weave it on a fly-shuttle loom which produces twice as much as the old loom. The Donegal peasant now has the whole world as a market for his homespuns and depends on this industry for his livelihood.[1]

The present position.

The following figures of the wool trade of the Punjab are instructive :—

Years.	Exports of raw wool.	Imports of woollen manufactures (excluding carpets and rugs).
1905-06 . .	136,667 maunds.	38,846 maunds.
1906-07 . .	100,312 „	31,071 „
1907-08 . .	91,917 „	28,751 „
1908-09 . .	129,818 „	32,264 „

There appears to be no valid reason why the raw wool sent out of the province should not be manufactured at least into yarn before export. It is true that raw wool is less in bulk and therefore costs less to export than yarn of the same weight, and the European spinner is more skilful than the Punjabi. But we must remember that Indian cotton yarn has established a firm market for itself in foreign countries in spite of similar difficulties.

Further, there would seem to be an opening in this province for the manufacture of "union" cloths and shawls of mixed wool and cotton to compete with the imported article. The cheap German or Paisley shawl often costs less than its own weight of raw

[1] *Indian Textile Journal*, May 1910, p. 265.

wool and cannot therefore contain much of that substance; but its popularity,[1] like that of the "garbi loi," indicates a vast future for mixed cotton and wool manufacture in Northern India. The cheap "shawl" has come to stay and might as well be made in India as in Europe.

The manufacture of carpets [2] is of comparatively small commercial importance in the Punjab. The average yearly export is only 5 lacs of rupees, whereas the total exports of all commodities in 1908-09 amounted to 1,530 lacs, of which 355 lacs were accounted for by wholly or partially manufactured articles. The industry is interesting from an artistic point of view, but with this aspect of local crafts we are not here concerned. Carpets.

The factory industry of carpet-making in the Punjab, now practically centred in Amritsar, owes its existence to the initiative of the jails. The Indian carpet was first brought to the notice of Europe at the London International Exhibition of 1851, but it was nott ill 1862 that the exhibits of the Lahore jail introduced the Punjab article to the world's market.

The Amritsar carpet trade is chiefly with the United

---

[1] The imports of "shawls" into India were as follows:—

Years.	Number.	Value in Rupees.
1904-05 . .	2,431,049 . .	61,12,427
1905-06 . .	112,858 . .	27,60,868
1906-07 . .	790,118 . .	15,89,424
1907-08 . .	1,203,372 . .	34,14,948
1908-09 . .	2,030,081 . .	52,87,945

There is a growing demand for fabrics of wool and mixed wool and cotton in Bagdad, which is the entrepôt for Mesopotamia. The demand is chiefly for smooth-surfaced cloths, both plain and with lines and checks.—*Indian Trade Journal*, June 30, 1910.

[2] For further information see Latimer, *Monog. on Carpet-making in the Punjab* (1905-06.)

States of America, and reached its present dimensions, which are probably normal, in 1898. An unexpected boom inflated it to twice this volume in the years 1900-01-02. The result was over-production and much bad work, with the consequence that the demand subsided and the mushroom factories that had sprung into existence went to the wall. The industry is safe at present in the hands of a few firms of standing, who practically monopolise it, and who fully understand that bad workmanship does not pay.

The leading manufacturers restrict themselves to the higher grades only, *i.e.*, from Rs. 12 per square yard (wholesale) upwards. There are six factories in Amritsar with about 200 looms altogether actually at work, and some of these have also branch establishments at Batala and Sujanpur in the Gurdaspur district, and Majitha and Jandiala in the Amritsar district. The system followed is that the manufacturer pays the master-weaver for different qualities of carpets at so much per 1,100 stitches as wages, and the latter in his turn engages his weavers, mostly boys and youths, between the ages of 10 and 20, at a daily or monthly wage. A master-weaver earns from Rs. 10 to 30 per mensem and a weaver from Rs. 4 to 15 per mensem. All the workmen are Mohammadans, the largest proportion of them, especially in the higher grades, being Kashmiris. Apprentices are, however, freely taken from other Mohammadan castes.

Woollen yarn, of which about 1,800 maunds are consumed yearly, is locally spun and dyed with vegetable colours. The ordinary grades cost from Rs. 40 to 45 per maund, but the finest, made of Bikaner wool, are Rs. 70 or more. The yarn of "*pashmina* carpets" is made of Ḳirmani wool[1] and averages Rs. 150 per maund. The dyeing adds from Rs. 20 to Rs. 25 per maund to the price of all these.

Considering the fact that only a few years ago eight hundred looms, employing from four to five thousand weavers, were busy in Amritsar, and there are less than a third of the number at work now, it is impossible there should be any real shortage of labour.

The carpet industry of Multan is a cottage industry of very old standing, and is historically distinct from that of Amritsar. It is, however, insignificant in extent, there being only 40 looms for carpets and 8 for *ásans* (small woollen rugs, 1½ to 3 feet square, used by Hindus for ceremonial purposes). Multan carpets have the merit of individuality, in spite of the fact that the colours are often glaring and ill-assorted and the patterns confused and ugly. They are made both of pure wool and of wool mixed with cotton and are usually 8 ft. by 4 ft. in size. They cost from Rs. 6 to Rs. 10 per square yard if aniline-dyed, and from Rs. 8 to Rs. 13 if dyed with vegetable colours. The *ásans* vary in price from 14 annas to Rs. 5-8 each, according to size and quality. **Multan.**

The industry is in a stable condition, as the weavers work with their own capital and find a steady market for their goods all over India. At the same time, the formation of a co-operative society would improve the present state of things, as the artisan would then be in a better position to know the changing tastes and requirements of the markets than he is now. The problem, however, is not of sufficient importance for Government interference.

---

[1] See page 45 *supra*.

Other Centres.

Half a dozen stray workmen weave carpets near the Ajmeri Gate at Delhi, and the craft is taught in the Arya Samaj orphanage at Bhiwani and in the Church of Scotland Mission School at Gujrat, both of which are glad to undertake orders. Carpets are also made in the Lahore, Delhi, Multan and Montgomery jails.

System of advances.

The bane of the industry in Amritsar is the system of advances, which is more or less prevalent all over Northern India in almost every craft. Under it the employer is compelled to advance large sums of money to his employees [1] without any hope of recovery. A workman will often take advances in one factory and then go over to another, leaving his first employer without any remedy except a costly and unprofitable action in the civil courts.

The only cure for this state of affairs—which is as degrading to the craftsman, whom it reduces to a state of life-long slavery, as it is damaging to the employer's purse—is legislation making all direct or indirect advances by a master to his employees beyond, say, two months' wages irrecoverable.[2] It will then be possible for an employer to refuse to make unreasonable advances to his work-people, well knowing that his rival will not outbid him. A general rise in wages, which, it may be mentioned, are low at present, will probably follow. But the rise will be fully compensated by an improvement in workmanship and the saving of the capital that now has to be sunk in advances.

Jail Competition.

The effect of jail competition on the industry may

---

[1] Advances are made not only to the master-weaver, but also to the weavers under him. The wages of the weavers are credited to their accounts and debited to the master-weaver, who is credited with his contract-wage for the whole carpet.

[2] It is, of course, not proposed that existing debts should be cancelled.

here be considered. In the first place, it is not true that the jails have crushed out a local craft. On the contrary, they have been its pioneers, and as such have encroached on no vested interests. It must be admitted that a Government department that originates a new industry is not justified in keeping a hold on it when private persons have taken it up. It is clearly the duty of Government, in all its branches, always to promote private enterprise. The case in question is, however, exceptional. The Punjab carpet industry is of little importance to the people, of whom it employs only a very insignificant portion. The output of the jails is comparatively very small and does not seriously compete with the enterprise of private firms, who are mostly engaged in the export trade, in which the jails have no share. On the other hand, carpet-making is peculiarly suitable for the employment of prisoners, and was indeed taken up by the jails for this reason. The only restriction that can be suggested is the fixing of minimum prices, below which the jails should not go.

Standardisation of colours.

The carpet-manufacturers of Amritsar would do well to standardise their colours. At present there is a great loss of custom because orders cannot be repeated, there being no guarantee that the customer will get what he wants. In 1908 £4,000 worth of carpets were returned from London, because they did not come up to sample as to their colour. This was not only an actual, but a still greater prospective loss to the industry generally.[1]

[1] It is understood that the leading firms of Amritsar do keep samples of every colour they use, and guarantee to match it after any number of years; nevertheless, the fact that there is no general standard of colours injures the industry as a whole. The shortcomings of the small manufacturer damage not only himself, but the big manufacturer, as well.

Pashm.

Pashm is the under-hair of a small breed of goats found only in the higher parts of Yarkand and the Tibetan table-land. It is brought to Ludhiana and Amritsar from Western Tibet *viâ* Kashmir, Ladakh, and Rampur on the Sutlej.[1] The breed is also found in Eastern Tibet, but there the value of *pashm* is unknown and thousands of maunds are wasted every year.[2]

The Indian shawl, the only article of importance made of real *pashm*, went out of fashion in Europe after the Franco-German war of 1870, and since that date the export trade has steadily declined almost to the vanishing point. The Indian aristocracy prize it chiefly in the form of *jâmawârs* and *jórás*,[3] but their custom is limited and must diminish with the gradual, but inevitable, adoption of Western habits of living by the upper classes in this country.

The chief centres of what still survives of the *pashmina*[4] industry are Ludhiana and Amritsar, the former with 200 looms which turn out *Rampur chadars*

---

[1] About 300 maunds of *pashm* pass through Kulu, and 150 through Rampur every year.

[2] Waddell, *Lhasa and its Mysteries*, 1905, pp. 476-7. Mr. Waddell suggests that *pashm* could be imported *viâ* the Chumbi and Nepalese passes.

The under-hair of certain breeds of dogs and ponies in Tibet is very like *pashm* and could, no doubt, be used for industrial purposes in Europe.

[3] A *jâmawâr* is a shawl, usually 3 by 1½ yards, covered with floral work. It is used in the United Provinces and Hyderabad (Deccan) for making *shirwânis* (a kind of dress worn by the upper classes). The term *jórá* literally means 'a pair' and may be applied to any pair of *pashm* shawls. It specially denotes, however, a pair of shawls with woven borders and ends.

[4] *Pashmína* is the Persian term for all *pashm* goods.

and *alwáns*,[1] and the latter with about 100 looms for plain and 25 for flowered shawls. The weavers are partly Kashmiris by descent, and partly Julahas, Mochis and others, who earn from Rs. 8 to 15 per month. The work is slow, as the loom has to be manipulated with very great care. The yarn is spun by women, who generally buy raw *pashm*, sort it and sell the finished article at from Rs. 15 to Rs. 30 a seer. Their profits are very low, never more than a couple of annas a day.

Shawls are also made for export to the Amritsar market in Nurpur (Kangra), which has 65 looms worked by Kashmiris.

The prices of genuine Amritsar shawls run high and vary with their quality. In addition, however, to a certain quantity of plain embroidered shawls, shawl-cloth[2] of the value of about Rs. 7,00,000 is annually imported from Germany, to be embroidered in the city and sold as inferior Amritsar "shawls."[3] The *Rampur chadars* of Ludhiana, measuring usually 4 yards by from 1½ to 2 yards, cost from Rs. 20 to Rs. 32. More expensive ones are made to order—but very rarely.

---

1 *Alwán* is a serge-like stuff in plain colours used for making articles of clothing. The *Rampur chadar* is made of finer material than the *alwan*, and is used as a wrapper by men in Bengal, to which province there is a large export.

A variety of the Rampur *chadar* is the one made with *pashm* warp and silk weft. It costs from Rs. 15 to Rs. 20 for a piece 3 by 1½ yards, and is exported to Bengal and Madras.

Both kinds are very suitable for dress-material for European ladies.

2 This "shawl" material is made of ordinary wool or mixed wool and cotton.

3 Cotton pieces imported from Manchester are also embroidered in Amritsar with cotton thread for 12 annas a pair, and are then called cotton shawls.

The embroiderer's or *toppagar's* art is closely connected with that of the shawl-weaver, whose manufactures he finally prepares for the market by working up the borders with home-spun *pashm* or imported woollen yarn. The craft is flourishing in Amritsar, where it gives employment to about 1,000 men, women and children, and there are a few hundred more scattered through the villages of the district. The charge for embroidering the borders of a pair of shawls, including the cost of the thread, is from Rs. 5 to Rs. 20.

Eighty Kashmiri embroiderers also ply the needle in Dera Nanak and a few in Ludhiana, but these are less thriving than their brethren of Amritsar.

The case of the genuine shawl industry is almost hopeless, but one may suggest as a palliative that the shawl-merchants of Amritsar and Ludhiana should combine, with the help of their municipal committees, to set up a kind of assay office where the various grades of shawls should be hall-marked. At present many rich people, especially foreign tourists, will not buy shawls because they are afraid of being cheated.

Goat-hair. There are about 4 million goats in the Punjab, a fair proportion of which are regularly clipped once a year, yielding half a seer of hair per head.[1] The hair sells at three to six seers a rupee and is used in most districts for coarse sacks, ropes and mattings. It is usually prepared for spinning by being beaten with a stick, but in some places it is scutched with a bowstring tied to a peg on the ground and alternately tightened and slackened by the operator. It is spun into thread with

[1] 15,866 maunds of goat's hair were exported from Karachi in 1909-10, chiefly to Marseilles, Hamburg and Liverpool.

the spindle or the *dherna*[1] and then woven on a small loom.

Goat-hair is used in Europe as a substitute for horse-hair. The longer hairs are employed in the manufacture of hair-cloth for upholstery, while the shorter ones are made into curled hair for stuffing purposes. It is also said to be used in the manufacture of cheap carpets.

Camel-hair.

The camel abounds in the Hissar, Ferozepur, Muzaffargarh, Multan, Dera Ghazi Khan and Mianwali districts in this order, the total number in the whole province being over 270,000. Like the goat, it is clipped once a year and yields about 2 seers of hair. The under-hair is of a light brown colour. It is chiefly used in the Punjab for ropes, and, mixed with goat's hair, for sacks. In Hissar, it is mixed with cotton and made into a cloth locally known as *bhakla*. In Europe, it is made into warm, soft and waterproof fabrics, which are used for many purposes[2]. It is often mixed with wool for special qualities of tweeds, etc.

The long hairs, used in Europe for rugs, carpets, beltings and artists' brushes, are entirely wasted in the Punjab. There is a possibility here of a useful minor industry.

Horse-hair, etc.

The hair of the mane and tail of the horse, and of the tail of the ox or the buffalo is of considerable commercial importance. It is employed in Europe

[1] For a description of the *dherna*, see *Monog. on Woollen Manufactures in the Punjab*, p. 5.

[2] J. de Cordenoy, *Les produits coloniaux d'orgine animale* (Paris 1903) p. 117.

The European supplies come chiefly from Russia and China. The present prices of Russian hair are from 7*d*. to 9*d*. per lb., according to quality, delivered at English ports, while the Chinese product realises from 10½*d*. to 12½*d*.

for the manufacture of sieves, strainers and various coarse fabrics, and is of equal importance to upholsterers, mattress-makers, and coach-builders.[1] Horse-hair is plaited into summer hats in China, and, amongst other things, is cut into short lengths for tooth, hat, shoe and clothes brushes of a rather inferior kind.[2]

Here there is very little organised trade in this material, which seems as a rule to be wasted.[3] It can be had in small quantities at six to ten annas a seer in Lahore, where it is used for making strainers and *chowries*, but the two or three dealers in Amritsar who use it for brushes, complain that they can never rely on getting a constant and adequate supply.

Bristles.

A few firms in Lahore and Delhi make brushes of bristles. The raw material is imported chiefly from the United Provinces, only a small quantity being locally available.

Pigs are bred in this country by the lowest and most ignorant orders of the people, and, as may be expected, very little care is bestowed on scientific details. Bristles should be pulled out from the live animal, as is done in the United Provinces, and not from the dead carcass. An authority states that it would pay to set up a piggery for the purpose of getting the bristles alone, as is done in China, which produces the highest grades of the material.

Squirrels' tails.

There does not appear to be any trade or industry connected with squirrels' tails in any district, save in Gujrat City, where painters make them into brushes for their own use. The tails are in demand in Europe.

---

[1] *Ibid*, p. 115.

[2] Consul-General Hosie, *Report on the Province of Ssuch'uan*, Blue Book, China, No. 5 (1904) p. 83.

[3] Only 16 maunds were exported from Karachi in 1909-10.

CHAPTER VI.

VEGETABLE FIBRES AND THEIR PRODUCTS.

The Punjab abounds with fibre-yielding plants which have not yet been sufficiently turned to account. In most districts the cultivators utilise the more plentiful and easily worked ones for baskets, ropes, mats, etc., for their own use, but there are very few people who make their living exclusively by this industry. Nor is there much systematic cultivation of the raw material, the total area for the whole province (exclusive of cotton) being only about 70,000 acres.

Sann or Indian Hemp.

While the United Provinces yearly raise about 150,000 acres of *sann* [1] of which they export 400,000 maunds,[2] the Punjab grows only 50,000 acres, chiefly in small plots of an eighth of an acre for home consumption.[3] Most of it is found in the submontane tract of the province, especially in the Hoshiarpur, Jullundur, Ludhiana and Sialkot districts, each of which has 5,000 acres or over.

The cultivation of this plant is considered less profitable than that of the other autumn crops, because of the tedious retting and defibring processes involved,

---

1 *Sann* (Corotolaria juncea) is called *sani* in Karnal.

2 *Agr. Journ. Ind.*, Oct. 1909, p. 347.

3 The crop is generally sown for the fibre, but in Hoshiarpur 10 per cent. of it is used, as a rule, for green manuring.

which are a serious consideration in a province where labour is comparatively dear. If simpler and cheaper methods are ever discovered, an important addition will be made to the list of the more valuable crops.

The chief points in favour of *sann* are the following [2] :—

1. Its cultivation is very cheap and easy. It needs neither hoeing nor manure, as it draws the nitrogen from the air.
2. It grows very rapidly, being ready for harvesting in 3 or 4 months.
3. It grows well on poor land.
4. It enriches the soil for other crops, and is therefore a good crop to grow in rotation with others.
5. It can be used as green manure.
6. It is profitable to grow, an acre yielding as much as Rs. 28 profit.[3]

The fibre can be put to the same uses as true hemp, *i.e.*, for ropes and canvas, the combings and sweepings going to the paper-mills. In the Punjab it is usually made into ropes, twine, and sackcloth,[4] and in the hills also into shoes.[5] In Sind and some other parts of India its most important use by far is for the

[1] For a brief account of the indigenous process, see Duthie and Fuller, *Field and Garden Crops of the N.-W. P. and Oudh*. 1882 pp. 83-84.

[2] *Indian Agriculturist*, Dec. 1st, 1909, p. 379; see also the *Ann. Rep. Lyallpur Agric. Stn.*, 1909-10, p. 12.

[3] In the Pabna district, the profit comes to Rs. 33, *Agr. Ledger*, 1908-09, No. 7, p. 135.

[4] Locally known as *tat-patti.*

[5] *Kangra Dist. Gazetteer*, Vol. II., 1899, pp. 84-85 and 98.

cordage of fishing-nets, while in Madras it is woven into fabrics used for buckets, curtains, cots, etc.[1]

The Hoshiarpur staple, though not equal to that of Jubbulpore,[2] is still the best in the Punjab. It costs Rs. 6 per maund in Hoshiarpur, where it is collected for export to the Amritsar market, both raw and as twine or sackcloth.

Gharota, in the Gurdaspur district, is another well-known centre of the industry, and is said to send out every year Rs. 2,000 worth of twine, and Rs. 1,000 worth of an inferior grade of sackcloth, made of *sann* brought from the Nurpur Tahsil of the Kangra district. Shahpur Kandi, also in the Gurdaspur district, obtains the raw material from the surrounding villages, and yearly exports Rs. 5,000 worth of twine, in addition to a quantity of the fibre.

The Punjab fibre industry is at present devoid of method or organisation. The fibre is retted in muddy water which discolours it, and is then sent out without proper scutching. A Rawalpindi firm complains that out of one maund of Hoshiarpur *sann* they get only 20 seers of clean fibre, while the other 20 seers, on which they pay full freight and other charges, consists of dirt and waste material. The same firm prefers to import sackcloth from Partabgarh and Mirzapore in the United Provinces, because the Hoshiarpur article is too uneven in quality. Hoshiarpur twine is

---

[1] *Madras Agr. Dept. Bulletin*, No. 59, on *Sann*, p. 11. The stalks after being divested of the fibre can be used as fuel and for thatching roofs, where they will last 4 years. The seed is given to buffaloes and is also used for making poultices. The flowers are cooked in curry.

[2] *Ibid*, p. 12. Only Jubbulpore *Sann* can pass the standard test of 4 tons for a 4-inch rope.

disliked, in spite of the excellent material of which it is made, because of the large amount of sand put into it. In the Ludhiana bazaars, for example, it sells at Rs. 16 per maund, whereas the locally made article, which is purer, fetches Rs. 19.

There appears to be an opening for a fibre factory run on modern business lines at Hoshiarpur,[1] and probably also at Shahpur Kandi,[2] near which places the raw material is abundant, and would be still more so if a regular demand arose.

The factory should, in the first instance, grade the raw material properly and adopt suitable methods of retting and scutching. The next step would be to prepare yarn,[3] strands, and twine, and finally canvas, sack-cloth, etc., of a uniform quality. As the raw fibre costs Rs. 6 per maund and the twine sells for at least Rs. 16, there is an ample margin of profit.

The machinery required for such a factory is very simple. The heckling tool consists only of a few iron spikes, arranged on a table like the teeth of a comb, through which the *sann* is dragged by the hand. The yarn is spun on a hand-driven wheel, with hooks attached to its circumference, which could be made by any village carpenter.

The only factory of the kind in the Punjab is the ropery set up by a local contractor at Rawalpindi in

---

[1] Shortly to be connected with Jullundur by rail.

[2] Shahpur Kandi is connected with Pathankot by eight miles of unmetalled but good road, which is troublesome only during the rains. Means of transport are abundant. Gharota, which is ten miles from Pathankot to the south, does not appear to be suitable.

[3] A single firm in Rawalpindi expressed willingness to buy 1,000 maunds of properly-made Hoshiarpur *sann* yarn every year, if available.

1905.[1] So far only ropes and cords are being made but it is intended to take up the manufacture of sack-cloth as soon as suitable local workmen are available. The rope-makers, originally imported from Calcutta, have now been replaced by Hindustanis, who are found more satisfactory.

An ample market for the better qualities of *sann* could easily be created in Europe if a good uniform supply were assured.[2] As now shipped, it fetches from £20 to £30 a ton, but if the fibres were in good unentangled lengths, they would command double this amount.[3]

The local Department of Agriculture is devoting serious attention to *sann*, which is much more deserving of encouragement than jute, the success of which is doubtful in the Punjab. In addition to improving the local varieties, it would be well if research were directed towards discovering better methods of extracting the fibre. This, more than anything else, is the great problem of the industry.

Sankukra or patsan[4] (*Hibiscus cannabinus*) yields a glossy fibre, which, though not so strong as *sann*, is almost as good as jute, for which it is sometimes substituted. It occurs in the same area as *sann*, being usually grown as a hedge-plant round sugarcane, maize, and cotton, but never as a separate crop. *Sankukra.*

The fibre is extracted by retting followed by beating with a stick, and is usually twisted into ropes,

---

[1] It has been worked by steam power since 1907.

[2] See Watt, *Comm. Prod. Ind.*, pp. 435 *et seq.*

[3] *Tropical Agriculturist*, March 1905, p. 567.

[4] Called *san* in Karnal.

though it can also be made into a coarse sack-cloth, and, in Bengal, is said to be used in paper-making and for fishing-nets. For this last purpose, however, it hardly appears suitable, as it will not long resist water.[1]

Sankukra costs about Rs. 5 per maund in Hoshiarpur where, however, only a limited quantity can be had. The cultivation might be largely extended with profit.[2] Properly treated, "Bimlipatam jute," as it is called, is likely to fetch a price equal to that of jute of medium quality in the London market, *i.e.*, from £11 to £12 a ton.

Munj. *Munj* (*Saccharum arundinaceum, var. ciliare*) is, with its varieties, the commonest and best known of the Punjab fibres. It is of rapid growth, and abounds in sandy soils in the neighbourhood of lakes and rivers, as for example, in the Gurdaspur and Hoshiarpur districts. It has come into prominence in the Chenab Colony with the canals, and is found on the banks of watercourses.

Munj is popular with the cultivator, as it is easily collected, and, unlike *sann*, needs no retting. It is put away in bundles after cutting until the slack season comes round, when the spathes are beaten with a wooden mallet to extract the fibre. About five seers is the daily outturn of an ordinary labourer.

The fibre is twisted into a strong and elastic rope which withstands moisture wonderfully well. *Munj* matting, largely manufactured at Delhi and elsewhere,

---

[1] The leaves are eaten as a vegetable and the seeds given to cattle in Poona. The latter have also been exported to England as an oil-seed.

[2] *Agr. Journ. Ind.*, October 1909, p. 356.

is said to be proof against the white ant, but is uncomfortable for the feet.[1]

Prepared *munj* fibre costs from Rs. 1-4 to 2-8 per maund in Hoshiarpur, and string from Rs. 5 to 13 per maund, according to its fineness.[2]

Bhabar (*Ischæmum angustifolium*) is a grass common in many parts of the Sewalik tract and the outer Himalayas at 2,300 to 4,000 feet, up to the Indus.[3] It is largely used for rope, string and matting, and for the construction of rope-bridges. *Bhabar ban* or string sells in Panipat and Rewari at Rs. 3 to Rs. 4 per maund. *Bhabar.*

Bagar (*Eriophorum comosum*) is a coarse, sedge-like herb often found associated with the above, with which it is generally confused. It flourishes in the Sewalik tract and the Salt Range. *Bagar.*

Its fibre is less esteemed than that of the other, for which it is often substituted.

The *dib* (*Typha spp.*) is common in water-logged lands in the plains, especially near hill torrents, and in the alluvial lands of the Indus. Its leaves are used for matting, and both leaves and culms are also made *Dib* or Bulrush.

---

[1] The coarse leaves at the base of the reed are used for thatching, while the *sarkanda*, or stem proper, is made into chicks, stools, and *hukka* tubes. The smooth thinner part of the stem (*tili*) is worked into fine chicks, baskets and sieves. The tapering flower-stalk (*sirki*) serves for covering hay-stacks and roofs.

[2] 10,000 maunds of cleaned *munj* fibre is reported to be available annually at Garh Muktesar station (Meerut). A few thousand maunds could be bought in the Moradabad district also, at Rs. 3 per maund.

[3] 4,000 maunds, at about 13 annas a maund, are reported to be available annually at Jawalapur Station (Saharanpur).

into sieves, rope and thatch.[1] It is about the best thatch grass available.

Panni Grass.

Panni (Vetiveria zizanioides)[2] is a grass that thrives in the Delhi Division, especially in Hissar[3] and Karnal, though it occurs also in other districts of the Punjab. It yields a good fibre and is also used for thatching, but it is best known for its root, called *khas,* of which "tatties"[4] are made. It has been suggested as a paper material.[5]

Bichua or Himalayan nettle.

The Himalayan nettle (*Girardinia heterophylla*) is found in many places in the hill districts and states from 2,500 to 7,000 feet. Its fibre is obtained by retting, and is worked up by hand into strands which are used for ropes, fishing nets and shoes. In Nepal and Sikkim it is woven into an exceptionally strong cloth called *bangra*. The Imperial Institute of London has reported on samples sent for trial that the product is of excellent quality and likely to take a high place among the textile fibres if available on a commercial scale. A London fibre-broker valued it at £20 per ton,

---

[1] The pollen is baked and eaten on the Indus, where it is an important article of food. The young shoots and tender roots are also eaten. The down of the ripe fruit is mixed with mortar as a binding material.

[2] Watt, *Comm. Prod. Ind.*, p. 1106. Coldstream, *Grasses of the Southern Punjab*, No. 18 (under *Andropogon muricatus*).

[3] In the Hissar district *Panni* grass chiefly grows in the *nali* villages of the Sirsa and Fatehabad tahsils. At a rough guess the yearly produce is from 20,000 to 30,000 maunds. It is not sold at all; anybody requiring it can have it cut before October, when the grass is burned to prepare the land for the autumn sowings. The wages for cutting it are about one rupee for ten maunds.

[4] Aromatic scented mats hung in doorways, and kept wet to cool the atmosphere by evaporation.

[5] Liotard, *Materials in India suitable for Paper*, 1880, p. 27.

but the value would, of course, largely depend on the state of preparation.[1]

Date-leaves are well adapted for plaiting into mats, though too tough to be split up into individual fibres. Date-leaf matting fetches about Rs. 6 per 100 square feet. In many places, especially the large cities, Delhi, Lahore, Amritsar and Sialkot, the leaves are also made into fans, baskets, well-ropes and twine, as well as mats. **Date-leaves.**

The close vascular network of the inside of the well-known *ghia-turai*,[2] (*Luffa ægyptiaca*) is a cheap, sanitary and effective substitute for the ordinary sponge, and is much used in Europe as a flesh-brush. It can also be worked up into useful and ornamental articles, such as hats and baskets, while the people of Korea sew it into their socks to keep their feet cool in summer. Japan yearly exports over a million loofahs, chiefly to London, Havre, Hamburg, San Francisco and New York.[3] **Loofah.**

The *turai* creeper is plentiful everywhere on the Punjab plains and is easily grown as a hedge plant or otherwise.[4] After the fruit has been dried on the tree, the sponge should be carefully cleansed of the incrusting material and also relieved of the seeds. An export trade in these, at all events, could easily be started.[5]

---

[1] For further information see *Sel. Rep. from the Scient. and Tech. Dept. of the Imp. Inst., I. Fibres* (cd. 4588) p. 55.

[2] Also known as the "towel gourd" and "sponge cucumber" in West Africa and the West Indies.

[3] Dodge, *Useful Fibre Plants of the World*, 1897, p. 230.

[4] Stewart, *Punjab Plants*, p. 98.

[5] For further information on loofahs, see Appendix II.

Wheat and Barley straw.

Wheat and barley straw is used to a small extent in Lahore, Gujrat, Panipat and a few other places for plaiting and basket work.[1] In Lahore, for example, over a hundred women are engaged in their homes in the preparation of plaits of ordinary straw. These are sold to the eight or ten men in "Mohammad Shafi's Sarai," who sew them up into caps for wearing under the turban, and occasionally into hats of European pattern. The former are often very prettily designed, and not only supply a large local demand, but are exported to out-stations as far as Peshawar. The hats are cheap and well made, but lack finish and shape. European Schools, such as the Lawrence Military Asylum at Sanawar, are the chief consumers.

The work could, no doubt, be adapted to a great many other useful purposes, such as the manufacture of ladies' work-boxes, waste-paper baskets, etc. The great possibilities of the industry are illustrated by its development in Central Europe and Japan.

Straw-plaiting gives employment to between 20,000 and 30,000 persons in Saxony and Bohemia, chiefly females, who all work in their homes. The material used is mainly wheat straw and bast, or, more properly speaking, chips or wood-shavings. These are extremely thin strips, ½ to ¼ inch wide, chiefly prepared from Russian aspen wood.

Great importance is attached to the production of suitable straw. The plaiter, who gets it almost in its natural state, draws each straw between a piece of leather, about the size of a boot-heel, and a curved knife, which flatten as well as straighten it. He

---

[1] For an account of the Hazara industry, see *Hazara District Gazetteer*, 1907, p. 79.

then splits it into several strips by passing it between the piece of leather and a toothed steel plate. The material is either used in its natural colour, or is bleached in sulphur fumes by the workmen themselves, as desired. Dyed straw, which requires special skill to prepare, is furnished by the dealers.

The plaiting itself is very simple, the only tools used being the workmen's deft fingers. The further processes of manufacture, such as washing and polishing the plaits, removing defects, sewing them together into straw hats, etc., are carried out by the manufacturers of straw hats and similar goods.

Itinerant buyers go round the cottages at fixed seasons, and buy up plaits for sale to the export merchants, who despatch them chiefly to the manufacturers in England and the United States. The industry has to keep in the closest touch with changing fashions, which are watched by the export merchants. These procure their patterns every year from Paris and other centres, and leave their orders with the middlemen, who in their turn communicate with the cottagers.

Straw-plaiting was introduced into Saxony from the Italian provinces of the Austrian Empire through the medium of two schools set up to teach it. Its progress affords a good example of the influence of properly conducted trade schools on industries.[1]

---

[1] For information on the industry, see the *Journ. of the Society of Arts*, October 8th, 1897, pp. 1133 *et seq.* For an account of the Tuscan straw-plaiting industry, and methods of bleaching straw, see *ibid.* July 2nd, 1897, p. 736, and Spon, *Workshop Receipts*, Vol. I. Art. *Bleaching*, p. 143. In Tuscany a kind of straw, *triticum æstivum*, which will only grow in certain localities, is specially raised for this purpose. The straw must have a certain length between the knots, must possess a clear golden colour, and not be too brittle.

No less than 250,000 persons, chiefly, women and children, are engaged in Japan in the manufacture of plaits and other articles from straw and the shavings of the wood of *abies sachalinensis* and various species of poplar. Most of these are exported.[1]

The Salvation Army and other missionary bodies in touch with London or New York might take up this industry with advantage. Not only is it possible for the province to share in the great world-trade in plaits, but also to go a step further, and develop, under proper instruction, the manufacture of straw hats, baskets and other articles for the European market.

The Forest Research Institute at Dehra Dun might investigate the question of an Indian substitute for the woods used in Europe and Japan.[2]

Rice straw. There is no industry worth mentioning connected with rice straw. In its natural state it serves occasionally as a roofing material, but its chief use is for spreading on the floor, and as fodder for cattle in time of famine. In Japan, the cultivators largely employ it not only for coarse matting, but also for ropes, rice-bags and sandals. The yearly export from Japan of articles of rice straw is valued at no less than 15 lacs of rupees.[3]

Alsi or flax. *Alsi* or linseed is grown in this province for its valuable oil-seed, and not on account of the fibre, which in the local variety is not usable. The experiments made by the Punjab Agricultural Department at Lyallpur with Russian flax, have, it is believed,

[1] A brief account of the Japanese industry will be found on p. 53 of Shimooka, *Agriculture in Japan* (Tokyo, 1910), page 79.

[2] Mr. A. J. Gibson, I.F.S., suggests *Populus ciliata*, *Abies Webbiana* and *Pindrow*, and possibly *Picca Morinda*.

[3] Shimooka, *op. cit.* p. 80, see also p. 87 *infra*.

produced good fibre material. The chief difficulty, however, is that of retting, which is under investigation. It is practically certain that the fibre-producing varieties would grow all over the province.

In 1861 a company was started to encourage flax cultivation in the Sialkot district. For a time it had good prospects of success, as the fibre locally grown from imported seed was pronounced equal to the best Irish. In spite of a substantial Government subsidy, however, the enterprise came to grief, because of the difficulty of procuring seed from Europe in good condition, and the apathy of the cultivators, who would not persevere in improved methods.[1]

There are few districts in the Punjab where the *ak* plant (*Calotropis gigantea*) is not indigenous. It thrives on barren soils, and covers vast tracts that will not bear any other kind of vegetation. The plant yields two species of fibre: the fibre of the stem and the floss of the pod. *Ak* fibre.

The former is finer than flax, of which it has many of the qualities, and its strength, gloss and softness, render it suitable for many purposes.[2] When nitrated it can hardly be distinguished from silk, and would then seem to be so valuable, that it could well afford to bear even an expensive process of extraction.[3]

The great difficulties in the way of the commercial utilisation of this material are: (1) the small proportion of its weight (about 2 per cent.) to that of the stems; (2) the shortness of its staple; and (3) the

[1] *Sialkot District Gazetteer* 1894-95, pp. 132-133.

[2] The bast fibre is actually used by fishermen for making fishing-lines and nets. It makes a very strong and durable string.

[3] See Crosse and Bevan, *Report on Indian Fibres*, 1887, pp. 25-27. For further information, see *Sel. Rep. from the Scient. and Tech. Dept. of the Imp. Inst. I. Fibres*, pp. 117-118.

present impossibility of separating it cheaply and rapidly. The discovery of a suitable chemical method of extracting the fibre would be a great boon to the agriculturist, who would then be able to utilise what is now a pest, as a regular crop for poor soils.[1]

The floss of the *ak* is soft and very white, with a fine silky gloss. Though considered too light for ordinary textile purposes, it enters largely into the manufacture of the so-called "mercerised silk,"[2] which is now extensively used by the weavers everywhere in the province,[3] and is also valued as a stuffing for quilts and pillows. It is further stated to be used for adulterating cotton by some cotton mills.

About 300 maunds of dried floss are exported annually from Rewari to Bombay, and a certain amount has also been reported to go from Bhiwani

---

[1] The milky juice of the stems is much used by the tanners of goat-skins in the Punjab. It can also be made into a substance with many of the properties of gutta-percha. The root is useful as a medicine. Further, the plant is said to be a powerful agent in the reclamation of *kallar* land.

[2] 47,578 lbs. of "mercerised silk," valued at Rs. 52,514, were imported into Karachi in 1909-10. The import into Bombay was about 1,950,000 lbs., valued at about 30 lacs, in the calendar year 1909, and about 1,410,000 lbs., valued at about 21 lacs, in the first seven months of 1910. It is not known what it is all made of, but average samples picked up by the writer in the bazaar of Multan (where it is much used by hand-weavers under the name of *Golâ*), were examined microscopically and chemically by the Reporter on Economic Products, with the following result:—

1. White (Rs. 12-8 per seer) consisted almost entirely of silk mixed with a little vegetable fibre, probably hemp.

2. Green (Rs. 12-8 per seer) was mainly composed of the floss of *Calotropis gigantea*, mixed with some hemp fibre.

3. Crimson (Rs. 4 per seer) was mostly made of the floss of *Calotropis gigantea*, with an admixture of hemp fibre.

[3] The Director of Commercial Intelligence, Calcutta, has the address of a German company which claims to have invented a process for spinning the floss into yarn, and is ready to negotiate with cotton mills, etc., desiring to purchase licenses to work the process in India.

and other places. It sells at Rs. 6 per maund in Rewari, but would realise as much as Rs. 20 to 25 in London, if an even and regular supply were assured.[1]

The Javanese plant is said to yield much better fibre and floss than ours. The *ak* of the Punjab has so far been held to be beneath serious notice, but there seems to be no reason why it should not be developed into a valuable fibre-plant by selection, hybridisation, and the other methods that succeed so well with plants held in higher esteem.

Cryptostegia grandiflora (*chharrá chábúk*) is an extensive climber, growing freely everywhere in the Punjab. In Lahore it flourishes on poor soil, while in Delhi it is found in rank profusion in the swampy *belás* by the river, and also on the stony ridge. It is almost a pest in Karnal. Cryptostegia grandiflora.

The stems, after steeping in water for three days, easily yield a fine, white, and strong fibre, from 16 inches to 20 inches (ultimately 1·2 inches) long, average samples of which were valued in London at £80 a ton. If prepared for export, the long and short filaments should be kept separate and as good a length preserved as possible.

The floss of the pods produces a "cotton" said to be worth 4*d*. a pound in London.[2]

---

[1] *Bullet. Imp. Inst.* (1903), Vol. I. p. 172.

[2] The milky juice of the plant yields from 50 to 80 per cent. of an elastic rubber of very fair quality, that has recently excited some interest. The Punjab Agricultural Chemist reports that cultivation for rubber alone is likely to be profitable, and that with best Para rubber at Rs. 10 per lb. (April 1910) the product of the Karnal creeper is likely to realise at least Rs. 6 per lb. A company is being floated in Karnal for making the rubber, and the Agricultural, Forest and Canal Departments propose to experiment on a small scale in suitable localities. A bullock-driven cane-crusher is the only machine required at the start. For further information see *Bullet. Imp. Inst.* (1907), Vol. V. p. 371, Watt, *Dict. Econ. Prod.*, Vol. II. p. 625, and the printed Report of the Punjab Agricultural Dept. on the subject.

Paper mulberry.

The paper-mulberry (*Broussonetia papyrifera*)[1] is a small tree, introduced into India from the Far East, which affords a singular instance of a plant able to thrive in tropical as well as temperate climes. In Japan it is cultivated on hill-sides and river banks, which are unsuitable for any other kind of cultivation. In Saharanpur it is now found as a weed, and it is also abundant near the water in the public gardens of Lahore. It yields a long, very strong and easily-extracted fibre, which holds the chief position among the materials used by the Japanese paper-maker, who makes it into a strong though somewhat coarse-grained paper.

The shrub produces suckers in abundance, coppices well, and grows fast. It is worth trying in the Hoshiarpur and Gurdaspur districts, especially in localities where sericulture is being attempted. Its leaves are excellent food for the silk-worm, while it would pay to use the annual prunings of the twigs for the extraction of the fibre.

Semul cotton.

The inner bark of the *semul* tree (*Bombax malabaricum*), which is common in the lower hills of Kangra and Hoshiarpur, yields a good fibre suitable for cordage and also for making paint and whitewash brushes and dusters.[2]

---

[1] Watt, *Comml. Prod. Ind.*, p. 186; Shimooka, *Agriculture in Japan*, p. 54; Rein, *Industries of Japan* (1889) pp. 393 *et seq.*; *Sel. Rep. from the Scient. and Tech. Dept. of the Imp. Inst. I. Fibres (cd.* 4588*)* pp. 126-128.

[2] The latter use is mentioned by a writer in the *Tropical Agriculturist* of May 15th, 1905, who refers to the bark of the *Bombax ceiba* (=*B. malabaricum, Flor. Br. Ind.*, I, 349).

The tree also yields a gum, which is used in medicine as an astringent, and its flower-buds are eaten as a pot herb. The roots and leaves are also used for food.

The so-called *semul* cotton is obtained from the pods. It is too short and soft to be spun, and too smooth to be felted: hence it could only be used to mix with other fibres to give them a silky gloss. It is useful, however, for stuffing pillows, though said to become lumpy after a time.[1] A small amount is imported into Simla in the summer for this purpose from the Arki, Ghana and Dhami States, but in Kangra it is practically unused.

Among other useful fibres may be mentioned those of the agave[2] and the plantain[3] tree, which are not, however, found in sufficient quantities in this province to detain us. *Marsdenia Roylei*,[4] a climber found in the outer hills and in the Salt Range, yields a material from which excellent fishing nets and strong ropes are manufactured, while the barks of several trees, *e.g.*, birch (*Betula utilis*)[5] and the various species of *Daphne* and *Grewia*, are used in the hills for ropes, paper-making, and similar purposes.[6] The fibre of the roots of the *seen* grass (*Elionorus hirsutus*) is made into weavers' sizing brushes in Bikaner.[7]

---

[1] *Semul*-cotton deserves a trial by the local furniture-makers for upholstering purposes.

[2] See Art. *Agave* in Watt, *Comml. Prod. Ind.*, p. 30. *Agave americana* and its varieties have been largely introduced into the Central Provinces as hedge plants or forest boundary lines, and pay well. They grow on poor soil and are easy to cultivate.

[3] *Ibid.* p. 786, Art. *Musa.*

[4] Stewart, *Punjab Plants*, p. 145.

[5] Watt, *Comml. Prod. Ind.*, p. 131. Found abundantly in the Punjab Himalayas, from 7,000 feet up to highest limit of vegetation. (Stewart, *op. cit.*, p. 198).

[6] See Gee, *Monog. on the Fibrous Manufactures of the Punjab*, 1891.

[7] Known as *sewan* or *shewan* in Sirsa and Bikaner. It abounds in the sandy soil of the Bágar tract of the Hissar district and in the Bikaner State. Its seed, mixed with bajra, is much eaten by the people of Bikaner. (Coldstream, *Grasses of the Southern Punjab*, No. 13; Tod's *Rajasthan*, II. 286.)

Paper. The indigenous paper industry of the Punjab, brought from China by the Moslems a thousand years ago, is on its death-bed, and cannot be saved. In the suburbs of Sialkot, where it was first set up on the bank of the *Aik,* and where eight lacs-worth of paper was made annually in the days of the Moguls, there are now only 28 miserable "factories" with a yearly outturn of barely twenty thousand rupees. A few artisans in Delhi, and five factories at Jalalpur Pirwala in Multan, complete the tale of the industry as it now exists outside the jails.[1]

Amongst the causes that have contributed to its downfall, the most important are the foundation of modern mills in the United Provinces and Bengal, and the flooding of the market with cheap wood-pulp paper from Europe. The *coup de grâce,* however, was dealt to the industry by the Jail Department which first took up the manufacture of country paper in 1870, and has since monopolised the patronage of Government, by far the largest consumer.

The annual imports of paper and pasteboard into the province, amount to about 82,000 maunds, valued at a little short of ten lacs of rupees, of which over 50 per cent. is supplied by the Lucknow and Bengal Mills.

---

[1] For an account of the indigenous paper industry, which now has little more than a historical interest, see Emerson, *Monog. on Paper-making in the Punjab,* 1907-08, pp. 3-22. Country paper is made in some quantity at Malerkotla for export to various places in the province.

It is noteworthy that in Japan the manufacture of paper is chiefly carried on by the farmers who raise the raw material. The 170,000 persons engaged in the industry in 1907 produced 7½ crores worth of paper. (Shimooka, *Agriculture in Japan,* 1910, p. 81.)

There are eight paper-mills altogether in India,[1] with a total capital of 53 lacs. Their output rose from Rs. 63·11 lacs in 1906 to Rs. 72·9 lacs in 1907, the largest on record.[2] The fact that some of them are not very flourishing is ascribed to the following causes[3] :—

1. The shortage of raw material, such as hemp, rags, etc., at sufficiently cheap rates.

This is due to two reasons : (*a*) want of enterprise in some places in organising an industry in fibre-growing, (*b*) heavy transit freights. A distance of a few hundred miles, usually a matter of small importance, is prohibitive in the supply of paper-fibre. The cost of land near the places where paper-mills are set up, precludes the special cultivation of the raw material.

2. The chemicals and other materials used by the mills have to be imported, and are a heavy item of expense. These include caustic soda, bleaching powder, gelatin, china clay, alum, and colophony. The last two are locally available, but their quality has been too uncertain for up-to-date factories.

3. Low quality of the unskilled labour. The paper-mills do not seem to have been more successful with the educated apprentice either.

4. The heavy coal-bill of such of the mills as are outside Bengal.

---

[1] The Punjab has none, but Bengal and the Bombay Presidency have three each. There is one at Lucknow, and another at Gwalior (Morar). The last is now closed down.

[2] *Statistics of British India for 1907-08*, Pt. I. (Industrial) p. 55.

[3] See *Outlook of the Paper Industry in India*, by J. Imms of the Upper India Couper Paper Mills, Lucknow, in the *Modern Review*, April 1908.

The ideal material must be cheap, abundant and easily accessible. An Indian mill, with an outturn of 137,000 maunds of paper, for example, is known to use about 220,000 maunds yearly of *bhabar* grass,[1] (at a cost of Re. 1-3 a maund) and, in addition, 23,000 maunds of imported wood-pulp, and even so is not very flourishing.

Further, the material should, like old *munj* and hemp twine, be fit for almost immediate use after an easy separation of the fibres and reduction to pulp. Paper-making cannot bear the cost of separation and preparation from the raw state, of even a very cheap fibre like jute. The most important paper fibres locally available are *bhabar* and *munj*, which are largely used by the Punjab jails, as well as by steam mills in other parts of India. Their use is limited only by the extent to which they can be supplied at a remunerative price. Hemp in the form of old gunny-bags, ropes, etc., is also in much demand. Other promising materials are *panni* grass and the fibres of *Calotropis gigantea* and *Broussonetia papyrifera.*[2]

Rice straw, if available in sufficient quantities, would be very suitable, as its feeding value is small,[3] while the stems and leaves of the maize plant are actually

---

[1] *Ischæmum angustifolium*, p. 73 *supra*.

[2] For all these fibres, see pp. 72-82 *supra*.

[3] "Some few experiments with rice straw proved that this raw material could be easily converted into paper-pulp. The pulp was fairly tough, bleached to a good colour, and would work up into good paper. If only partially boiled, the pulp proved to be hard and tenacious, very suitable for the manufacture of a tough cardboard for box-making purposes."—Sindall, *Report on the Manufacture of Paper and Paper-pulp in Burma*, 1906, p. 26.

used in America for the manufacture of paper said to be suitable for bank-notes.[1]

Megass, or the refuse of sugar-cane, is a very promising material which is, however, still in the experimental stage. It is said to have been made into excellent printing and writing paper in Maine (U.S.A.), while in 1908, it was reported that a fine wrapping paper had been produced on a commercial scale in Trinidad with 30 per cent. megass, 20 per cent. bamboo, and 50 per cent. Para grass.

The difficulty of megass is that it contains only a small amount of cellulose, and a large proportion of lignin, to remove which a large quantity of soda

---

[1] Watt, *Comml. Prod. Ind.*, p. 1138. The disadvantage of rice straw or maize leaves is that they will not bear heavy freight charges. The subjoined table gives average acreages in some districts within a hundred-mile radius of Jagadhri or Sialkot. The latter place, it may be noted, could obtain 500 electric H.P. from Jammu all the year round, except in January and February.

Districts.	*Rice.*	*Maize.*	*Districts.*	*Rice.*	*Maize.*
Ambala	62,875	81,264	Sialkot	51,801	64,570
Karnal	66,903	38,032	Gurdaspur	52,877	65,596
Saharanpur	120,372	79,810	Gujranwala	37,734	30,808
Muzaffarnagar	49,343	49,961	Amritsar	35,242	54,558
Bijnor	173,978	—	Lahore	34,651	65,548
Meerut	20,000	121,847			

The average outturn of rice straw or maize leaves may be taken to be 25 maunds per acre, but the supply available would depend on local agricultural conditions. There is no trade in maize leaves, which, it appears, are always consumed locally as fodder. As to rice straw, 40,000 maunds are stated to be available annually at Karnal station and 6,000 at Garh Muktesar station (Meerut) at 4 annas a maund, besides several thousand maunds in the Moradabad district at 5½ annas. 30,000 maunds at 8 annas is reported at Begowala Ghartal station (Sialkot), and the same quantity at Kathunangal station (Amritsar) at 4 annas. The material is said to be abundant at Gohlwar Varpal station (Amritsar) at 5½ annas.

is required.[1] This is likely to make the cost of manufacture prohibitive, except in places which possess, in combination, a cheap and plentiful supply of power, and chemicals, and water, as may be the fortune of Jagadhri some day.[2] For the present, India might safely wait and see what the very enterprising Javanese sugar companies do in the matter.[3]

Mention may finally be made of cotton stalks, of sugar-cane leaves,[4] of the straw of the *alsi*, and of the short cotton fibres that adhere to delinted cotton-seed, all of which, like megass, await the final judgment of practical experts.[5]

Wood-pulp. Wood-pulp, which enters largely into all the cheaper grades of paper now used, has a future before it in Northern India. Heavy freight rates will stand in the way of its transport to the sea-board for export, but the vast and ever-growing local demand for cheap paper is sufficient for all the wood-pulp ever likely to be produced from the Himalayan forests.

There are two main kinds of wood-pulp, mechanical and chemical, of which the latter is subdivided into soda-pulp and sulphite-pulp. Mechanical pulp is made by grinding billets of suitable wood on a rotating stone, large quantities of water being used in the process. It has very little felting power, and is

1 Prinsen Geerling, *Cane-sugar and its Manufacture*, 1909, p. 128, *West India Committee Circular*, Vol. XXXIII. 1908, pp. 73-74.

2 See chapter X *infra*.

3 It will be practicable to use megass for paper only where some cheaper fuel can be found to take its place. It is very doubtful if this will ever be the case in the Punjab.

4 Sugar-cane leaves (*patti*) do not seem to have been seriously tried. Large quantities are available at a low rate in the cane-growing districts.

5 See *Indian Trade Journal*, Sept. 8, 1910, p. 250.

suitable only for admixture, to the extent of 30 per cent. for inferior papers. Sulphite pulp may be left out of account for the present, as it needs a far more expensive plant than soda-pulp.[1]

The caustic soda process consists in chopping up the wood, boiling in a 77 per cent. solution of caustic soda for 10 to 15 hours, washing and beating for 6 to 8 hours, screening the pulp, and, after extracting the water, rolling it into sheets. The amount of caustic soda (recovery of soda included) may be from 400 to 600 lbs. per ton of raw material.

Two species, very suitable for pulp-making, *viz.*, spruce (*Picea Morinda*), and silver fir (*Abies Pindrow*),[2] are available in vast quantities in the valleys of the five Punjab rivers and in the Jaunsar Forest Division of the United Provinces. The problem, however, is whether the wood could be delivered at 2½ annas per cubic foot, which is perhaps the most a pulp factory could afford to pay.

---

[1] Galena or sulphide of lead occurs around Chaba, on the Sutlej, near the power-station of the Simla Hydro-Electric Works. It has been suggested that, if found in sufficient quantities it should be converted into sulphate of lime by means of the limestone abundant in the neighbourhood, and used for the manufacture of sulphite pulp from the spruce and silver fir that could be floated down the Sutlej. It is believed, however, that these woods could not be landed cheaply enough at Chaba for a wood-pulp factory to pay.

Calcium sulphite liquors for wood-pulp could, perhaps, be made more satisfactorily with lime-water and sulphur dioxide generated from the sodium sulphate that largely enters into the composition of *reh* soils in several parts of the Punjab. (See under Sodium Sulphate in Ch. X.). The Agricultural Chemist might inquire into this matter, when he takes up the study of *reh* soils.

[2] Of the two, spruce makes the best pulp, and is the easier to float. Bamboo is quite out of the question in the Punjab, as there is not enough of it.

Among suitable sites might be mentioned Jagadhri which has also been suggested for pencil, match,[1] and caustic soda[2] manufacture.

Celluloid.

Celluloid is a cheap substitute for ivory and bone, and is used for numerous purposes, of which the best known is the manufacture of combs, toys and umbrella handles. Its base consists of cellulose in its various forms, such as wood-pulp, paper and rice straw. These are first treated with nitric and sulphuric acids, then cleansed of all traces of either, and finally dissolved in acetone, or wood-naphtha, or a mixture of spirit and camphor. The resulting mass, called pyroxylin or nitro-cellulose, is thoroughly kneaded, and then moulded into the required shapes. The addition of a little castor-oil makes it flexible, while shellac or copal makes it hard. Manganese or zinc chloride reduces its combustibility.

Camphor is important to the manufacture, as it is not only a good solvent itself, but increases the action of the other solvents. It is not a heavy item of expense, and could be imported, as in Germany, where enormous quantities of celluloid goods are made.

It is hoped that the industry may be started some day in conjunction with the manufacture of wood-pulp.[3]

---

[1] *See* Chapter XV. [2] *See* Chapter X.

[3] For an account of the processes, see Thorpe, *Dict. Appl. Chem.*, Vol. I, Art. *Celluloid*, and Vol. III, Art. *Photography*, p. 206.

CHAPTER VII.

DYEING AND CALICO PRINTING.

The dyer's craft boasts of great antiquity in this country, and was flourishing till about forty years ago, when synthetic colours first began to be imported. These have steadily gained in popularity on account of their cheapness and handiness, and have ended by driving the indigenous dye-stuffs almost entirely out of the Indian market.[1]

The local dyeing industry is rightly divided into distinct classes, each of which deals only with cotton, silk or wool. Of these, cotton-dyers are ubiquitous; in fact, many cotton-weavers dye their own yarn. Silk-dyers or *patrangs* exist only at the larger centres of silk-weaving, such as Amritsar, Jullundur, Multan and Lahore. Wool and *pashm* dyers, chiefly Kashmiris, are found in Amritsar, Lahore and Multan. The silk and wool dyers are the best paid of all, earning as much as from eight annas to a rupee a day.

Outside the carpet factories of Amritsar,[2] the only vegetable colours which still maintain the unequal

---

[1] The reasons for a corresponding change in Europe are not far to seek. Synthetic dyes can be had in standard qualities and in a state of guaranteed purity, whereas the vegetable dyes vary in character and composition, and have often to undergo tedious refining processes before they are fit for use. Further, synthetic dyes are not inferior in fastness or beauty, provided the dyer knows how to use them.

[2] P. 58 *Supra*.

struggle on cotton, wool or silk, are cutch, indigo,[1] and, to a much smaller extent, lac-dye, cochineal and safflower.[2] Cutch gives to cotton the well-known *khaki* shade, which, it is said, is unequal for fastness to light, acid, alkali, and other reagents, by anything the chemist has yet been able to produce. Indigo still holds its own on wool,[3] though on cotton it is being rapidly supplanted by indanthrene, immedial indone, and other "sulphur blues,"[4] which, though giving slightly different tints, are cheaper and far easier to manipulate.

Of the others, lac-dye is only employed in very small quantities by tanners of goat-skins in the districts. Cochineal, as yet without a rival for fastness to light and perspiration, is still used in some places on silk,[5] while safflower owes a precarious footing to the fact that it is considered semi-sacred, and obligatory for wedding garments, by a section of the Hindu population. It is grown chiefly in Gujrat, which contained 3,800 acres out of the provincial total of about 4,580 acres in the period 1904-09.[6] Its chief use in this

[1] The average area under indigo in the province, during the five years 1904-09, was 50,247 acres. Of this, 27,530 acres were in the Multan District, 12,693 in Muzaffargarh, and 6,317 in Dera Ghazi Khan.

[2] *Kasumba* (*Carthamus tinctorius*). For an account of the process of manufacturing the dye, see Watt, *Comm. Prod. Ind.*, pp. 279 *et seq.*

[3] Indigo is a difficult material to handle, and sulphate of indigo, which is directly soluble in water and dyes wool and silk from a slightly acid bath, is sometimes employed in its stead. The use of the latter dye-stuff is to be condemned, as it is not at all fast in sunlight. The manufacturers of synthetic indigo do not admit its inferiority to the natural product even on wool.

[4] These can only be used on cotton.

[5] Cochineal is still used in England for army clothing.

[6] These figures apply to all dye-stuffs, such as safflower, *henna*, etc., but mainly safflower.

district, however, is for fodder. Madder is said to be regarded with favour in a few out-of-the-way places by old-fashioned calico-printers.

The substitutes for lac and cochineal are various alizarine dyes where fastness is required, and aniline ones where it is not. Safflower has given place to safranine, and madder to synthetic alizarine, which gives purer shades and is equal to the vegetable product in every respect.[1]

The triumph of chemical dye-stuffs has been viewed with general disfavour by all lovers of Indian art. It is stated that they have injured the artistic sense of the people by introducing amongst them a taste for glaring and ill-assorted colours. They are also said to be much less fast than the older materials they have displaced, and, lastly, to damage many of the fabrics on which they are used.

On the first point it might be observed that there are over two thousand artificial colours, which give a far wider field to the artistic sense than the natural ones ever could. The patrons of the more offensive aniline dyes are the poorer classes, who in the olden days could not afford to wear any colours at all, and hence never learnt how to wear them wisely and well. They never had any artistic sense to lose, so cannot have lost it. Had they possessed such a sense, they would never have fallen such facile victims to the cheaper products of German chemistry.

---

1 For a complete account of the methods of dyeing with vegetable colours in Northern India, see Sayad Mohd. Hadi's *Monog. on Dyes and Dyeing in the United Provinces* (1896).

For further information on indigenous dyes, the *Technical Reports and Scientific Papers* of the Imperial Institute, Part II, pp. 213-222, and the reports of Mr. A G. Perkin in the *Agr. Ledger* should be consulted.

The objection that artificial colours are not as "fast" as vegetable ones is absurd, for two reasons. In the first place, the term "fast," if used in a general sense, is vague, as a colour may be fast for one purpose and not for another. Thus, cochineal is faster to sunlight and perspiration than the azo-scarlets, but is more sensitive than the latter to soap and alkalies. Secondly, the origin of a dye-stuff has nothing to do with its properties, which depend on its chemical composition. For example, there is no *essential* difference between the alizarine obtained from anthracene, and the alizarine that constitutes the colouring principle of madder, a vegetable product.

The third objection is equally groundless. Wool, cotton, and silk are substances differing in chemical composition, and different chemical substances will have different effects, harmful or beneficial, upon them. Some colouring matters, for example, the "sulphur blues," are suitable for cotton, but will ruin silk or wool. Others, such as the acid and eosine dyes, will give good results on silk or wool, but will not fix on cotton at all. Moreover, some of these colours involve the use of acids and alkalis which must not only be correctly manipulated, but also thoroughly washed out after the dyeing process is over, else they will gradually destroy the fibre of the material. It is the dyer's errors of omission and commission that often give rise to the idea that artificial colours are in themselves harmful.

The European, American, or Japanese dyer keeps himself informed through the technical papers, about the various dye-stuffs available, tests them for himself, and selects what suits him. If his Indian confrère cannot or will not do the same, if he will buy only what is cheapest in the bazaars, and if he will rely for information solely on the pictures on the box-label, it is surely the workman, and not his tools, that are to blame. There was a time when this workman knew how to produce some exquisite effects by simple methods. The very simplicity of the modern dye-stuffs has now undone him. Not that *he* thinks so. Unfortunately for himself he has not yet taken the first step to knowledge, *i.e.*, to know that he knows nothing. He thinks he knows all and will not learn.

It is not, however, the Indian artisan alone who is in fault. Competition is very keen and profits are very low. The public is all for cheapness, and considers nothing else. It is hopeless for the Indian dyer to improve under present circumstances, even if he would.

It is very necessary that both the Government and the more intelligent section of the public should bestir themselves in the matter. The former might establish a school for dyers, under an expert, in connection with the Central Weaving School which has been suggested in previous pages of this work.[1] The importers of chemical dyes do what they can to bring the use of their products to the knowledge of the public, but they cannot reach the individual artisan. They would, however, be willing to help the Government in its efforts to diffuse better methods among the classes beyond their own reach.

For the public, it is high time to realise that dyeing with artificial colours is by no means a simple task, and that to be served well they must pay well. Failure to grasp this fact has led to the ruin of many a costly

[1] P. 13 *supra*.

fabric at the hands of some ignorant dyer who used the wrong chemical combination.

Dyeing factories.

The dyeing industry is very much specialised. It is divided, in the first place, into three main branches, concerned respectively with cotton, wool and silk, which cannot be profitably combined. In any one of these, *e.g.*, cotton, it will be found that one set of processes and machinery is required for the treatment of yarns, and another for the treatment of cloths. The specialisation often goes a step further, and one comes across establishments, such as the flourishing ones started by educated youths in Madura,[1] which engage solely in the Turkey-red dyeing of yarns.

There seems to be room for modern dyeing factories in places like Delhi, Lahore, and Amritsar, especially in connection with the existing cotton mills.[2] It may be mentioned that the Dhariwal Woollen Mills have a very well-equipped department of this kind in charge of an expert.

Calico printing.

The art of calico printing is closely allied to that of dyeing; and its decline, though due to a different cause, has coincided with that of the latter. The Punjab never had a reputation for its calico beyond its own borders, although before the era of cheap chintz, it made practically all it wanted for home consumption. The prints of Kamália in Montgomery have long been distinguished by a certain rude quaintness of pattern and brightness of colour,[3] and have enjoyed

[1] Madura-dyed yarn finds its way even to Northern India. (Chatterjee, *Industries of the United Provinces*, p. 67).

[2] A factory of this sort can be set up for Rs. 20,000.

[3] "The pattern, after being stamped all over, is elaborated by coloured patches or bands, which are brought up to the required shade by hand-painting the large patches." (Watt, *Indian Art at Delhi*, 1903, p. 244.)

a reputation that is more than local. The same may be said of the productions of Sultanpur in the Kapurthala State and of Lahore, Amritsar, and, to a less extent, of Panipat.[1] None of these, however, can rival the exquisite and elaborate productions of Farrukhabad and Lucknow, where the patterns often contain as many as a dozen colours and require several thousand applications of the block on a single curtain.

The calico-printer still plies his trade in all the cities of the province, but he can only look to the diminishing custom of the poorer village and hill folk to earn his four to eight annas a day. All the other classes of the people use Manchester chintz. Calico is still popular, however, amongst rich and poor for curtains, floor cloths, quilts, bedspreads and similar uses, but those who can afford it, get their wants supplied by the more artistic craftsmen of the United Provinces.

As in the dyeing industry, chemical colours have displaced all vegetable ones, except indigo. Madder and turmeric are, however, alleged to be still used to a small and diminishing extent in some of the by-ways of the province, such as Gurgaon and Hoshiarpur.

The two branches of calico-printing, the industrial and the artistic, are often confused in practice, but must nevertheless be kept distinct in our minds to enable us to devise a policy for the future. The former deals with a class of fabrics on which the same pattern is repeated at short and regular intervals, and can therefore be turned out better and cheaper by machinery. Here the final defeat of the hand-printer is only

---

[1] For a further account of the art in the Punjab, see *ibid.* It must be noted, however, that there is no calico-printing worth mentioning in the Gurdaspur district.

a question of time. Artistic calico-printing, on the other hand, includes not only prints where the craftsman's individuality comes largely into play with brush or block, but all those which have a complex arrangement of shades and designs, which it is impossible to produce economically by machinery. This branch of the craft finds its best expression at Lucknow and Farrukhabad in the neighbouring province. It will never die out any more than the art of painting has died out in consequence of the discovery of photography. In a country like Switzerland, where labour is dearer than in the Punjab, a considerable hand-printing industry still holds its own against the competition of Manchester, thanks to the originality and sheer excellence of its products.[1]

What even individuals can do to promote artistic calico-printing is illustrated by the development of the craft in Jehangirabad and Fatehpur, in the United Provinces, through the efforts of Mr. F. S. Growse, I.C.S., Collector, successively, of the Bulandshahar and Fatehpur districts.[2] In the Madras Presidency a similar feat was performed by M. Kalianasundara Mudaliar, Tahsildar of Ponneri, where an industry of considerable merit had died out in 1880. The Tahsildar discovered in 1908 three old men who had been calico-printers in their younger days, and further got together, with infinite pains, a fine collection of blocks. The three veterans were encouraged to produce the

[1] It may be mentioned, however, that of late years the Swiss industry has suffered some decline. But the causes that are at work there, do not yet exist in the Punjab.

[2] Hadi, *Monog. on Dyes and Dyeing in the United Provinces*, 1896, p. 44. See Watt, *Indian Art at Delhi*, p. 248, for an account of the industry.

very best they could, and were paid handsome prices. They at last saw that their art was good and taught it to their sons and their sons' sons, so that now from thirty to forty men are busy at calico-printing in Ponneri. The work is sold chiefly to Europeans through the Principal of the Madras School of Arts, who often gives the artisans new blocks and suggests but never dictates new designs. It may be mentioned that a fair portion of the patterns are sketched by hand and then filled in with a brush.

Much may be done in the Punjab on similar lines. The Deputy Commissioners of Montgomery, Karnal and other districts where calico-printers exist in fair numbers might induce their District Boards to subsidise artists of Farrukhabad or Lucknow to come over for two or three years to teach their art to the local craftsmen. They might, in addition, suggest to the producers new patterns likely to appeal to the European and Indian public for table and wall covers, curtains, etc., and help them to get into touch with private persons as well as with the dealers in Amritsar and Delhi. The latter would, no doubt, be able to sell the goods to tourists as well as residents.

CHAPTER VIII.

TANNING AND LEATHER-WORK.

The tanner's craft has always held an assured, though not an honoured, position in the economic organisation of this country, but it is now suffering a rapid decline in the face of European competition. In few other industries have Western science and organisation gained so signal a victory over the rude traditional methods of an ancient civilisation.

The raw material.

Not that there can be any complaint as to the lack of raw material in a province possessing 10½ million cows and bullocks, 3¾ million buffaloes, 4½ million sheep, and 4 million goats. Assuming, with Sir George Watt, that 40 per cent. of the agricultural stock dies or is slaughtered every year, the yield of hides and skins must be very considerable.

Most of these, however, go out of the Province untanned. A large proportion of the hides has always been exported in the raw state, but it is only during the last few years that the trade in skins has been completely revolutionised. This is almost entirely the effect of the heavy duties levied on tanned, as distinguished from raw, pelts by most of the importing countries, which have thus helped to throttle a defenceless Indian industry.[1]

---

[1] Free trade in hides and skins can only be established by the imposition of an adequate export duty on the *raw* material, to counterbalance that levied abroad on Indian *leather*.

The following figures will show how the state of affairs has been altered during the last decade :—

—	1899—1900.[1]		1909—1910.	
Export of Hides.	Maunds.	Rupees.	Maunds.	Rupees.
Dressed or tanned .	66,640	20,90,830	658	21,358
Raw	295.664	71,69,609	146,168	51,15,043
Export of Skins.				
Dressed or tanned .	86,771	20,22,405	9,240	4,66,934
Raw	77,854	21,40,988	201,446	68,55,717

The local hide is inferior, its defects being due to the fact that Indian cattle are lean, heavily branded, seldom cared for, and killed only when too old to breed or give milk. Of the several varieties, buffalo-hide (*májá*) is very durable, but too thick and stiff to be suitable for every purpose. It is mainly used for the thick soles of country shoes, and, with ox-hide, for harness, saddlery, *hukkás*, *charsás*, etc. The hides of cows and bullocks, on the other hand, are made into good leather, which is much esteemed for boot and shoe uppers. Hides.

India is compensated for the inferiority of its hides by an abundant supply of goat-skins, which, though somewhat coarse in grain, are not less serviceable than those produced by any other country. The world-demand for *glacé* skins, in particular, is rapidly rising ; but, unfortunately, all attempts to manufacture them in India for the European market have so far failed through lack of the necessary skill, knowledge, and machinery, all of which mean capital. Skins.

[1] The figures for 1899-1900 include the exports from the districts severed from the Punjab in 1901, and now constituting the N.-W. Frontier Province.

Goat-skins (*khál*) are larger, stronger, and of much better texture than sheep-skins (*méshá*), but the leather made from both is softer and finer than that from hides, and is much used for the uppers of shoes and book-binding.

Tanning materials.

Hides and skins are converted into leather by the action of tannin, and it will be useful to summarise here the existing information on the more important tanning materials of the Punjab. It would be a great boon to the industry if the Forest Department published full details of its resources in this respect.

The chief of these is the bark of the *kikar* (*Acacia arabica*), which can be had in abundance at Ambala, Sialkot, Multan, Rawalpindi, and other places, at prices ranging between Re. 1-4 and Re. 1-8 per maund. The larger the tree, the greater the tannin-content of the bark, which will, in a full-grown tree, yield as much as 20 per cent., while the branches and twigs give 10 per cent. The material can be used for all classes of leather, except that intended for export, to which it gives too red a colour.[1]

Though the supply is, for the present, ample, it is not unlimited, and will assuredly fall further and further behind the growing demand, as it has done in the neighbourhood of Cawnpore, where prices have risen 125 per cent. during the last few years. In districts where the consumption is increasing, fellings should be regulated, and the landholders encouraged to plant the tree, which grows well in sour, clayey soils not profitable for cultivation.

---

[1] Guthrie, *Rep. on the Tanning Ind. of the Bom. Pres.* (1910), § 31.

The bark and leaves of *Rhus Cotinus*,[1] too, are in some demand. The shrub is fairly common in the low-lying scrub forests of the Kangra hills, though it never occurs in large masses, and it also thrives all along the Punjab Himalayas from the Jumna to Hazara, being commonest in the last-named district. It is also much in evidence all about the hills below Simla at about 4,000 to 5,000 feet, but is rarely seen in the villages, as the cultivators cut it down.

Among other tanning agents may be mentioned the leaves of the *dhau* (*Anogeissus latifolia*), and the barks of the *amaltás* (*Cassia Fistula*), the *chíl* (*Pinus longifolia*) and the *kreu* (*Quercus semecarpifolia*) used in Kangra, and of the *rhin* (*Q. incana*) and the Himalayan spruce (*Picea Morinda*) employed in the Kulu subdivision. Near Murree, tanners prefer the *ailan* *Pieris ovalifolia*)[2] and the *barin* (*Quercus glauca*), when they can get them, taking *Q. incana* only as a *pis aller*. Small quantities of fruits and leaves of the *ámlá* (*Phyllanthus Emblica*), the *harrar* (*Terminalia Chebula*)[3] and the *bahera* (*T. belerica*), are imported into the Hoshiarpur district from the neighbouring hills to be used with *kikar*, while the same purpose is served in some places by the barks of the *bér* (*Zizyphus Jujuba*), the *siris* (*Albizzia Lebbek*), the *jáman* (*Eugenia jambolana*) and occasionally, for special purposes, the rather expensive rind of the

---

1 *Rhus Cotinus*, Eng. Wig plant, Vern., *padn*, *bhán*, *manu*, *banlhra*, *tugang*, *titri*, *tung*.

2 *Pieris ovalifolia*, Vern *ailan*, *arúr*, *ailaur rattankdt*, *eran*, *erana*, *ellal*, *bhel*, *ayatta*.

3 *Harrar* is produced in the Hamirpur and Palampur tahsils of Kangra. It sells from 8 to 20 seers a rupee and is mostly exported to Amritsar. The annual outturn is estimated at 180 and 100 maunds, respectively.

pomegranate (*naspál*). Finally, mention may be made of the barks of *Bauhinia variegata,*[1] *B. purpurea,*[2] and *Mallotus philippinensis,*[3] small trees which occur in the Salt Range, and are very common in the sub-Himalayan tract and Lower Himalaya from the Indus eastwards.[4]

Turning now to the men who use these materials, we find that an industry which commands the highest knowledge and technical skill in Europe, is here the monopoly of the meanest, poorest and most degraded orders of the people. The very touch of the tanner pollutes : his bare presence is an abomination even to a Sudra, a member of the lowest of the four main castes. An aristocracy may, however, exist among the impure, and laws of precedence even amongst the lowly and down-trodden : and we find the artisans who handle skins and hides marked off into social ranks by barriers as impassable as those which guard the privileges, or check the pretensions, of castes within the pale of orthodox Hinduism itself. In Sirsa, for example, the Nánkia chamár, who makes shoes, holds his head higher than the ordinary chamár who merely cobbles them ; and both in their turn must perforce admit the superiority of the *Raigar*, who only dyes leather. Again, in some districts, the Jútia

[1] *Bauhinia variegata*, Vern *kachnár, kolár, koliár, padriáu, karár purál.*

[2] *B. purpurea*, Vern. *koirál, karár, karalli, gray.*

[3] *Mallotus philippinensis*, Eng. Monkey-face tree, Vern , *kameta, kamal, kambal, kúmila.* See *Agric. Ledger*, 1905, No. 4, pp. 53, 70.

[4] This list is by no means exhaustive. For a detailed account of the Indian tanning materials, see *Agric. Ledger*, 1902, No. 1. The extent to which a given tree or plant occurs in this Province can easily be ascertained by reference to Stewart, *Punjab Plants* ; Brandis, *Indian Trees*, and Gamble, *Indian Timbers.*

chamar can have no social dealings with the Chandar chamar, who prepares the hides of impure animals.[1] The khatík, or tanner of goat and sheep skins, is either a Hindu or a Mohammadan, and stands everywhere in a class quite apart from the chamar.

Further, from an economic point of view, the position of the town worker is very different from that of his brother in the village. The former is a free agent, buying his raw materials and selling his finished products in the open market. Village tanners and shoe-makers, on the other hand, are divided, respectively, into two different classes, the one working for their own hand as ordinaryartisans, and the other governed by custom as menials of the village community in whose midst they live. Even the last-mentioned, however, are changing with the spirit of the times, and developing from status to contract, so that we find that though in Ludhiana their customary obligations are respected, yet in Dera Ismail Khan, Rawalpindi and other districts they are almost entirely independent. Many village chamars add to their earnings by subsidiary occupations, such as carrying clay, plastering houses, and weaving cotton and wool, in addition to their hereditary calling. In Karnal and other parts of the Delhi division, indeed, they are the "coolies of the tract."

The tanners and shoe-makers are ubiquitous, and with their dependents constitute 4·1 per cent. of the population of the province. They are, however,

---

[1] These remarks do not apply to Mohammadan tanners and workers in leather, who are by no means a degraded class. In the western districts there are no chamars, and the Mohammadan shoemakers usually also tan leather.

unevenly distributed, the ratio of their number to the rest of the population being highest in the Delhi and Jullundur divisions, but diminishing as we travel westward, until it sinks to 2 per cent. in Muzaffargarh. As distinguished from the leather manufacture, which will be treated subsequently, the tanning industry is nowhere centralised, save to a certain extent in Lahore and Jullundur, and in the region around Sialkot.

Tanning. The methods of the chamar are, as has repeatedly been proclaimed from the housetops, primitive in the extreme, and include all possible errors of omission and commission, which cause an enormous waste of raw material.[1] Some of these errors are undoubtedly to be ascribed to the artisan's stupidity, ignorance and lack of moral backbone, but too much stress cannot be laid on the fact that the main weakness of his position is the lack of capital. From a purely household craft, tanning has developed, under modern conditions, into a highly specialised factory industry. The quality and finish which European and American consumers have been taught to expect can only be attained by long and expensive processes, absolutely beyond the means of the Indian tanner.

The ultimate ruin of the native tanner is merely a question of time, and the Government can do nothing, nor is it in the public interest to do anything, directly to save him. The only course to follow is, in general, to offer every reasonable encouragement to large tanneries, and, in particular, to subsidise, in accordance

---

[1] The processes of tanning hides and skins, respectively, are distinct. For an account of the former see the *Monograph on the Punjab Leather Industries*, pp. 17-19, and for the latter, *ibid.* pp. 19-20.

with the precedent of the Ambala Glass Works, a suitable factory, to enable the promoters to set up a laboratory, and engage competent experts. The chamars trained in these establishments will carry with them the more elementary principles of modern tanning to the backyards of the Punjab villages, and help to postpone the final downfall of their fraternity.

It will not be out of place to mention here that the method of flaying cattle, practised in this country, leaves a great deal to be desired, and is in no small degree responsible for the low quality of the hides. Nothing probably could be done in the villages, but in the large municipal abattoirs, influential dealers, with the help of the local authorities, should make arrangements to teach better ways to the butchers, and encourage them to persevere in them by the offer of better prices. This plan has been adopted by the British tanning industry to the general advantage of every one concerned.[1]

Modern tanneries.

The efforts made to establish modern tanneries, that is to say, tanneries producing what is known as "Cawnpore leather," in the Punjab will now be reviewed. The difference between "Cawnpore" and *desi* methods is hard to define, but the superiority of the former over the latter may be said to be due to greater attention to hygiene, and the fact that a pelt is

[1] The deputation which waited on Lord Carrington some time ago, estimated that the annual loss to the United Kingdom, through bad flaying, amounted to no less than half a million sterling. *Ind. Tr. Journ.*, July 7th, 1910, p. 9. What then must be India's loss every year? The same article proceeds to give an account of an ingenious flaying machine worked by electric power, which, it is claimed, will flay a bullock in half the time now taken by an ordinary butcher. Its chief feature, however, is that it is impossible to score or damage a hide with it.

put through a long series of graduated tannin baths, and is finally subjected to finishing processes which are more or less trade secrets.

The Punjab Tannery Co., Ld., Rawalpindi.

The Rawalpindi tannery is owned by a few Hindu gentlemen. They started working with hand-labour in 1908, and have now (1911) set up modern machinery for both bark and chrome tanning, as well as boot-making and leather-work generally. The manager is stated to have been trained in Madras and Cawnpore, and has under him factory-trained chamars from the latter place. Local tanners have proved apt pupils and are learning modern methods.

Other tanneries.

A Khoja in Sialkot, and another in Wazirabad, also employ Hindustanis, and have partially introduced "Cawnpore" processes into their factories, apparently with success. Another has set up an improved tannery in Jullundur with a capital of Rs. 3,000, while the sons of a Mohammadan Extra Assistant Commissioner are trying, under many difficulties, to work a small one in Ferozpur. In general, very great interest is shown in the matter all over the Punjab, and a spirit of enterprise is abroad, which deserves friendly encouragement.

Time and patience and, above all, much capital are, however, needed to make a tannery successful in the Punjab. There is a fair local market for good unwrought leather,[1] and the demand is certain to

[1] The value of the imports of wrought and unwrought leather, into the Punjab, is as follows :—

	Wrought leather.	Unwrought leather.
1904-05	Rs. 16,54,604	Rs. 1,41,355
1905-06	" 30,21,633	" 1,29,114
1906-07	" 17,28,302	" 3,29,677
1907-08	" 18,52,325	" 4,97,829
1908-09	" 16,85,383	" 3,33,566

develop with the supply of the material ; but the prejudice in favour of real "Cawnpore" is strong, and the new factories will have to make a hard fight to oust their long-established rivals. It would appear advisable, in any case, that all such factories should also have a department for leather-work, to use up soft leather for boots, and hard for trunks and similar articles. The North-West Tannery Co. of Cawnpore were in low water until they began to manufacture their well-known saddlery and footwear.

In establishing a tannery, care should be taken to select a place well supplied not only with hides and skins[1] and tanning materials, but also with suitable water. All these requirements are not always present together. Delhi, for example, is a large hide-market, but lacks good water ; Ambala has an abundance of *kikar* bark and has no water at all.

Hides must dry slowly during the various tanning operations if they are to be converted into the best leather. A great drawback in Northern India is that, in the hot weather, the surface dries up before the interior is at all affected by the heat. This could, no doubt, be obviated by the system of regulating

---

[1] The following table gives the export of hides and skins by rail from the chief stations:—

	1906-07		1907-08		1908-09	
Amritsar .	203,018	maunds.	138,669	maunds.	157,707	maunds.
Delhi . .	103,614	"	57,759	"	94,170	"
Lahore . .	48,176	"	36,933	"	45,711	"
Multan . .	43,748	"	11,603	"	23,275	"
Rawalpindi .	23,437	"	20,911	"	15,757	"
Kasur . .	26,427	"	18,099	"	19,330	"
Jullundur .	16,338	"	9,176	"	9,058	"
Gujranwalla .	16,132	"	8,434	"	5,230	"

temperature and humidity adopted by the Empress Mills at Nagpore.

Most of all is it necessary that a modern tannery should be put in charge of a practical expert, who must not only be familiar with the various processes, but must know enough chemistry to understand their principles. He must, at the same time, be a man of business, have some knowledge of machinery and tannery construction, and be able to handle the men under him.

Leather-work. Country shoes.

The shoemaker plies his trade in every village, but there are a few towns which have earned an Indian reputation for plain as well as embroidered country footwear. Chief of these is Delhi, with over 2,500 artisans, mainly chamars, who are said to produce seven lacs of rupees' worth of goods every year, of which five lacs' worth are exported all over Northern India, and even to the Nizam's Dominions. Leather tanned in Delhi itself is inferior, and Ludhiana and some places in the United Provinces, which are more fortunate in this respect, are cutting into the trade.

The two thousand shoemakers of Multan are almost all Mohammadans of miscellaneous castes, from Syeds to Telis and Mochis proper. The export is chiefly westward, *i.e.*, to the North-West Frontier Province, Sind, Baluchistan, Afghanistan, and even distant Bokhara, but the trade is declining, as the Amir's subjects no longer bring in large quantities of dried fruits to exchange for Multan shoes. Besides, the *powinda* has discovered the superior lasting qualities of Cawnpore footwear, and even taken to buying old army boots, on which he can make a larger profit.

There are 1,000 shoemakers in Lahore, who cater chiefly for local needs. Amritsar follows with 400, while Ludhiana and Hoshiarpur have a hundred shops each. Shoes from the last-named place, the handiwork of the *Sirajes* as they are called, are exported to the value of Rs. 30,000 to 40,000 yearly, and are in demand as far as Hyderabad (Deccan).

The maker of country shoes appears to be doing fairly well in most places, except Multan, where he has been hard hit by the loss of the lucrative trans-frontier trade. An ordinary worker is said to earn from eight annas to a rupee per diem in Delhi and Lahore, and from six to twelve annas in Multan, but these figures include the wages of his womenfolk, who help him very materially in embroidering and otherwise finishing his goods. It must be admitted that, as a type, the mochi is thriftless and ignorant, and is everywhere under the thumb of the Khoja shopkeeper, whose profits, including the gains of usury (euphemistically termed *munafa)*, are said to be very large.

The prospects of the country shoe industry are by no means bright, as the European boot is increasingly affected by all classes who have been touched in any manner by the rays of European culture, from the graduate to the *khidmatgar*. Much of this new demand is, at present, satisfied by Cawnpore, but small factories working with imported leather are springing up in every large town.

Lahore, for example, has as many as 40 shops, while Delhi and Ludhiana have 15 and 7, respectively. A Colony of Hindustani chamars in Karnal, a relic of the old cantonment, export their boots and shoes all over the Punjab and the Frontier Province.

A number of men of education have interested themselves in this craft, chiefly as employers of Hindustani artisans, and it is a hopeful sign of the time that some of them have been at pains to become practical shoemakers themselves. A young Khattri, the son of a station-master, has established a factory in Delhi, to which he hopes to attach a tannery, while his brother, now at school, has made up his mind to learn tanning at Madras and Cawnpore. Two Mohammadans, relatives of the well-known Allibhoy Valliji of Multan, make very good boots in Ferozpur Cantonment, and obtained a gold medal at the Lahore Exhibition. One of them is a water-colour artist, and the other a photographer of some merit, but they believe that there is more money in their present profession. A Kashmiri Pandit makes footwear to order in Amritsar, and claims that he has himself a practical knowledge of his craft. A retired Mohammadan Inspector of Schools has set up a boot factory in Gujrat in charge of his eldest son, and has decided to bring up his second son with a practical knowledge of leather-work. Similar workshops have been opened in Sialkot. As has been mentioned above, a boot factory is attached to the Rawalpindi Tannery, while the Doaba Leather Works, Ld., of Jullundur, a company with a capital of Rs 15,000, hope to possess one shortly.

Business training and connections, in addition to an artistic eye, are necessary in this industry, which otherwise appears to be suitable in every way for men of education. Only large and well-equipped establishments, however, could hope to succeed in the end, as boot-making, no less than tanning, has now become essentially a factory industry. With machinery for fifty pairs of hands, more boots can be produced than by five hundred hand-workers.

Boots and shoes are, of course, not the only leather manufacture of the Punjab. The simple wants of the zamindar and his menials are supplied by his village môchi, who provides them with all articles of daily use, such as thongs and whips, *bókás, charsás*[1] and bellows. The demand for country harness and saddlery is declining with the change of fashions, and towns such as Kalanaur in Rohtak, and Dinanagar in Gurdaspur, which used to be seats of their manufacture, have already given way to Cawnpore and Meerut. Drums (*daf*) and timbrels, as also leather *hukka* bowls, however, still continue to be made in most districts. In Lahore, Gujrat and Sirsa, the last-named are richly ornamented with brass or silver, and the leather is often given a brilliant polish. Khoja firms in Lahore, Wazirabad, and Gujrat have taken up the manufacture of leather belting for machinery. Leather manufacture.

In 1909-10 the Punjab imported, chiefly from Cawnpore, a little over two lacs of wrought-leather goods, such as trunks, saddlery and straps, which are becoming more popular every year. There is hardly room yet for a separate leather factory, but, as has already been suggested, the industry could conveniently be attached to an up-to-date tannery.

The main difficulty of all branches of the leather, as well as the tanning industry, is the dearth of skilled and reliable workmen. The artisans, recruited at

---

[1] The *bóká* and the *charsá* are each a kind of bucket for drawing water from wells.

present mostly from the United Provinces, are drunken, thriftless and generally unsatisfactory; moreover, they refuse to teach their craft to the natives of the Punjab.

General education, free, universal and compulsory, has been suggested as a panacea. If, however, we remember that "education" in India rarely means anything beyond "instruction," and does not connote any sort of moral training, it is difficult to believe that a degraded and despised class will improve in anything but cunning by being merely "educated." It is hopeless to expect any improvement in the moral standard of the "depressed classes" until their self-respect is raised by promotion to a higher social status, or until another Ravi Das[1] is born amongst them to illumine their minds with the light of higher ideals.

Industrial education, on the other hand, not only teaches a craft, but imparts a higher gift, namely, the habit of steady and regular manual work, which cannot but raise the learner in the moral scale. Small schools, in suitable localities, to teach boot-making, would do much to ease the present situation. In Sialkot, in particular, the sons of the Kashmiri weavers, who are fast losing their inherited trade, will hasten to learn a more profitable industry, while the mochis of Multan, always more pushful and intelligent than their custom-bound brethren further east, are anxious to teach their children to make European

---

[1] Bhagat Ravi Das, or Ravdas, or Raidas, a saint of the chamars, was, according to some accounts, a disciple of Ramanand, and according to others, lived in the time of Akbar.—Maclagan, *Punjab Census Report* (1892), Vol. I. p. 145.

boots and shoes, which now command an expanding market on both sides of the Indus.

Joint action is familiar to the artisans with whom we are here concerned, especially to the chamars, who usually tan leather in combination, hence the co-operative movement has every chance of success amongst them. Societies for co-operative production and sale should be started among the shoemakers of Delhi, Ludhiana and other places, under the auspices of the district authorities.[1] The Delhi artisans, in particular, seem to include some intelligent and literate men, and appear to be fairly well organised under their *chowdhries*. **Co-operation.**

The art of book-binding is at present monopolised by a rather unsatisfactory class of workmen, but offers a fair opening to educated youths who do not consider themselves above earning fifty rupees a month by the labour of their hands. In fact, there is every chance that the profits will rise, as there is a steadily increasing demand for good work. The art is not difficult to learn, and could be acquired by apprenticeship to one of the larger firms in Bombay or Calcutta. It should certainly be taught in one of the Lahore industrial schools. **Miscellaneous industries: Book-binding.**

Goat, sheep, calf and other skins can be converted into a substance resembling leather, though essentially different from it, by a process called "tawing," which involves the use of ammonia-alum or potash-alum and salt.[2] The drying has to be very rapid, hence **Alum tannage or "tawing."**

[1] There are six societies of shoemakers and three of tanners in the Bombay Presidency, and seven of shoemakers in Bengal.

[2] For a description of the process, see Proctor, *Leather Manufacture*, pp. 184 *et seq.* See also *Shoe and Leather Trader*, May 1910, pp. 10, 191, 196.

the industry would appear to be specially suited to Northern India.

Alum leather is much used for whip-lashes, boot-laces and "skivers" for capping chemists' bottles, but it is in special demand for *glacé* gloves, on account of its exceptional elasticity and resistance.

Raw hide industry.

Drums, ropes, scale-pans and, above all, oil-jars and bottles (*kuppás* and *kuppis*), are made in Jhang-Maghiana, Lahore, Panipat, Fatehabad and a few other places, from the raw hides of cattle, horses, and camels, and the skins of sheep and goats. Consequent on the general rise in prices, camel-hide softened by a thorough soaking in water, and, for smaller wares, occasionally the intestinal integuments of cattle reduced to a glutinous mass by boiling, are the only materials used. The process[1] consists in stretching the hide, or applying the glutinous mass on a clay model of the required shape. The small jars made in Jhang and Lahore are often made into fantastic forms, and are ornamented with bits of foil or parchment, which are covered over with a thin transparent layer of skin.

The kerosene-oil tin has almost killed this unsavoury industry, and in Jhang alone does one find as many as fifteen men engaged in it.

Camel-hide.

Camel-hides are not tanned in this country,[2] but if properly prepared, they make good and durable leather, which is useful for many purposes. England,

---

[1] For the process, see *Monog. on the Punjab Leather Industries*, pp. 21 and 25. Watt, *Dict. Econ. Prod.* Vol. II. p. 63. Hoey, *Manufac. of N. India* (1880) p. 138.

[2] 3,715 pieces of camel-hide, mostly from the Punjab, were exported from Karachi in 1909-10. They were all shipped to Marseilles. The Punjab has over 270,000 camels.

for example, regularly imports them from Egypt in a dry and dry-salted condition. The London price for Egyptian raw hide, which is shipped in a very dirty and wasteful condition, is 2½*d.* to 2¾*d.* per lb., but, if properly trimmed and quite dry, it would fetch as much as 5*d.*

Horse-hides are tanned, to a small extent, in Lahore, and made into shoes, but their chief use, with donkey-hides, is in the manufacture of shagreen at Delhi. They are largely in demand throughout Europe for leather, which is mostly used for boot uppers, enamels, and buffs, but not much for soles. Horse-leather is usually split, or well shaved down, the flesh side of the split being used for cheap leathers, razor strops, whips, thongs, etc. Horse-hide.

Horse-hides for the European market must be classified and sized. It is useless to send any but good ones, as they must compete with the excellent "fresh" hides of the South American wild horse.[1]

Donkey-hides are a regular article of trade in Delhi, where, with horse-hides, they are made into shagreen (*kimakht*).[2] The work is done in seven workshops owned by Mohammedans, who are said to turn out altogether Rs. 250 to Rs. 350 worth of the material a day.[3] Shagreen costs from Rs. 12 to 17 per maund, Donkey-hide.

---

1 2,740 pieces were exported from Karachi to Hamburg, Marseilles and Hull in 1909-10. There are 358,000 horses and ponies in the Punjab.

2 2,740 pieces of donkey-hide were exported from Karachi to Hamburg, Marseilles and Hull in 1909-10. There are 582,000 donkeys in the Punjab.

3 For a description of the process, which involves the use of copper filings and chloride of ammonia, see *Monog. on the Punjab Leather Industries*, pp. 20-21.

and is used by the book-binder, and also by the shoemaker for the toe and back of the country shoe. The industry is said to be declining, the workers barely earning six annas a day.

Deer-skin. Lálwán, in Hoshiarpur, is the only place where deer-skins are tanned regularly and on a considerable scale. The work is done by 30 to 35 Ramdásia families, who procure the skins from the waste country in the neighbourhood of Ferozpur and Ludhiana, and prepare them, and also the skins of young buffaloes, into a soft dark-coloured wash-leather, locally known as *sábar*, and used for buskins, hawking gloves, and breeches.

Dog-skins. Most of the so-called "dog-skin" gloves are made from Cape sheep and lamb-skins, and other small skins suitable for light leather. Nevertheless, the skin of the dog has such a fine texture, flexibility, and beauty of grain, that, despite its being harsh and flabby on the flesh side, it is largely in demand, particularly on the Continent of Europe, for gloves and pocket-books. The skins of big dogs would be very suitable for shoes.

The difficulties in the way of dressing and tanning dog-skins are great in India, as even the chamar will not touch them, but the industry may commend itself to missions amongst the submerged classes. Unlike his mangy cousin of the towns, the village pariah dog is sleek and well fed, and ought to yield very good material.

Raw dog-skins should be very carefully disinfected before export, and be well preserved and packed in salt, so that the grain is not injured in any way. The price likely to be realised, even for perfect pieces (which alone should be sent), in the London market is very uncertain, but may be put down at 12 annas to Re. 1-2 each. Tanned skins, on the other hand, should be worth from 12 annas to Re. 1-2 per lb., if they are clean, dry leather, with a fair grain.

The iguana (*góh*), a kind of lizard, is occasionally hunted in Gujrat, Jullundur and Multan for its flesh and fat, and its skin is said to make excellent shoes.[1] There is a growing demand for rat[2] and squirrel-skins[3] in Europe for ladies' purses, hand-bags and similar fancy articles. Miscellaneous.

---

[1] See also Watt, *Dict. Econ. Prod.*, Vol. VI. Pt. I. p. 434. The Singalese also use these skins for shoes. The animal is often infested with a parasitic insect, which has to be removed carefully.

[2] Rats must be trapped, not poisoned, to obtain the best skins.

[3] See also p. 66 *supra*.

CHAPTER IX.

Miscellaneous Animal Products.

This chapter deals with several industries likely to be offensive to orthodox Hindus, but they merit the careful attention of the enterprising Khoja community, who largely control the trade in slaughter-house products in the province. Religious prejudice, combined with a lack of scientific imagination, is responsible for an enormous wastage of animal products in the Punjab. It will be observed that in some cases valuable raw material is actually thrown away.

Blood. Few municipalities derive any profit from the blood of animals. Delhi gets a paltry sum of Rs. 300 every year for the blood of 20,000 cattle and 160,000 goats and sheep,[1] while in Lahore, Multan, Sialkot and a few other places it is used for manure.[2]

Dried blood is a valuable substance that can be put to numerous industrial uses, the most important of which is the manufacture of cyanide of potassium. It is also commonly employed as a decoloriser in the

---

[1] The contractor is said to boil the blood and export it to Bombay.

[2] Blood is a very rich manure, being more productive of nitrogen and ammonia than even flesh. When dried blood is used as a fertiliser, it should, to obtain the best results, be mixed with wood-ashes and powdered charcoal and applied to the ground in wet weather (Koller, *Waste Products*, p. 35).

manufacture of tannin extracts,[1] and as a fixing agent in alizarin dyeing.[2] Blood-meal is useful for poultry, and is largely prepared for this purpose at Melbourne.[3]

The most important industry, however, that could be started in connection with the larger municipal slaughter-houses of the Punjab is the manufacture of albumen, a substance useful for food as well as for industrial purposes.

The process consists in defebrinising blood by whipping,[4] and then subjecting the residue to the action of slightly acidulated methyl alcohol or acetone or both.[5]

The fibrin is obtained in the form of threads. It is washed with distilled water till quite white and is then either dried, or treated wet with pyrolusite[6] and sulphuric acid. The product is butyric acid, which enters into the manufacture of butyric ester, much used in combination with other esters and with spirit in the preparation of fruit essences, *e.g.*, of apricots, peaches, etc.

Even if the municipalities fail to set up industries in blood, it is not too much to expect them to bestir themselves to stop the daily waste in their abattoirs, by carefully collecting and exporting the raw material.

It is easy to prepare blood for transport in gunny bags, to any distance, provided all the processes are carried through as quickly as possible to prevent

---

1 Proctor, *Leather Manufacture* (1903), p. 337.

2 Notter & Firth, *Theory and Practice of Hygiene* (1896), p. 803.

3 *Jour. Agr. Dept., Australia*, Vol. XVI., March 16, 1908, p. 106.

4 *Jour. Soc. Chem. Industries.* Vol. XII. (1893), p. 500.

5 *Ibid.* p. 459.

6 On the occurrence of pyrolusite in India, see *Manganese-ore Deposits in India* in *Mem. Geol. Surv. Ind.* (1909), Vol. XXXVII.

decomposition. Blood is coagulated by boiling, the coagulated part being removed as it rises by means of a scoop and dried very thoroughly in the air.[1] To produce the best results, however, the concentration should be effected in a steam-jacketed boiler. There is also another process for drying and preserving blood which involves the use of lime.[2]

Bone. About 22,450 tons of bones, valued at Rs. 12·44 lacs,[3] are exported annually from Karachi after being crushed by a Greek firm that has secured an absolute monopoly of the trade. With the exception of camel-bone, which is sometimes substituted for ivory in Hoshiarpur inlay work,[4] and is made into toys and other fancy articles by a few artisans in Delhi, the material is not utilised in any craft in the province.

The possibilities of a domestic industry in ox, camel, and buffalo-bone, apart from its use as manure, may be realised from what is done in China.[5] After carefully removing the marrow for use as food, the Chinaman boils the bones to recover their fat, which he sells to the candle-shops. He then turns all the large and

[1] Simmonds, *Waste Products* (1876), p. 76. A thorough drying is absolutely essential.

[2] For an account of this process, see Koller, *Waste Products*, p. 29.

[3] Bones fetch about Re. 1-4 per maund delivered at the railway stations.

[4] *Hoshiarpur Gazetteer* (1904), p. 148. There are a few men at Lucknow and Saharanpur in the U. P. who make paper-knives, pen-holders, etc., of bone, and sell them at the railway stations [Chatterjee, *Industries of the United Provinces*, p. 193.]. Artistic *surmâdânis* (antimony-boxes) are made of camel-bone in Peshawar, and the same material is used for the white bosses on the lac work of Dera Ismail Khan.

[5] Consul-General Hosie, *Report on the Province of Ssuch'uan* (Blue Book, China, No. 5, 1904), p. 83.

hollow ones on a lathe, and makes them into opium-cups, which he polishes first with a wet braid of the stalks of *Equisetum Hiemale L.*, and then with dry bone-shavings. Flat bones, useless for cups, are planed and made into dice, brush-backs, buttons, etc., and waste pieces are pounded up for manure. The material is similarly utilised in Chicago in connection with the meat-packing industry, enormous quantities of knife-handles made of it being shipped to England every year. A man in that city knows a secret process by which he makes bone-dust into billiard-balls.[1]

A few men in Delhi make combs of horn, otherwise this material is not put to any industrial use in the province.[2] **Horn.**

Horns of all kinds, chiefly those of the buffalo, are annually exported by the hundred thousand from India to Europe for manufacturing purposes.[3] In Germany, for example, they are made into an enormous number of articles, such as paper-knives, spoons, combs,[4] scale-pans, shoe-horns and pen-holders,[5]

---

[1] *Dip. and Cons. Rep., Ann. Ser.*, 2,566 (1901), *Trade of Chicago for 1900*, pp. 29-30.

[2] One Fateh Muhammad, an ordinary shopkeeper in Malerkotla, can make horn buttons to order. For an account of the industry in other parts of India, see Watt, *Indian Art at Delhi*, *passim*, and Chatterjee, *Industries of the United Provinces*, pp. 191-2.

[3] The Punjab exported 6,812 maunds, valued at Rs. 39,167, in 1909-10, almost all to the United Provinces.

[4] A set of foot-driven machines to manufacture combs of horn, wood, celluloid, etc., costs Rs. 825 (C. I. F. Nürenberg, Germany). About 120 to 400 combs can be made per day, according to size of combs and capacity of workman.

[5] A complete plant to manufacture from 60 to 110 gross of ordinary pen-holders, such as are largely sold to schoolboys in India, in 10 hours, working partly by hand and partly by power, costs Rs. 4,000 (C. I. F. Nürenberg). Power required about 5 H.P.

by individual artisans, working with simple implements in their homes. Not a particle of a horn is thrown away. Even the waste pieces, when solid enough, are softened by heat or treated with a saturated solution of potash and lime, and pressed into buttons, pipes, etc., which are finished by carving with a knife. Refuse unfit for any other purpose is used as manure.[1]

There are various processes for working this material. The English method is to soften it by a preliminary immersion in cold, or sometimes hot, water, and afterwards in an acid bath for about two weeks. In Ratnagiri, pieces of horn are kept moist in cocoanut oil, and heated before a fire for an hour or more till they become almost as soft as wax. They are then fashioned by hand or in moulds, and finished with a lathe and some other simple tools. The polishing is done with the moistened dry leaves of a tree found in the locality.[2]

The latter is undoubtedly the best process, as the heated oil saves the horn from becoming charred or discoloured. Further, a small portion of the oil is absorbed and helps to consolidate permanently the fibrous structure of the material, at the same time giving the finished articles an exceptional translucency.[3]

The industry, if organised on proper business lines, ought to succeed in the Punjab, where the raw material is most abundant. There is, besides, a wide and expanding market for the finished products,

---

[1] In Sambhalpore (Moradabad District, U. P.), it is used as a manure for potatoes.

[2] *Ficus gibbosa* var. *parasitica*.

[3] See *Agricultural Ledger*, 1897, No. 10, pp. 2-3; Koller, *Waste Products*, pp. 118-9, describes various processes.

which, if well finished, could profitably be exported, not only to the other provinces of India, but to Europe.

The hoofs of cattle are universally wasted, as it has not occurred to any one even to collect and export them. One exception, however, must be mentioned. The blacksmiths of Multan use a mixture of salt and the ashes obtained by burning the hoofs, as a kind of flux to prevent the oxidation and softening of iron tools during the process of heating.[1] Hoofs.

Great quantities of hoofs used once to be sent from the United States to Japan, where they were put to various uses. A heavy export duty stopped this drain,[2] and now they are made into buttons and knife-handles in Chicago, the waste being used in the manufacture of cyanide of potassium.[3]

The gut or intestines of every living creature can be made into a string of immense strength and wearing qualities, commercially known as catgut. Catgut.

In this province the guts of bullocks and buffaloes are as a rule thrown away, the edible portions being occasionally sold for food. Those of sheep and goats, on the other hand, are everywhere made into strings for musical instruments, cotton-cleaners' bows, and, above all, sporting requisites, and, packed in salt, are also exported to Europe.[4] Raigars engage in the industry

---

1 The ashes of the horns and hoofs of animals and common salt are used in Europe in the manufacture of steel. The process is known as "case-hardening."

2 *Dip. and Consul. Rep., Misc. Ser.*, No. 581 (1902), *Cattle and Meat Trade of the U. S.*, p. 20.

3 *Dip. and Cons. Rep., Ann. Ser.*, No. 2566 (1901), U. S., *Trade of Chicago for the year 1900*, pp. 29-30.

4 269 maunds of sheep-gut were exported from Karachi in 1909-10.

in Hissar, Delhi and Gurgaon, Pinjas and Mirasis in Ambala, and Chuhras and Kashmiris in Sialkot. Except in the last-named place, the workers are scattered and entirely without organisation.

The Sialkot industry.

About Rs. 5,000 worth of gut is annually consumed in Sialkot city in the manufacture of tennis and badminton rackets, etc. The gut-makers, financed by the large firms, purchase the intestines of sheep and goats (*ronda*), locally or from other cities, at Re. 1-4 to 1-8 per hundred, and subject them to a primitive process of preparation. The material is first soaked in water for 12 hours, and then scraped continuously with a shell for two days in the summer, and eight in the winter months. The pieces are finally joined together, twisted and dyed.

Besides *ronda* catgut at from 16 to 45 yards for a rupee, an inferior variety, known to the trade as "white Sialkot gut," which sells at from 35 to 70 yards, is obtained from *patha*, or the flesh of the back of old cows and bullocks. The raw material is obtained in strips about two feet long, and is prepared in the same way as goats' intestines, except that the soaking takes longer.

The industry has been highly developed in Europe, where the intestines, not only of goats and sheep, but of every species of cattle are utilised. The largest are everywhere used for sausages, while in France a very strong cord is made from the intestines of horses, donkeys and mules, to be used with light machinery in place of leather belting.

The process followed is almost as simple as in India, but far greater care is devoted to hygienic details and the manipulation of the raw material.

The intestines are first cleaned and then scraped with a small plate of copper with a smooth semi-circular hole. This removes the external membranes, which are used for the cords of battledores and rackets, and for sewing together the ends of intestines. The scraped gut itself is either spun to the required thickness on an ordinary spinning wheel, or dried for exportation by stretching over frames in an artificially heated chamber.

Few chemicals are used. For ordinary gut, all that is wanted is a solution of two ounces of crude carbonate of potash in a gallon of water, but for violin-strings, four ounces each of caustic potash and carbonate of potash are dissolved in 3 to 4 gallons of water. Common salt and bleaching powder are used to prevent the guts from putrefying.[1]

The leaner the sheep the stronger the gut, so it is not surprising that the emaciated flocks of Italy supply three-fourths of Europe's demand for the material. The Indian animal excels even the Italian in leanness, and ought therefore to yield the best catgut in the world. The industry is commended to the notice of men with little capital, but plenty of energy and enterprise.

Glue. Glue[2] is made from various nitrogenous animal tissues, such as clippings of hides and skins, waste pieces of leather and old shoes, bones, sinews[3] and

[1] For further information on catgut generally, see Spon's *Workshop Receipts*, Vol. I. Art. *Catgut*.

[2] On the subject generally, see Sadtler, *Industrial Organic Chemistry* (1908), pp. 338 *et seq.* Spon, *Workshop Receipts*, Vol. II. Art. *Glue*. Koller, *Waste Products* (1902), pp. 42-45, 83-84 and 132-135.

[3] 65,281 maunds of sinews and other refuse used for the manufacture of glue, known to the trade as bone-sinews, were shipped from Karachi in 1909-10. The exports were almost entirely to Antwerp and Hamburg.

entrails, the bony cores of horns, and the skins of cats, dogs, and other animals.

Glue and gelatine are merely varieties of the same material, the difference lying in the greater adhesive power of the former, and the purity of the latter. Glue is chiefly made from tannery waste and leather, and is used by the carpenter and the joiner. Gelatine, usually extracted from bones by a very careful treatment, is much used in European kitchens and is also put to many medicinal and industrial uses such as the manufacture of capsules, court-plaster for wounds, and bromide and chloride of silver emulsions for photographic dry plates. Mixed with glycerine it makes an elastic mass used for hectographs and printers' rolls.

Glue-fat, or lime-soap, consists of the fatty parts of the raw materials saponified by lime. It is a useful product of glue manufacture, as mixed with mineral oil, it can be made into machinery-grease.[1] Another by-product is the residue of the boiling process, called "scutch," which is a valuable manure.

The Hindus consider glue impure, and use it very sparingly, but a certain amount is manufactured in Lahore, Amritsar and Delhi, by Mohammedans, and sold at about Rs. 10 to 18 per maund. It is a very inferior product, and has to be rejected in favour of the imported commodity for all the better kinds of work. English glue costs Rs. 28-5 per maund in Sialkot, where from 60 to 70 maunds of it are yearly consumed by makers of sporting requisites alone.

There is no difficulty in making glue in India, but the manufacture of gelatine is a highly specialised

[1] Koller, *Waste Products*, pp. 138–9.

industry, requiring much experience rather than scientific knowledge. There would appear to be an opening for an up-to-date glue-factory at such places as Rawalpindi, Sialkot, Amritsar, and Delhi.[1]

Ivory.

The ivory industry of the province is very unimportant.[2] It falls into three divisions: ivory-carving proper, inlaying and turning. The first is practised in a single workshop in Delhi, where the craft has been developed to a high pitch of artistic merit, and by a few artisans in Amritsar, who make small figures, boxes and combs. The art of inlaying wood with ivory is the monopoly of Jullundur and Hoshiarpur, but bangle-turning is general throughout the province. A few workmen at Ludhiana and Jagraon make billiard-balls for export.

The raw material used for the best articles comes from Africa, and costs from Rs. 19 to 25 per seer in Amritsar. Inferior work, such as Hoshiarpur inlay, is done with Indian ivory costing from Rs. 6 to Rs. 15 per seer.

Shell.

The manufacture of shell buttons and rings in Malsian and Nurmahal, in the Jullundur district, is of interest as illustrating the possibilities of small cottage industries in this country. A blacksmith of Malsian is said to have learnt the craft in Madras and America, and introduced it into his native village, about fifteen years ago.

---

[1] A complete factory handling daily five tons of bone for glue could be established for about Rs. 33,000 (C. I. F. Altona, Germany). The products obtained would be coarse bone-meal about 50%, waste 16%, fat 14%, and water 20%. About 20% of glue would be recovered from the bone-meal.

[2] For a complete account of the ivory industry of the province, see Ellis, *Monog. on Ivory Carving in the Punjab*, 1900

The processes are simple. Shells collected from the Beni river and elsewhere are first boiled, and then washed with lime and pounded glass. They are finally cut, polished and drilled, with the aid of some dozen implements, among which are a *katira* or clipping tool, three varieties of drills for making cavities and holes, a *kirkāra* for working designs on buttons and rings, and a grindstone for polishing and smoothing the edges.

The shells cost a rupee for 16 to 32 seers. The buttons sell at one-eighth of an anna to six annas a dozen, and the rings at three to twelve annas a dozen. An average artisan earns six annas a day.

There was a time when fifty persons earned their livelihood in Malsian by button-making, but their number has now dwindled down to sixteen. These goods have ceased to be popular because they have neither finish nor durability. The entire output, perhaps Rs. 150 per month at present, is usually bought up by one of the artisans, who hawks the articles all over Northern India from Peshawar to Shillong, taking care not to go to any customer twice.[1]

Feathers. Peacocks' tails are occasionally made into fans and similar fancy objects; but a more modern industry has sprung up in white fowls' feathers, which are extensively used for shuttlecocks in Sialkot, a single firm consuming as many as 102,000 annually. A fowl yields on an average 25 feathers, which sell for an anna

---

[1] Besides bad buttons, Malsian is also noted for false coins, current as well as ancient. It is notorious as the headquarters of a tribe of Mohammadan goldsmiths who counterfeit His Majesty's coin in many of the principal cities of India.—*Jullundur District Gazetteer* (1904), p. 202.

and a half? It may be possible to bleach the coloured ones, which are now wasted, by one of the numerous chemical processes given in *Spon's Workshop Receipts.*[1]

Large quantities of fowls' feathers are imported into the United Kingdom, about two-thirds coming from China and the rest from Japan, Germany, France and the United States. They are chiefly used for stuffing beds and cushions.

Feathers for the English market must be soft and downy, hence the shafts and barbs must be separated from the larger ones and rejected. Dirt and foreign matter should also be removed, as far as possible, before pressing into bales. The present London prices for Japanese feathers are as follows : ordinary dark, 1¾*d.* per lb.; light yellowish, 2¼*d.* per lb.; white, 5½*d.* per lb.; c. f. and i. terms. It is probable that Indian feathers would have about the same value, but it is impossible to state this definitely until their quality is known.

---

[1] Vol. I. Art. *Bleaching*, p. 130.

CHAPTER X.

CHEMICAL INDUSTRIES.

Various substances used in the arts, such as alum, sal-ammoniac, etc., are manufactured by crude and primitive methods in the Punjab, but their quality is generally inferior and the output comparatively insignificant. Chemical industries in the European sense of the term can hardly be said to exist, though the essential conditions—supply of the raw material and market for the manufactured products—are present in many cases.

Before passing on to details, however, a warning must be recorded. Many young men are at present under the impression that if they gain some knowledge of manufacturing processes in India or in Europe, they will forthwith be in a position to organise, if not to create, some branch of chemical industry. Now, the difficulties involved in many of the more important manufactures, such as that of acids and alkalis, have been worked out in such detail, that, except in cases where keen competition demands supervision of an exceptionally high order, science has really little further to say on the matter. It is impossible to insist too strongly on the importance of business capacity, training and connections in the creation of chemical industries.

The base of all these industries is sulphuric acid, and until this can be produced cheaply in India, many raw materials must remain unused, or be exported to be utilised in more fortunate countries. Copper pyrites, one of its commonest sources, occurs, as already mentioned, in some of the Simla hill-states and in Kulu, but the extent and the commercial value of the deposits have yet to be determined.[1] Unless rich ore-bodies are discovered very close to acid factories, the actual freight on pyrites per sulphur unit will probably be much higher than the freight on Sicilian sulphur, and the difficulty both of burning the former and of getting rid of the waste products will more than balance the cost of Sicilian sulphur.

Sulphuric acid.

There are two sulphuric acid factories at Delhi, one of which has only recently been started, with an annual outturn of 50,000 and 125,000 lbs., respectively. This is chiefly consumed in the city itself by the coppersmiths and, before the new carbonic acid gas works[2] were set up, was also in demand by soda-water makers.

Two factories are also at work in Lahore, the larger one producing about 56,000 lbs. and the other 48,000 lbs. yearly. The former has arrangements for turning out 160,000 lbs., if there is sufficient demand, and manufactures besides small quantities of hydrochloric acid, nitric acid and ferrous sulphate (*kasis*).

[1] The pyritic shale which occurs above and below the Dandot colliery, in the Salt Range, is unsuitable because of the large proportion of organic matter it contains. [*Rec. Geol. Surv. Ind.*, Vol. XXXVIII. (1909-10), p. 34.]

The survey of the sulphide ores of the Punjab forms part of the programme of the Geological Survey for 1910-11.

[2] See p. 136 *infra*.

The chief customers for the sulphuric acid are the soda-water factories of Lahore and out-stations, while sulphate of potash, the by-product of the industry, is sold as manure for tea at Rs. 3-8 a maund.

There is no reason why India should not produce all the sulphuric acid she requires.[1] While freights on Sicilian sulphur are comparatively low, both shipping and railway rates for carrying the acid are so heavy, and the conditions as to packing, etc., so severe, that, thanks to their protection, the Indian manufacturer can afford to use comparatively primitive methods and yet make his business pay in the seaports as well as at the large inland centres. A minor obstacle in the way of the industry is the lack of suitable acid-proof jars,[2] but the real difficulty is a commercial one. Manufacturers must learn to push their product on the market and to control the rate of production so as to keep pace with the supply.

A capital of about three lacs is required for an up-to-date sulphuric acid factory.[3]

Alum. The Indian alum industry was formerly considerable, but the importation of the cheap European

---

[1] The average yearly imports of the acid into India amount to 60,255 cwts., valued at Rs. 6,17,547.

[2] Cf. Chapter XIX.

[3] The "contact" process of making sulphuric acid, *i.e.*, by passing sulphur dioxide and air over platinized asbestos, is now in vogue in Germany. Given a cheap supply of sulphur and careful management, this method can be made to yield a large profit, as it requires very little fuel and not much capital. Pyrites may be used as a source of sulphur, and catalysts other than platinum, *e.g.*, ferric oxide, may be employed. For further information, see Roscoe and Schörlemmer, *Inorg. Chem.*, I. p. 428, and Lunge, Sulphuric Acid and Alkali, 3rd ed.

On sulphuric acid in India generally, see *Rec. Geol. Surv. Ind.*, Vol. XXXIX. (1910), pp. 276 *et seq.*

product, chiefly from the United Kingdom, has practically destroyed it. Alum is, however, still extracted from pyritous shale at Kalabagh, where there is one factory, and at Kotki, 11½ miles off, where there are three. These four together turn out about 7,000 maunds per annum, valued at Rs. 30,000, which is exported to various tanning centres. The price at Kalabagh varies between Rs. 4-8 and Rs. 6 per maund.

The raw material is mined in a very desultory fashion, and the process of manufacture is primitive. Improvements are specially desirable in the manner of roasting the shale, which is now done in the open, thus causing considerable loss, and also in the construction of the fire-chamber for the boiling pans. Great care is necessary to regulate the heat, as an excess of it is very wasteful. What is of even greater importance is the substitution of gypsum, which is abundant in the neighbourhood, for lime in the lining of the various tanks. In the present process, the lime destroys over Rs. 6 worth of alum daily in each factory.[1]

Alum is largely used not only in tanning, but also in dyeing, as a size and weighting material for paper, and mixed with sawdust, as a fireproof material for safes.[2] Kalabagh alum is unsuitable for most of these purposes on account of the large quantity of iron it contains. For the more delicate dyes, for

---

[1] For a complete account of the industry, see Daru, *Alum Manufacture at Katabagh*, in *Rec. Geol. Surv. Ind.* (1910), Vol. XL. pp. 265 *et seq.*

[2] An average quantity of 15,364 cwts. of alum a year valued at Rs. 69,795 was imported at Karachi during the period 1904-09. The average yearly import into India during the same period was 68,048 cwts., valued at Rs. 3,06,515.

example, the chemical must be of extreme purity, the presence of less than ·001% of iron rendering it unsuitable. Kalabagh alum could, no doubt, be purified to the required standard by suitable methods. It may be possible, for example, to precipitate the iron as basic iron sulphate and allow it to settle after the alum liquor has been concentrated to a specific gravity of 1·40. But the process appears to be practicable only in a properly equipped factory.

There is possibly an opening for an alum factory at Dandot, which is nearer the markets than Kalabagh and has abundant deposits of shale with a large sulphur content.[1] The success of this industry hinges, however, on the possibility of underselling the imported article in the large industrial centres, freight rates to which are heavy. Dandot alum would further have to compete with alum manufactured from the aluminous laterites of Katni and other more favourably situated centres.[2]

Carbonic acid gas.

Carbonic acid gas, for the use of aerated water and ice factories, is made at Sujanpur by the Sugar Works from jaggery and molasses. A branch factory of the Sardar Carbonic Gas Co., Ld., of Bombay, has also been set up at Delhi. The producers, gas-engine, absorbers, purifiers and compressors of the Delhi works are stated to be of the most modern type, and to be capable of producing 1,600 lbs. of liquid gas per diem, without smoke, smell, or noise. The raw material

---

[1] In this connection *cf.* Appendix VI.

[2] A considerable proportion of the alumina manufactured at the Larne works of the British Aluminium Co. is used for the manufacture of alum in Manchester and other places.

used is charcoal, 1,200 lbs. of which not only yields the daily quota of gas, but also produces the 60 H.P. necessary for driving the machinery.

Ammonium Chloride.

Ammonium chloride or sal-ammoniac (*naushadar*) is used in pharmacy, as well as for various industrial purposes, such as the tinning and soldering of metals, the operation of forging the compound iron used for country gun-barrels, and lastly, as a freezing mixture with nitre and water. It has been made for ages by the potters in the Kaithal and Guhla circles of the Karnal district by a primitive process. Bricks are made of the slime of certain ponds and burnt. The material found encrusted on the burnt bricks is sold to the shopkeepers who submit it to sublimation in glass retorts. The annual outturn of naushadar is estimated at 2,300 maunds. It sells at about Rs. 15 a maund[1] and is exported to Amritsar, Ferozpur, and various cities in the United Provinces.

Carbonate of potash.

Crude carbonate of potash (*jao-khár*) is much used in India in medicine and the arts. In Europe the pure salt is essential in the manufacture of potash-glass and in various textile and dyeing processes. After being causticised, it is largely employed in soap-making.

In the Punjab it is manufactured from the ashes of various trees and plants, the chief of which are[2] :—

Butea frondosa (*dhâk*)	Hordeum vulgare (*jao*)
Calotropis gigantea (*ak*)	Luffa aegyptiaca (*turai*)
Cassia Fistula (*amaltâs*)	Cedrus Deodara (*deodar*)

---

[1] The portion of the naushadar which is formed in the mouth of the retort is distinctively called *phûl*. It is used in the preparation of *surma* for the eyes, and is sold at Rs. 40 per maund.

[2] Baden-Powell, *Punjab Products*, p. 97.

Large tracts of mountain lands, as for example in the Simla Hills and in Bashahar, are covered with various species of wormwood (Artemisia), the ashes of which contain a high percentage of carbonate of potash, but are not used except as manure. Without being so sanguine about large profits as Sir George Watt,[1] one might suggest the extraction of the salt to the hill-folk as a profitable industry during the long winter months, when they have very little else to do.

Potassium nitrate.

Potassium nitrate (saltpetre, nitre, *shórá*) occurs largely as a saline efflorescence in most districts in the Punjab, chiefly near rivers and deserted village sites. It is recovered by exhausting the saline matter in the nitre-bearing earth by the percolation of water through it, and by the evaporation of the liquor so obtained by heat.[2] The crude saltpetre thus obtained is taken to the refinery.

1,085 licenses were issued in the Punjab in 1908-09 for the manufacture of crude saltpetre, which was handled by 29 refineries. The total exports by rail amounted to 154,317 maunds, valued at Rs. 8,10,158, and of this about 60,000 maunds went to Calcutta for shipment to Europe.[3]

Hissar, Gurgaon and Montgomery are the principal saltpetre-producing districts of the Punjab. In Karnal, too, there is a considerable industry, about 4,000 maunds being exported every year from

---

1 See his *Comm. Prod. Ind.*, p. 50.

2 For an account of the process, see Watt, *Comm. Prod. Ind.*, p. 973.

3 *Administration Report, N. I. Salt Revenue Dep.* (1908-09), p. 28. The figures on page 15 do not appear to have been checked by those given in the *Punjab Internal Trade Report.*

the refineries at Karnal, Panipat and Kaithal. The Gujranwala district has a factory at Chhapanwali (*tahsil* Khangarh Dogran) with an output of 5,000 maunds per annum, valued at Rs. 31,000. There are seven works at Kamar Masháni in the Miánwáli district.[1]

The use of saltpetre for preserving meat and fish is not unknown in India, but the mineral is chiefly employed in lac and cochineal dyeing, as a flux in glass-making, and, above all, in the manufacture of fireworks. The Agricultural Department is now making experiments to determine its value as a fertiliser. Formerly it was largely exported to Europe, where it was in great demand for the preparation of gunpowder as well as of nitric acid. But other explosive compounds have now been discovered, and for nitric acid the potassium nitrate of India has been displaced by the sodium nitrate of Chili, which is found to be more economical.

The chief Punjab salt-deposits are at Khewra, Warcha and Nurpur in the Shahpur district, and at Kalabagh on the Indus ; but about 26,000 maunds are manufactured in a group of villages known as the Sultanpur Mahals in the Rohtak and Gurgaon districts, by the evaporation of brine raised from wells.[2] An impure salt containing only from 60 to 70% of sodium chloride is obtained from open quarries at

Common salt.

---

[1] There are two large factories in the Bahawalpur State with a total annual outturn of about 8,000 maunds. Mr. Bose reported to the Durbar in 1904 that the manufacture of saltpetre was capable of expansion in the Sadikabad Tahsil of the State.

[2] For a description of the process, see the *Gurgaon District Gazetteer*, now in the press.

Guma and Drang in the Mandi State for consumption in the hills.

The Mayo mines at Khewra have an inexhaustible supply of the purest rock-salt, of which 30 lacs of maunds are annually extracted. This does not include the large quantities of salt in a powdered state, which has so far had no market. Part of this powder is utilised for filling in old workings, while the rest is heaped outside and becomes a nuisance to the surrounding fields, where it is often carried by the rain.

The Salt Department is prepared to deliver annually about two lacs of maunds of this waste salt in wagons at Khewra station at six pies per maund, free of duty, for industrial purposes. This charge does not, of course, include the cost of picking, screening and other operations which might be undertaken at the request of the purchaser. If a larger quantity is required, it can be supplied from the waste in the Depôt enclosure at the same price plus the cost of digging out the weathered portions.

Sodium sulphate.

The production of sodium sulphate (Glauber's salt) from common salt by the action of sulphuric acid is the first stage in the Le Blanc process of soda manufacture. It is called *khári* in the Punjab, where it is obtained from *réh*, an efflorescence on the surface of the earth consisting of varying proportions of sodium sulphate, sodium carbonate and ammonia salts.[1]

The process is very similar to that pursued with crude saltpetre.

---

[1] Mr. Bose reported to the Bahawalpur Durbar in 1904, that in extensive tracts of kallar land in the State the soil contains as much as 33% of sodium chloride (common salt) and also a large proportion of sulphate of soda, which could probably be utilised.

The best sodium sulphate produced in India is that of Behar, called *patna khári*. It is universally preferred to common salt for the curing of hides. Sodium sulphate is chiefly used in Europe in the manufacture of wood pulp.

Sodium carbonate is obtained in the Punjab in a crude form called *sajji* from *réh* or soda-soils by washing. It is also recovered from the ashes of the *láná* plant (*Salsola fœtida*) in the Jhang, Montgomery, and Multan districts, and from those of the *kangan khár* (*Haloxylon recurvum*) in Shahpur and in the Bahawalpur State.[1] Sodium Carbonate.

In Europe it is a product of the ammonia-soda process preparatory to the manufacture of caustic soda. In the electrolytic process it is obtained by passing carbon dioxide through caustic soda.[2]

Crude carbonate of soda is of much importance in the Indian arts. It is used in dyeing, bleaching, and glass and paper-making, and also, to a small extent still, in the manufacture of country soap. The cultivator often neutralises with it the organic acids in cane-juice when boiling it for making jaggery.[3]

Caustic soda is largely consumed in the Punjab in the manufacture of soap. Amongst its possible important uses are the refining of oils, the preparation of wood-pulp[4] and the extraction of alumina from bauxite.[5] Caustic soda.

---

1 For an account of the process, see Watt, *Comm. Prod. Ind.*, p. 113.

2 See *infra*.

3 Watt, *Comm. Prod. Ind.*, p. 55.

4 See p. 89 *supra*.

5 Holland, *Indian Bauxites*, in *Rec. Geol. Surv. Ind*, Vol. XXXII. (1905).

The production of caustic soda, the raw material for which, *viz.*, salt, is abundant in the Punjab, would seem to offer a great opening to capitalists. A cheap supply of the chemical would not only give an immense impetus to several existing industries, but also lead to the establishment of many new ones in the province. There are only two suitable methods of manufacture that need be considered—the ammonia-soda process and the various electrolytic processes. The Le Blanc is out of court, if only because of the large quantity of fuel as well as of sulphuric acid required.

The electrolytic processes, of which the Kastner-Kellner is the most economical, are simple, and consist in subjecting a solution of common salt to electrolysis. They all require cheap power and an unfailing supply of lime and salt. The products are caustic soda and chlorine, the latter in sufficient quantity to yield 2·1 tons of bleaching powder to 1 ton of caustic. There is very little demand for bleaching powder in India so far, but large quantities [1] of it would be required for the manufacture of wood-pulp, and it could also be used with great advantage as a disinfectant in Indian cities. Chlorine is used in the extraction of gold from the "tailings" of the goldfields, and the South Indian miners would probably be glad to obtain a cheap supply of the gas.

The electrolytic process pays at Niagara, where electrical energy costs about 4·4 pies per unit of kilowatt-hour. At Jagadhri, electrical energy would

---

[1] The yearly imports in all India averaged 47,794 cwts., valued at Rs. 2,54,295 in the period 1904-09.

be available from the Jumna at 4·25 pies per unit,[1] limestone from Dehra Dun at 5½ annas and waste salt from Khewra at 5¼ annas per maund.[2]

The ammonia-soda process consists in adding to a saturated solution of common salt about one-fifth of its quantity of full-strength ammonia and then passing carbon dioxide through it. Sodium bicarbonate is produced, which on heating gives carbonate of soda. The advantages of the process are that fuel and power are minor factors, and the output of each of the soda compounds can be adjusted to the requirements of the market.[3] The ammonia used would be obtained from ammonium sulphate[4] or

---

[1] See notes in Chapter XVIII. At Rasul, power may be available at an anna per unit or even less when the Upper and Lower Jhelum Canals are completed some years hence. The disadvantage of this source will be the irregular working of the Lower Jhelum Canal, which is expected to run only 13 days in the month. It will further be liable to uncertain stoppages, dependent on the flooding of the three hill-torrents that cross the track of the Upper Jhelum Canal.

[2] See pp. 139-140 *supra*, for salt. There are extensive deposits of tufacious as well as dolomitic limestone at Dehra Dun. The freight on limestone from Dehra Dun is about 1½ annas per maund, and on salt from Khewra 4¾ annas per maund. The rate is capable of reduction in either case.

[3] The yearly imports into India for the period 1904-09 averaged :—

	Cwts.	Rs.
Bicarbonate of soda	74,661	4,37,157
Caustic soda	84,557	7,28,157
Other soda compounds	124,707	5,13,335

[4] At Giridih the E. I. Ry. manufacture about 180 tons of sulphate of ammonia per annum which can be delivered at Delhi at Rs. 193-7-9 per ton (latest quotation). The price varies with the English market, that quoted at Giridih being the English price less freight and port dues. The chemical is guaranteed to contain 24% ammonia (NH_3). It is said to be of a good grey colour and entirely free from arsenic and cyanide. At present most of it goes to Japan.

ammonium chloride, which would have to be imported, but the item is not very heavy, as a good deal of it would be recovered with the aid of limestone. The great difficulty, however, is the necessity of keeping the temperature of the ammonia below 30°C. which would prevent a factory on the plains from working in the hot weather.

It has been estimated that the cost of setting up an ammonia soda factory in Madras, to produce 3,000 tons per annum, would be Rs. 3,50,000, and the cost of producing a ton of carbonate of soda as follows :—

	Rs.	a.	p.
Salt, 2 tons	10	8	0
Lime, 1·2 tons	14	0	0
Fuel, 2 tons (wood and charcoal)	12	0	0
Ammonium sulphate. say	5	0	0
Interest on capital and depreciation	18	0	0
Working expenses	30	0	0
Total	89	8	0

The cost of management, which would in no case be less than Rs. 15,000, would raise this figure to Rs. 95 per ton. This would still leave a margin of Rs. 17 per ton on the present price of the chemical in Madras.

The safest way to start the industry would be to set it up in conjunction with the manufacture of some other product of which it furnishes the raw material, such as chemical wood-pulp or soap, thus ensuring a minimum demand, and safety from destructive competition.

Borax.

Sodium biborate or borax (*sohágá* or *tinkal*) is found on the shores of certain lakes in Tibet and is deposited with sulphur by hot springs in the Puga valley of Ladakh. Jagadhri is the great entrepôt of the trade for the Punjab and annually imports about 4,000 maunds by way of the Naini Tal district or Simla.

The material is purified in one of the four refineries[1] and then railed to Delhi and Amritsar for distribution. In former years there was a large export to Europe through Bombay, but this has ceased in consequence of the discovery of limitless deposits of the mineral in Nevada and California.

The price of the unrefined borax at Jagadhri averages Rs. 7-8 per maund, and of refined about Rs. 11.

Borax is extensively used in this country in medicine and as a mordant in dyeing and calico-printing. It is indispensable to brass-founders and the makers of glass beads. The candle-maker treats his wicks with it in Europe. In India, as in Europe, it enters largely into pottery glazes and enamels for metallic surfaces.

Copper sulphate, obtained by dissolving copper in sulphuric acid, is in much demand in India, especially with dyers and calico-printers, and is used directly or indirectly in most pigments containing copper. It would pay to manufacture it from the copper and brass filings and metalliferous refuse that can easily be procured from the workshops in the larger centres. Taking the raw material at Rs. 45 per maund,[2] the following is the cost of the process :— Copper sulphate.

One maund of copper	Rs.	45	0	0
Two maunds of sulphuric acid	„	10	0	0
Other expenses	„	5	0	0
Total	Rs.	60	0	0

[1] The refining process is very simple and consists in dissolving the crude borax in water in large iron pans which are heated over a fire. The borax solution is decanted into earthenware pots and allowed to crystallize.

[2] In Lahore, waste copper is sold at Rs. 30 per maund and in Gujranwala for less.

The result is about four maunds of copper sulphate crystals[1] worth from Rs. 72 to 80 and giving a profit of 20 to 33% on the outlay.[2]

An enterprising amateur chemist of Amritsar[3] makes some profit by the manufacture of copper sulphate from the copper nitrate liquors which he obtains from the refiners of silver. He recovers the free nitric acid from the liquors by distillation, and then converts the remaining copper nitrate into the sulphate by the addition of some sulphuric acid. The supply of the raw material is, however, very limited.

Copper nitrate when ignited gives copper oxide, a substance used to some extent as a pigment, and also in the manufacture of green and blue glass.

Lead Oxide. Half-a-dozen persons in Jagadhri earn from 12 annas to Re. 1-4 a day by the manufacture of oxide of lead (litharge or *murda sang*) by a crude process which consists simply in roasting lead with saltpetre.[4] Lead is imported from Bombay at Rs. 11 per maund by the shopkeepers, who supply it to the workmen on a piece wage. Oxide of lead sells at Rs. 12 a maund

---

1 A certain quantity of water enters into the composition of the crystals, hence the increase in weight.

2 The estimate does not take into account the cost of the apparatus, which would be about Rs. 500, and of the labour, which would be the chemist's own with perhaps a couple of coolies.

3 L. Shambhoo Nath, a *sunár* by birth. After passing the Anglo-Vernacular Middle Examination, he joined the district office as a copyist, a post which he subsequently resigned on being refused special promotion. He took up privately the study of chemistry, for which he seems to have talents of a very high order, and now makes a living by the manufacture of various chemicals with apparatus largely devised by himself. He invented and patented the "Shambhoo gold-testing balance," the rights of which were recently bought by a local firm for Rs. 8,000.

4 For an account of the process, see Baden-Powell, *Punjab Products*, p. 103.

wholesale in Jagadhri, and Rs. 16 in Bombay, Calcutta and Karachi, to which places almost all of it is exported for use as an ointment (*marham*) for wounds and a waterproof paint for ships. The annual output is estimated at 500 maunds. The industry originated in the days when lead was imported from the hills, but it is strange that it should survive, under present conditions, at such a distance from the markets. We have here an illustration of the way in which commerce often persists in its time-worn channels.

Carbonate of lime occurs in two main groups in the Punjab: (*a*) as *kankar* or concretionary lime, and (*b*) as limestone and dolomite. **Carbonate of lime.**

Kankar is widely distributed, and is much used for road-building. It yields an excellent and somewhat hydraulic cement.[1]

Limestone occurs in immense profusion in the Salt Range as well as in the Narnaul district of the Patiala State,[2] and in fair quantities in many other parts of the province.

Lime, obtained by burning limestone, is very generally used in the dyeing and tanning industries, and in sugar manufacture. It is most important as an ingredient of mortar, which is a cement made of lime, sand, and water.[3]

Portland cement, or hydraulic cement, is obtainable from certain limestones naturally containing the requisite ingredients, or may be prepared artificially by

---

1 A hydraulic cement is one that will set under water.

2 A black limestone, well suited for lime, occurs four miles south-east of Narnaul. It sells at the high price of eight annas a maund in Delhi.—Bose, *Geol. and Minl. Resources of the Narnaul State* in *Rec. Geol. Surv. Ind.*, Vol. XXXIII. (1906), p. 59.

3 For other uses of lime, see p. 142.

mixing due proportions of pure lime with suitable river mud or clay.

The principal constituents of Portland cement are lime, silica, alumina and iron oxide. These vary considerably, but, roughly speaking, are found in the following proportions :—

	Per cent.
Lime	60 to 64
Silica	20 „ 24
Alumina	6 „ 10
Iron oxide	3 „ 5

These four constituents amount as a rule to 99 per cent., the remainder being small quantities of magnesia, alkalies, etc.

There are two processes of manufacture, the wet and the dry. In the former the materials are mixed by the agency of water, and in the latter by grinding in the dry state.

Each process consists of three operations, all of which must be very carefully performed. These are:—

(1) Intimate blending or mechanical mixing of the raw materials ;

(2) The conversion of this mixture into a chemical compound by calcination ; and

(3) Pulverisation of the calcined product.[1]

It is very desirable that the clays in the neighbourhood of Dandot and other convenient centres where limestone is abundant should be tested as to their suitability for the manufacture of Portland cement.[2]

---

[1] See Art. on the manufacture of Portland Cement in *Ind. Tr. Journ.*, Aug. 26, 1909, pp. 257 *et seq.*

[2] See Appendix IV. Deposits of a pale buff-coloured limestone occur at Madh and Palana in the Bikaner State, and of a chocolate brown clay at Bhinasar, near Bikaner City. Experiments made with these materials in England show that superior Portland cement can be made by mixing them.

A good deal of money will have to be spent on experiments, but considering the great importance of the subject it will be worth while to do so.

Gypsum. Gypsum or sulphate of lime is found generally in a very pure form, and in enormous quantities, in the Salt Range in association with salt marl.[1] There are considerable deposits of it also in the Murree hills,[2] as well as in the Kohat district,[3] where it can be obtained in any quantity by open quarrying.

The best known use of gypsum is the manufacture of plaster of Paris by calcination. It is in large demand, however, in Europe and America as a manure for leguminous plants as well as for tobacco, potatoes and clover.[4] In Northern India it is largely used for whitewashing, for which purpose it is exported from Dandot and Khewra.

Borate of lime. Borate of lime is a most useful glaze for earthenware, and can easily be made by adding borax to the chloride, nitrate, or any other very soluble salt of lime.

---

[1] Wynne, *Geol. of the Salt Range*, in *Mem. Geol. Surv.*, 1878, Vol. XIV. p. 300.

[2] *Rawalpindi Gazetteer* (1907), p. 169.

[3] Ball, *Econ. Geol. Ind.*, p. 452.

Gypsum of very good quality is found at Jamsar and other places in the Bikaner State. Plaster of Paris of average quality can be made from it, and in the opinion of Mr. Hooper it is very suitable for agricultural purposes, as it would cost so little to grind. It can be had at Jamsar railway station at Rs. 3-10 per ton. Selenite, a form of gypsum, is found at Lunkaransar.

Gypsum is not likely to be of general use as a manure in the Punjab at present, as the Doab soils contain a fairly large quantity of it. It might serve as a corrective to black *kallar* soils, provided it could be delivered cheap.

[4] Mukerji, *Handbook of Ind. Agric.* (1901), pp. 569 *et seq.* For other crops, see the *Proc. Bd. Agri. Ind.* (1907), pp. 126-7.

Pharmaceutical chemistry.

Pharmaceutical chemistry is hardly a subject for a layman, and a few remarks will be sufficient.

There are two distinct classes who purchase Indian drugs—the *hakim* and the *vaid* on the one hand, and the doctor on the other. The former have so far been the best customers, but the latter, too, is now beginning to extend his patronage to the local article. Many products in high favour with the former class, however, are ignored or despised by the latter and *vice versa*, while some are used by both.

Among the exclusively Indian drugs may be mentioned *Fumaria parviflora*, known as *pit pápra* to *vaids* and *shahtara* to *hakims*, the knowledge of which came to India with the Moslems. It was once much valued by physicians in Europe, but is not now used by them. It is one of the commonest weeds in the Punjab, infesting, in particular, fields sown with wheat, and the dried plant sells at 1¼ annas per seer in the Delhi bazaar. The extract is largely used as an aperient and febrifuge.

The Punjab produces an interesting variety of drugs, many of which deserve to be better known to the trade. The seeds of *Withania coagulans*, locally known as *panir band*, contain a curdling ferment which should be further popularised in the country. The roots of the *ratanjot* (*Onosma echioides*) are used for colouring oils and fats, and have been found to contain the same dye-principle as that of the ancient alkanet root of commerce. *Harmal* (*Peganum Harmala*) seeds have been suggested as a substitute for quinine, and are now being investigated chemically in England to determine their active principle. Among medicinal extracts which might be prepared with profit for the Indian market, we may mention Aconite, Colchicum, Datura and Rhubarb, which have now to be imported.[1] It may be noted that the Saharanpur Botanical Gardens have, for some years past, prepared a very satisfactory extract of henbane (*Hyoscianus niger*) for the Medical Stores Department.

Further, there is a regular market in Europe for the fragrant roots of the *kut* (*Saussurea Lappa*), which not only form a source of costus root oil, but are also used as an insectifuge and packed with furs and clothes for this purpose. Similarly, the fruit of the *betar* (*Juniperus communis*) is in much request for the preparation of juniper oil and gin. The pulp of the fruit of the *khartúma* (*Citrullus colocynthis*) comes at present from Smyrna, France and Austria, but it might be possible for India to share in the trade. Finally, mention may be made of the root of the *wanwângan* (*Podophyllum Emodi*), which is more likely to be exported in quantity than any other drug named in this article.[2]

It should be kept in mind, however, that fewer drugs are used in Europe and America than formerly, and there is besides a tendency for synthetic medicines to displace the cruder ones yielded by the vegetable kingdom. There is now little demand save for a few staple products, such as rhubarb, jalap, opium, cinchona, podophyllum, etc. From a practical

---

1 *Cf.* the *Indian Agriculturist*, Nov. 1st, 1910, p. 322.

2 See Watt, *Comm. Prod. Ind.*, p. 904. The root also yields a valuable dye-stuff, quercetin, as a by-product.

The crop in the Hazara Forest Division in 1911 is estimated at 87 maunds, which the Department undertakes to deliver at Hassan Abdal station.

The plant is also common at Murree.

or commercial point of view, therefore, the examination of Indian drugs is generally useless, unless they exhibit physiological activity of a very marked kind, though it is often of the highest scientific interest to investigate the herbs and simples to which the experience of an ancient medical science ascribes highly beneficial properties.

It should be quite possible for retired officers of the Provincial Medical Service, who are often compelled by circumstances to pass their days in out-of-the-way places, where private practice is out of the question, to take up with profit the cultivation and preparation of the many drugs which still command a good market.[1]

Dry distillation of wood.

The dry distillation of wood is an industry with a future in the vast Indian forests of inferior timber. The subject is, for various reasons, already engaging the serious attention of the Government of India.

Charcoal,[2] which constitutes only one-fifth of the weight of wood, and which in reality ought to be

[1] For an account of Punjab drugs, see Baden-Powell, *Punjab Products*, pp. 318 *et seq.* Much useful work, however, has been done since by Dunstan, Watt, Hooper and others. In addition to the valuable information contained in various publications of the Imperial Institute of London, there is an abundance of well-digested material in Watt, *Dictionary of Economic Products* and *Commercial Products of India*, and Dymock, Warden and Hooper's *Pharmacographica Indica.*

[2] The consumption of charcoal in the Punjab is considerable, but difficult to estimate. It has its largest outlet in household cooking and in metal workshops. It is also used for the generation of carbonic acid gas (p. 136 *supra*) and for making gunpowder. In Europe it is employed in iron and steel works, copper foundries, sugar refineries, and for filtering drinking-water. It is the basis of the manufacture of carbon bisulphide, the demand for which is increasing, and has, besides, a future in suction gas engines. For an account of the different woods used in India for preparing charcoal for various purposes, see Troup, *Indian Forest Utilization*, p. 85.

only a by-product of dry distillation, is, in the primitive process locally practised, the only substance recovered. The other very valuable products, which in European countries are obtained by the use of brick and iron retorts, are entirely wasted in India. Amongst these products may be mentioned pyroligneous acid, from which by a brief chemical process are obtained acetic acid, acetone and the various acetates. Acetone is in much demand in Europe and, to a certain extent, in India, for the manufacture of cordite, chloroform and celluloid. The other commercial products of distillation are wood-pitch, wood-tar and wood-spirit (methyl alcohol). Wood-pitch mixed with 20 per cent. of colophony asphalt is sent into the market for use by shoemakers. Wood-tar is used for creosoting wood, roofing felts and as an antiseptic.

Wood-spirit is used for various purposes, the chief of which are, (1) the methylating of rectified spirits, and (2) the production of paints, varnishes, perfumes, formaldehyde, etc. As it is very much more volatile and powerful in action than methylated spirit, it has been suggested as a solvent in the manufacture of shellac.[1]

The two conditions of success for a wood-distillation factory are, (1) abundant supply of cheap and suitable wood, and (2) a good market for charcoal.

In Europe, beech and birch are considered best for the purpose. In India, acacia, oak and other hard species of wood, which are generally used only for fuel, would be the most suitable, as they yield the largest percentage of charcoal, methyl-alcohol and

[1] See under *lac* in chapter XI *infra*.

acetates of lime. No statistical information is so far available on these species, or on the economic prospects of the industry, but the Forest Research Institute is now endeavouring to collect it.

The industry has been highly developed in France, Germany, and the United States of America, and the actual balance sheet of a German factory will be of interest in the present inquiry. The stills are at work for three hundred days in the year and handle birch wood[1] (one mark=12 annas).

Cost of production :—

	Marks.
Wood, 530,000 c.f. (about 6,000 tons)	67,500
Coal, 900 tons at 15 mks.	13,500
Lime, 150 tons at 15 mks.	2,250
Labour, 8,400 shifts at 2·10 mks.	17,640
Repairs	4,000
Packages	6,000
General (including management)	17,300
Marks	128,190

Sales :—

	Marks.
Charcoal, 1,650 tons at 48 mks.	74,250
Wood-spirit, 91·75 tons at 592·9 mks.	54,450
Acetate of lime, 382 tons at 160 mks.	61,120
Wood tar	7,500
Marks	197,320
"	128,190
Gross profit, Marks	69,130

[1] The destructive distillation of wood may be taken to yield approximately :—

Charcoal	25 to 29 %
Water-free tar	5 %
Pyroligneous acid	1 %
Acetate of lime	6 %
Wood-spirit 80 %	2 %

Depreciations :—

	Marks.
1 per cent. on land (9,000 mks.)	90
2 per cent. on buildings (50,000 mks.) . . .	1,000
12 per cent. on plant (125,000 mks.)	15,000
Marks .	16,090

Net Profit, Mks. 53,120 per annum.

The capital of the factory is 184,000 marks and the return amounts therefore to 35 per cent.[1]

As has been said already, the industry has great possibilities, but it is not one for private persons to take up in the first instance. It would certainly be worth while for Government to spend a capital sum of three lacs of rupees on an experimental factory to treat 25,000 tons of wood yearly. The first step would be to send sample consignments of, say, ten tons each of all suitable varieties of wood to Europe, for expert opinion as to the value of their products. An officer of the Forest Department with the necessary qualifications might then be deputed to study wood-distillation methods in France, Germany, Austria and America, and then frame a scheme in consultation with the best manufacturers for setting up a factory in a selected forest area.

Writing Ink.

Writing ink is used more and more with the growth of education in this country, but, if we leave out of account a couple of small firms each in Rawalpindi, Lahore and Amritsar, its manufacture on

[1] The balance sheet is taken from a lecture by Mr. Max Muspratt, reported in the *Jour. Soc. Chem. Ind.*, Vol. XXIV. (April 29, 1905), pp. 372-74. It apparently leaves out of account interest on the floating capital. For an account of the industry as it exists in America, see *Chemical Method for Utilising Wood* (U. S. Dept. Agric. Bureau of Chemistry, Circular No. 36), and Harper, *Utilization of Wood Waste by Distillation*.

scientific principles is practically unknown in the Punjab.[1] A good ink must:

(1) Flow easily from the pen,

(2) Yield a deep black writing, either immediately or after a short time,

(3) Not corrode the pen nor destroy the paper, and

(4) Leave little or no sediment when kept in air-tight bottles.

Writing inks are of two kinds: (*a*) tannin inks, and (*b*) non-tannin inks. The former are undoubtedly the best, and their manufacture has a great future in India. It should not, however, be undertaken by any but men of education, preferably with a knowledge of science.

The following recipe will give an idea of the composition of tannin inks :—

Galls (*Máju phal*)[2]	3 parts.
Crystallised ferrous sulphate[3]	2 ,,
Gum arabic	2 ,,
Water	60 ,,

---

[1] "Indian ink," however, is made everywhere, though in diminishing quantities. At the census of 1901 a hundred ink-makers were enumerated in Amritsar and twenty in Delhi.

[2] The fruits of the *Quercus infectoria*, which is not indigenous to India, but is found in Greece, Bosnia, and Asia Minor. Some of the gall-nuts used in India are probably obtained from oak trees in the Kumaon, Garhwal and Bijnor forests. Watt, *Dict. Econ. Prod.*, Vol. VI. Pt. I. p. 338.

[3] Ferrous sulphate can easily be made by treating scrap iron with dilute sulphuric acid or by roasting iron pyrites and then oxidising it in the air. On the occurrence of ferrous sulphate in the Punjab, see Baden-Powell, *Punjab Products*, pp. 66-67. About 100 maunds of a substance, locally known as *káhi*, is yearly extracted from the hills near Kalabagh, the price at site being 10½ annas per maund. A sample analysed for the writer was found to be native sulphate of iron with some sulphate of alumina and insoluble matter.

Gall-nuts, which contain from 30 to 50 per cent. of tannin, are by far the best material for tannin inks; but their place could be taken by other materials abundant in India, amongst which may be mentioned myrobalans (*harrar*), containing about 30 per cent.; pomegranate rind, containing about 20 per cent.; the aqueous extract of the *khair* tree (*Acacia Catechu*), which contains 60 per cent.; the fruit of the *bahera* (*Terminalia belerica*), containing about 20 per cent., and others.[1] In the above recipe about double the weight of myrobalans could be substituted for gall-nuts, and a few experiments would show what proportion to use of the others.

For gum arabic one can substitute refined gum of the common *kikar* (*A. arabica*). Ink made with ferrous sulphate writes blue at first, but soon changes into black on exposure to the air. If ferric sulphate (oxidised ferrous sulphate) is substituted, it writes jet-black.

Carbolic acid in the proportion of 8 lbs. per 1,000 should always be added. The addition of a little indigo sulphate very much improves the quality of the ink.

Non-tannin inks can be made from aniline colours or from indigo carmine, which is easily prepared from indigo by the action of strong fuming sulphuric acid. The following simple recipe for blue ink may be cited.[2]

Indigo carmine	10	parts.
Gum arabic	5	,,
Water	50 to 100	,,

[1] See pp. 102-104 *supra*.

[2] For further information on the subject, and for a description of the processes of ink-manufacture, which should be carefully studied, the reader is referred to Lehner, *Inks*, and Thorpe, *Dict. Appl. Chem.*, Vol. II. Art. *Ink*.

CHAPTER XI.

Essential Oils, Resins and Allied Industries.

Essential oils[1] are almost all of vegetable origin and are extracted from flowers such as the rose, leaves such as those of the basil, the rind of fruits such as the orange, chips of wood such as deodar,[2] and the fruits of the umbelliferæ, *e.g.*, *ajwain*.

There are several methods of extraction, but the only one common in the Punjab is that of distillation. The material to be treated is boiled with water and the oil collected by condensation.

Perfumes.

Rose-water and otto of roses are made in Amritsar and Lahore, which grow the flower in large quantities, and also to a certain extent in Hoshiarpur.[3] The otto is prepared according to an ancient process by distilling rose-water with sandal-wood oil, over and over again, to the strength required. Sandal-wood oil imported from Bombay or Kanauj costs Rs. 20 per seer,

---

[1] Thorpe, *Dictionary of Applied Chemistry*, Vol. III. Art. *Oils (Essential)*; Sadtler, *Industrial Organic Chemistry*, pp. 44 *et seq*.

[2] See Troup's *Indian Forest Utilisation*, pp. 151, 225. Deodar oil, called *kelu-ka-tel*, is used for skin diseases and rheumatism and also for smearing over inflated skins used in crossing rivers (Baden-Powell, *Punjab Products*, p. 540. Atkinson, *Himalayan Districts*, 1882, p. 831). There is plenty of deodar in the Punjab.

[3] Hardly any perfume is made in Delhi itself which, however, is a great distributing centre. There are no flowers in the neighbourhood; but a certain amount of sesame-seed impregnated with various perfumes is imported to be crushed locally.

and roses Rs. 6 per maund,[1] while the otto sells at 8 annas to Rs. 2 per tola in the bazaar. The essences of *henna*[2] and *khas*,[3] the former noted for its cooling properties, are also distilled in Amritsar and Lahore. Oil or otto of *henna* is generally prepared with a sesame-oil base in the same manner as otto of roses, and sells at eight annas to a rupee a seer.

No special caste monopolises the industry in Lahore, but in Amritsar it is entirely in the hands of ten Hindu shopkeepers, each of whom employs half a dozen hill-men at 10 to 12 rupees a month. The perfumer's craft is distinctly on the decline, partly because he adulterates his perfumes, but chiefly for the reason that his products, as compared with European scents, are becoming less and less fashionable with men. About Rs. 25,000 worth of otto is, however, said to be still sent out annually from Amritsar city to all parts of the Punjab, and even to Siam, to which country there is a regular export.

The Punjab has a fair number of aromatic herbs and plants, and there seems to be room for an essential-oil factory on modern lines[4] at Lahore, Amritsar, Hos-

[1] 100,000 roses, or 100 lbs. of rose-leaves, yield 180 grains or 3 drachms of pure otto of roses, or 100 bottles of rose-water.

[2] *Henna* or *Mehndi* (*Lawsonia alba*) leaves cost about Rs. 5-8 per maund in Amritsar.

[3] *Khas*, the root of *Vetivera zizanioides*, Stapf, costs Rs. 5 per maund in Amritsar. It is abundant in the Karnal and Hissar districts (Coldstream, *Grasses of the Southern Punjab*, No. 18, under *Andropogon muricatus*) and also imported from Kahnuwan (Gurdaspur district), Jagadhri and Saharanpur. The oil is known in Europe as vetiver, and is used as a perfume and for flavouring sherbet. It commands a high price, but is hardly if ever exported from India. It is pressed in Europe from Indian roots or imported from Réunion.

[4] The capital required for buildings, machinery and cultivation need not exceed Rs. 30,000.

hiarpur [1] or some other convenient centre. Amongst the flowers that could be treated may be mentioned those of *Acacia Farnesiana*,[2] which can be made into an excellent pomade with some vegetable fat such as kokam butter (*Gracinia indica*) or Malabar tallow (*Vateria indica*) by the process of *enfleurage* practised at Cannes in France[3]. About twenty years ago a consignment of *cassie* pomade, as it is called, sent to London by a Naini Tal planter was pronounced superior to that of Cannes, but the industry unfortunately came to an end shortly after, at the death of its founder. A European capitalist has lately leased a forest of *Acacia Farnesiana* from the Balrampur estate (Gonda district, United Provinces). He treats about 1,000 maunds of flowers every year and exports the product to Europe.[4]

Other essences.

Mr. Puran Singh, of the Forest Research Institute, writes that in Lahore he once subjected the locally grown *sónf*[5] and *ajwain*[6] seeds to distillation with steam. From the former he obtained aniseed-oil or anethol which the Mian Mir medical department pronounced to be excellent and satisfying all the tests of the British Pharmacopœia. Anethol sells at Rs. 6 to

---

[1] A railway will shortly connect Hoshiarpur with Jullundur.

[2] *Wilayati kikar*, *Cassie*.

[3] See *Indian Essential Oils*, by Hooper, Indian Industrial Conference Report, 1906, p. 267, where the process is described. The annual yield per tree, when cultivated, is 2 pounds of flowers, worth from three to four annas per pound, which means from Rs. 450 to Rs. 600 per acre. The Saharanpur Botanical Gardens will shortly make experiments with these flowers.

[4] Chatterjee, *Industries of the United Provinces*, p 178.

[5] Anise, *Pimpinella anisum*.

[6] *Carum copticum*.

12 per lb. He also prepared thymol, the well-known antiseptic, from *ajwain* at a cost low enough to make the distillation profitable, considering that the by-product, ajwain-oil, is in great demand.[1] He found the green seeds of Punjab-grown *ajwain* richer in oil than those of other localities.

It has further to be noted that the by-products of the process include concentrated *'arks* (perfumed waters) which can be easily disposed of in the bazaars of the great cities. The price realised from their sale would add to the profits.

The other promising materials available in the Punjab for cultivation as well as manipulation by a modern factory include black and white caraway,[2] cumin,[3] fennel,[4] fenugreek,[5] marsh mint,[6] spearmint,[7] the roots, shoots and leaves of the *khawi*[8] and *rauns*[9]

---

[1] Besides thymol, a substance called thymene is obtained from *ajwain* oil and used as a soap-perfume.

[2] *Carum Bulbocastanum* and *C. Carui*, *zírá*.

[3] *Cuminum Cyminum*, also known as *zírá*.

[4] *Fœniculum vulgare*, *bari sonf*.

[5] *Trigonella Fœnum græcum*, *methi*.

[6] *Mentha arvensis*, *phudina*, Watt, *Dic. Econ. Prod. Ind.*, Vol. V. p. 228.

[7] *Mentha viridis*, *pahári phudína*. Ibid. p. 231.

[8] *Cymbopogon Schœnanthus*. This fragrant jungle grass is not found near cultivation, but is common on rocks, sand and hard loamy soil in some of the desert tracts from Karachi to Peshawar and Ludhiana, and is plentiful in the Hissar *bir*. Its red colour, when ripe, gives a special tinge to the landscape where it abounds. Coldstream, *Grasses of the Southern Punjab*, No. 18, under *Andropogon laniger*.

Watt (*Comm. Prod. Ind.* p. 461) states that an essential oil known in Europe as ginger-grass oil is sometimes expressed from the roots of C. Schœnanthus (C. Martinii) in the Punjab.

[9] *Cymbopogon Jwarancusa*, also called *buj* in Hissar, *ágyaghás* in the neighbourhood of Lahore, where it is common, and apparently known as *khawi* in some parts of the Punjab and in the United Provinces. It is the *Nardus indica* of the early writers. It has a peculiar fragrant smell, the perfume residing chiefly in the roots. In some parts of the country, *e.g.*, Rawalpindi district, it is especially aromatic, but it is nowhere very abundant. Coldstream, *op. cit.* No. 17, under *Andropogon Schœnanthus*.

grasses and the flowers or other parts of the well-known *motia*,[1] *henna*, *khas*,[2] *chambeli*[3] and *tulsi*.[4] It is suggested that the Agricultural Department might experiment in the cultivation of these and other fragrant grasses and plants.[5]

Turpentine oil and Colophony.

Turpentine oil is obtained by distilling the crude resin that exudes from various trees of which the *chir* (*Pinus longifolia*) alone is of commercial importance in the Punjab. What remains of the crude turpentine after the oil volatilises is strained and purified and then put on the market as rosin or colophony.

Turpentine oil is in great demand in many industries, chiefly in the manufacture of varnishes and paints. It is valuable as a cleansing agent and is also used to a small extent in medicine, in the preparation of rubber cements, artificial camphor, etc.

Colophony finds its principal application in the manufacture of cheap yellow household soaps and cheap varnishes. It is also used by calico-printers and paper-mills for stiffening machinery belts, for cements, and as a reducing agent in the soldering of metals. In pharmacy it is in request for many ointments and plasters.

---

[1] Also called *mógra*, the Arabian jasmine (*Jasminum Sambac*).

[2] See note 4, p. 74.

[3] The Spanish jasmine (*Jasminum grandiflorum*). At Grasse in Southern France, one acre planted with this is said to yield £250 yearly, but requires a good deal of work. See *Journal of the Society of Arts*, Nov. 20, 1908, p. 19.

[4] The sweet Basil (*Ocimum Basilicum*).

[5] In Europe, coriander (*dhania*, *Coriandrum sativum*) is valued for its oil, the Russian variety yielding as much as ·8 to 1 per cent. The Indian fruit is poor in oil, the proportion being ·15 to ·2 per cent. Coriander oil commands a high price in Europe, and an improvement of the Indian variety in this respect is much to be desired. Coriander oil is prepared in Lahore and sells at 8 annas to Re. 1 a seer in the bazaar.

When submitted to dry distillation, colophony yields two qualities of oil, the lighter or rosin-spirit, which comes off first, and the heavier, or rosin oil, which distils later. Rosin-spirit is used in varnish-making and as an adulterant of turpentine oil. It is an ingredient of printing inks and many useful metallic resinates that serve various industrial purposes.

The Forest Department has produced turpentine and colophony in the Punjab and United Provinces for some years, chiefly by way of experiment, but the considerable demand in India has almost entirely been met so far by imports from the United States of America.[1] The Punjab product is, however, quite suitable for local purposes if not for export, and its manufacture might be made lucrative by those who will profit by past experience.[2]

Amongst the difficulties in the way of the industry are the proper conduct and supervision of the tapping operations and the collection and transport of the crude turpentine to the factory. These have been successfully overcome at the Bhowali distillery near Naini Tal.

The chief obstacle, so far, has been the lack of a firm market, due to the uneven quality of the

---

[1] The annual imports of colophony into India average about 100,000 maunds, valued at 6¼ lacs of rupees, and of turpentine 200,000 gallons, valued at 5 lacs of rupees. To produce this locally would mean the collection of 200,000 maunds of crude resin yearly, and for the purpose over 1½ million of *Pinus longifolia* and *P. excelsa* trees would have to be tapped.

At present the combined Indian output does not exceed 14,000 maunds (of 80 lbs.) of crude resin per annum.

[2] That colophony of excellent quality and quite equal to the best French and American varieties can be made by careful distillation of Indian resin, is now beyond doubt. See *Indian Trade Journal*, Dec. 8, 1910, p. 274.

turpentine, and to a certain extent, also, to defective methods of packing for transport, and the absence of business-like arrangements for selling the products. The quality of the turpentine can be assured by the rather wasteful process of repeated distillation. Mr. Puran Singh of the Forest Research Institute has, however, been able to obtain a product which appears equal to the best American grades, by carrying on the distillation with the aid of acetic acid and methylated spirit at a much lower temperature than hitherto used. If this process is found to be a commercial success, it will no doubt be universally adopted. The Institute has further discovered that the clarification of colophony with crystalline alum over an open fire considerably reduces its colour. Experiments are still in progress to bring Indian colophony up to the standard of the imported article.

The Bhowali distillery, set up at a cost of Rs. 15,000, has yielded a regular profit of from 104 to 217 per cent. during the six years 1905-1910.[1] It has four stills, each still treating six maunds of crude turpentine per day of eight hours. It handles a little over 17,000 maunds of crude turpentine a year. As a *chir* tree yields between 3 and 3½ seers per annum, and must rest twenty years after being worked for five years, we must reckon that it takes a forest of rather more than a million to supply this quantity.

In the Punjab the Kangra, Bashahr and Rawalpindi forest divisions, and in the Frontier Province the Hazara division seem to be suitable for exploitation

---

[1] The profit leaves out of account the cost of the forest establishment to look after the tapping operations, and the royalty a private factory would have to pay to the Forest Department.

by a turpentine factory. The Kangra *chir* forests, in particular, cover vast tracts which yield but little revenue at present, and are besides a standing source of anxiety on account of their liability to fires. The trees themselves are gnarled, badly grown and fire-damaged, and not even in demand for fuel. The Forest Department, as is well known, set up a factory at Nurpur in this division[1] in 1899, but closed it down in 1905 for reasons other than commercial failure. An experimental factory, involving a capital expenditure of Rs. 60,000 has now been established at Shahdara. It will be supplied with the crude resin by the *chir* forests of Kangra, Bashahr, Hazara and Rawalpindi, and the *kail* forests of Kulu and Bashahr.

Lac is the resinous secretion of an insect on certain trees, of which the chief varieties in the Punjab are the *kikar* (*Acacia arabica*), the *ber* (*Zizyphus Jujuba*), the *dhák* (*Butea frondosa*), and, to a smaller extent, the *pipal* (*Ficus religiosa*) and other species of *Ficus*. The Hoshiarpur district is estimated to produce from 3,000 to 5,000 maunds of it annually, followed at a long distance by the Amballa district with about 300 maunds, the Hamirpur *tahsil* of the Kangra district with 160, and the Batala *tahsil* of Gurdaspur with 100. Small quantities are also collected, for local use Lac.

---

[1] Nurpur was declared to be ideal for the purpose. It is on the tonga road, six miles from Pathankote railway station, and has large fuel-producing areas within easy reach. It was estimated to command an annual supply of 10,000 maunds of crude turpentine, the cost of collection of which, plus transport to the distillery, was found by actual experience to amount to less than Rs. 2 a maund. See *Bullet. Impl. Inst.* 1906, Vol. IV. p. 226; also *Punjab Administration Report* (1904-05), pp. 14-15, and *Working Plan of Kangra Forest Division* pp. 37 *et seq.*

or export, in the Jullundur, Ludhiana and Amritsar districts, in the Chakwal *tahsil* of Jhelum, in parts of the Rawalpindi district, and of the districts of the Delhi division. The insect appears to be unknown, at all events to the general market, in the districts further to the west.

In Hoshiarpur alone do the advantages of systematic propagation and collection appear to be understood, and the lac crop held sufficiently valuable for private owners to lease land with suitable trees for lac cultivation, but even here the methods employed are extremely primitive and wasteful, and it must be rarely indeed that a single tree yields a profit, as is alleged, of as much as Rs. 12 a year.[1]

There is no regular lac refinery in the province, the major portion of the Punjab crop being exported to Mirzapur for further treatment.[2] The material is, however, often cleaned by individuals for their own use by rough and ready methods, and in Amritsar, in particular, there is a considerable trade in it.

Nothing has been done by the Government so far to promote an industry which yields such handsome profits in other provinces to every one concerned. Systematic lac cultivation could be taken up with advantage by the Forest and Canal departments, and

---

[1] The Hoshiarpur District Board derives an annual revenue of about Rs. 500 from the sale of lac on its road-side trees. Small sums are realised by the District Board of Ambala, and occasionally by that of Jullundur.

[2] The Provincial figures (in maunds) of the trade in lac are :—

	1904-05	1905-06	1906-07	1907-08	1908-09.
Imports	8,853	5,420	3,773	6,366	5,093
Exports	5,106	6,395	5,758	2,223	1,708

is as deserving of the attention of district officers as the rearing of the silkworm.[1]

Lac is put to numerous uses in India. Besides being the common ingredient of varnish, it is employed by the turner as a paint and polish, and by the cutler to cement the knife-blade to its handle. It is everywhere made into bangles for poor women, while it is of value to the goldsmith for the coloured ornamentation of his costly wares. In Europe, it enters not only into the composition of varnish and lithographic ink, but is also in much demand as a stiffening material for hats, for electrical work, and latterly for the manufacture of gramophone records.

Sealing-wax.

Sealing-wax is made with any quality of lac, mixed with colophony, turpentine, etc. The best and least brittle kinds are made of shellac *immediately* after its separation by fusion from stick or seed-lac. Hence sealing-wax properly prepared in India will necessarily be better than that made in countries into which the lac has to be imported.[2] The process of manufacture is fairly simple. The wax is first rolled out into round sticks on a slab and then cast in moulds. For red sealing-wax, for example, the following proportions are used :—

Turpentine	4
Shellac	$5\frac{1}{2}$
Colophony	$1\frac{1}{2}$
Cinnabar (for colour) . . .	$1\frac{1}{4}$

[1] For an excellent account of the industry, see Stebbing, *The Lac-insect* (*Ind. For. Mem.*), 1910, where the lines of future development are indicated. See also *Agric. Ledger*, No. 9 of 1901. To Mr. Puran Singh is due the credit of discovering how to extract, by the use of wood-spirit, the finest and purest quality of shellac from even the inferior grades now wasted. The practical value of the process depends, however, on a cheap supply of wood-spirit. See his *Manufacture of Pure Shellac* (*Ind. For. Mem.*), Calc. 1909.

[2] See Thorpe, *Dict. Appl. Chem.*, Vol. III. Art. *Sealing-wax.* For an account of the processes of manufacture see also Spon, *Workshop Receipts*, 1909, Vol. IV, Art *Sealing-wax.*

Sealing-wax is made by only one firm, employing half a dozen men, in the Punjab—at Amritsar. The industry is capable of great development. There is no reason why India, which has a monopoly of the raw material, should not supply the whole world with the manufactured commodity.

Boot-blacking. "Blacking" is a preservative varnish to give a polish to the uppers of boots, and protect them from wear and decay. The substance is now much used in this country and is being manufactured by a few amateur chemists in Lahore and Amritsar. The industry is simple in itself and would appear to be profitable, but the men engaged in it are handicapped by lack of capital and business connections.

The raw material is available locally in abundance. The base for boot-blacking, for example, is generally bone-charcoal mixed with substances which acquire a gloss by friction, such as sugar and oil. Harness-blacking is made differently, but is of equally simple composition.

Varnishes. Varnishes are of two kinds, oil-varnishes and spirit-varnishes. The former are mixtures of drying oils like linseed oil, and resins like copal, sandarach, colophony, stearin-pitch, or bone-oil pitch. Spirit-varnishes are made either of methylated spirit mixed with shellac, colophony and other resins, or of turpentine oil mixed with shellac, sandarach,[1] dammar,[2] etc.

---

[1] This is the valuable resin of the sandarach tree (*Callitris quadrivalvis*) of Algeria. Though Watt says the tree could be grown in India, no one has yet attempted to acclimatise it. The Forest Department might look into this.

[2] See Hurst, *Paints, Colours, Oils, and Varnishes*. For recipes, see Livache and McIntosh, *Varnishes*, etc.

Varnishes are used not only for ornamental purposes, but also with the object of preserving articles of wood, metal, glass, stone, leather, paper, etc., from the action of the weather and from the ravages of noxious insects, such as the white-ant.

Though varnishes of a kind are made in the Punjab, the industry is still in a very elementary stage, and the imported article is preferred in most places as being cheaper and better. In Gujarat a tolerable mixture is made of country shellac with 90 % overproof German alcohol.[1] An Amritsar firm makes a preparation of colophony and alcohol which finds a local sale.

The Hoshiarpur, Jullundur and Chiniot carpenters use *rál*[2] with linseed-oil, and shellac with spirits of wine, while those of Kartárpúr are satisfied with a more rough and ready mixture of colophony or *rál* with turpentine or even kerosene oil. The fine carved screens of Chiniot lose much of their charm because of the evil-smelling preparation applied to them.

The difficulty of the manufacture lies in discovering the proper proportion of the various ingredients for different kinds of work. This can only be found by experiment. The industry, however, has great possibilities before it in the Punjab, which abounds with all the raw materials, while in Europe they have to be imported from long distances.

Printing-ink is a very stiff, rapidly-drying varnish made of boiled linseed or poppy-seed oil mixed with lamp-black or finely ground charcoal. Rosin is also sometimes added to the composition, while for the Printing-ink.

---

[1] German alcohol costs Rs. 2-2-0 per gallon Formerly that of Shahjehanpur, at Rs. 3-4-0 per gallon, was used.

[2] Resinous exudation of the *sál* tree (*Shorea robusta*).

ink used for books, soap is necessary. The following recipes,[1] which are only two of many, will illustrate the proportion in which the different ingredients are used. The colouring material has, of course, to be added separately :—

Boiled oil	100
Rosin	25
Soap	4
Drying oil	6
	135

In inferior inks, rosin-oil takes the place of linseed oil, *e.g.* :—

Rosin oil	10
Rosin	4
Rosin soap	1
Ordinary soap	1
	16

Strange to say, no printing-ink is manufactured in the province, in spite of the large local demand.

Paints.

The manufacture of paints[2] is another industry that could be started here. Messrs. Olpherts and Co. of Jubbulpore, and Turner, Morrison and Co. of Calcutta, are the only two firms in India who have taken it up so far, and both are doing well. The former use the soft hæmatite of Jauli and yellow ochre from the Panna State, while the latter chiefly depend on imported raw material.[3]

Amongst the locally available materials for paint-making, besides linseed-oil, may be mentioned

---

[1] The recipes are cited from Livache and McIntosh, *op. cit.*, Vol. I. p. 67.

[2] See Thorpe, *Dict. Appl. Chem.*, Vol. III. Art. *Pigments* ; Spon, *Workshop Receipts*, Vol. III. Art. *Paints.*

[3] *Rec. Geol. Surv. Ind*, Vol. XXXIX. 1910, p. 263.

orpiment and cobalt[1] and the very good red oxide of iron[2] and yellow ochre of which there are abundant deposits in the Bikaner State.

---

[1] Cobalt is found at Babai (Shekhawati, Jeypore State) and is used by enamellers on the precious metals.

[2] It is estimated that the actual cost of quarrying and delivering the red oxide of iron at Palana Station would be Rs. 7 a ton. The figure does not, of course, include such royalties as the State may charge.

CHAPTER XII.

OILS, FATS AND ALLIED INDUSTRIES.

Oils are divided into two main classes, the fixed or fatty oils and the essential or volatile oils. The latter are distinguished from the former by a strong and characteristic smell and the habit of volatilising without decomposition and usually without any residue. This chapter treats of the former class only.

Taking the vegetable oils, we find that the net annual imports into the Punjab come to about 1,000 tons, whereas the net exports of oil-seeds, mostly to Europe *via* Karachi, amount to no less than 50,000 tons.[1] *Prima facie,* therefore, there ought to be an opening here for an oil-crushing industry of some magnitude. As a matter of fact, that which exists is by no means in a flourishing condition.

The relative importance of the various vegetable oils and oil-seeds produced in or imported into the province will appear from the following average figures for the five years 1904-09. The first three varieties on the list are common everywhere, but linseed is not cultivated to any extent worth mentioning, save in the Kangra hills and the submontane districts of Sialkot, Gurdaspur and Hoshiarpur. The castor plant is

[1] The average imports of vegetable oils for the five years 1904-09 were 2,519·5 tons, and exports 1,481·3 tons.

nowhere cultivated systematically, but grows wild on canal embankments chiefly in Jhelum and Gurgaon. The villagers pay no attention to it and do not use the seeds.

Name of Seeds.	*Crop acreage.*	*Net Imports (in mds.).* *Oil-seeds.*	*Oil.*
Rape, Taramira and Mustard	774,759	—	—
Toria	292,667	—	—
Til or Jinjli	116,532	—	—
Linseed	34,081	—	—
Castor-seed	—	19,566	10,329
Cocoanut	—	—	9,929
Earthnut	—	15,216	—
Poppy-seed	—	4,929	—
Others	1,871	—	29,346
Total	1,219,910	—	—

It will be useful to give a brief account of the nature of all the fixed oils and fats of present or prospective interest to the Punjab, with the uses to which they are put in India or in European countries.

I. The olive-oil group includes olive oil,[1] earthnut oil, almond oil, etc. Of these, olive oil is largely consumed in Europe in cooking and at table. Earthnut oil is a substitute for olive, neats-foot and other oils, and almond oil is useful for ointments and emulsions.

[1] There are large tracts covered with the wild olive (*Olea ferruginea*) in the Jhelum, Salt Range and Rawalpindi forest divisions. Experiments in grafting European varieties upon it have been commenced under Government auspices at Khairi Murat (Rawalpindi division) and at Sakesar, in areas free from rights of user. If, however, the industry is to be taken up on any considerable scale, the difficult question of the position of the right-holders in the larger forests will have to be solved. See the *Prog. Rep. on For. Admn. Punjab*, 1909, p. 19. The tree fruits abundantly in the Kohat district (N. W. Frontier Province), and the oil, which resembles the olive-kernel oil of Europe in all its properties, seems to be well adapted for table and domestic purposes. *Ann. Rep. Ind. Sec. Ind. Museum*, 1904-05, p. 25.

II. The rape-oil group[1] includes the oils of *sarso*, *tárámirá* and *tória*. In India they are used for cooking and lighting, and in Europe for lubricating machinery, greasing steel goods and soap-making. Rape oil is also used for illuminating in many places, notably the Jewish quarters of Galicia. After refining, it is used as an edible oil in Europe.

III. The cotton-oil group[2] includes the oils of cotton-seed, sesame, maize and soya-bean.[3] Cotton-oil is of sufficient importance at the present moment to be treated in a section by itself. Sesame or *til* oil is used in India for cooking and for the manufacture of soap and perfumed oils. The whole seed is used in sweetmeats, while the cake is in great demand as a cattle food and is even eaten by men in time of famine. In Europe the oil is largely used by the soap-maker, but it is also held to be the best table oil after olive, and usually the two are mixed. Maize oil, obtained from the germ of the seed, is valued for lighting, lubricating, soap-making and as a salad-oil. Soya-bean oil is used for the manufacture of soft soap, but when highly refined it often forms a foundation for table oils.

IV. The linseed-oil group. Linseed oil is the drying oil[4] *par excellence*. It is, however, used not only

---

[1] There is much confusion at present in the nomenclature of this group in the Punjab. *Sarsõ* is officially known as *Brassica campestris*. *Toria* is *Brassica campestris*, sub-species *Napus* var. *Toria*; *Taramira* is *Eruca sativa*. It is expected that the Economic Botanist will shortly take their scientific classification in hand.

[2] As cotton-seed oil is now more conveniently termed.

[3] On the soy-bean see *Agric. Ledger*, No. 8 of 1911, and Bulletin No. 197 of the Agric. Dept. of the U. S. A.

[4] A "drying oil" is a vegetable oil that has the property of gradually absorbing oxygen and changing eventually into a solid elastic substance, insoluble in the usual oil solvents. Such are the oils used by painters.

by the paint-maker, but also by the textile manufacturer and the maker of soft soap.

Poppy-seed oil, which also belongs to this series, is used for cooking, lighting and mixing with paints.

V. Castor oil, well known for its purgative properties, is also largely used in India as an illuminant on the railways. It is in demand with soap-makers and manufacturers of Turkey-red oil and is also a good lubricant for heavy machinery.

VI. The cocoanut-oil group. The chief members of this group are cocoanut-oil and *mahua* oil,[1] both largely used in India for cooking, lighting and soap-making. In Europe, cocoanut oil is also made into candles and "marine soap," *i. e.*, soap soluble in sea-water. It is now, however, chiefly refined by the deodorising process into cocoanut butter, which fetches as much as £55 a ton.

VII. The bone-grease group includes bone-grease and neats-foot oil. The former is extracted from bones by boiling [2] or the use of solvents, and is largely made into soaps of the cheaper kind, especially those used for industrial purposes. The latter is obtained by boiling the feet of various animals,[3] and is used for lubricating clocks and machinery exposed to low temperatures, and as a dressing for leather.

---

[1] Oil of the seeds of *Bassia malabarica*. The tree is found in the Kangra district, but it is not common and there is no trade in its products, though occasionally a man may express some oil for his own use. Besides the oil, it yields extremely valuable economic products, *viz.*, edible flowers, leaves for fodder, a gum, a dye, etc., and deserves to be encouraged in the province. (See Watt, *Comm. Prod. Ind.*, p. 118.)

[2] For the process, which is simple, see Koller, *Waste Products*, p. 72, Hurst, *Soaps*, p. 77. *Cf.* also note 5, on p. 122.

[3] Koller, *loc. cit.*

VIII. The tallow group includes fatty oils obtained from animals dead or alive. These are the fat[1] of the ox, sheep and horse, wool-fat [2] obtained from wool wash-water, and ordinary butter-fat and ghee from milk.[3] Of these, tallow and horse-fat are used for making soap and candles and for lubricating machinery. Wool-fat is usually made into candles or distilled with steam to obtain oleic and stearic acids, but it is also the most abundant source of cholesterin, which, after undergoing a process involving the use of caustic soda, becomes the "lanolin" of commerce, valuable as a drug and also as a dressing for leather.

IX. *Waxes* [4].—Of these one need only mention bees-wax, which is used for various purposes in commerce,

---

[1] The extraction of animal oils and fats such as tallow from the covering tissues is known as "rendering," a simple process described in Hurst, *Soaps*, pp. 68 *et seq.*

There is a fair local trade in animal tallow, which is, however, nowhere properly "rendered." The operation would largely increase its value in the European market as a candle-material. It could also be locally treated for obtaining margarine, which could be exported for use as a substitute for butter.

Fat is locally used for soap-making. It is also used for cooking by those who cannot afford *ghee.* It sells at Rs. 10 to Rs. 14 a maund.

[2] See note 2, p. 49 *supra*, and Thorpe, *Dict. Appl. Chem.*, Arts. *Cholesterin* and *Lanolin.*

A plant dealing with a few tons of "yolk" per day would cost about Rs. 10,000.

[3] On the extraction of fat from animal offal, see Koller, *Waste Products*, p. 40.

[4] Bee-culture and the collection of wild honey is limited to the hill and submontane districts of the province. An attempt is being made to promote scientific apiculture in Kangra. It can be made into a profitable and interesting industry by educated men in their leisure hours in localities such as Hoshiarpur, where there is an abundant supply of flowers suitable for bees. For a detailed account of Indian bees-wax, see *Agric. Ledger*, No. 7, of 1904.

such as moulding, and also as a resist in certain stages of dyeing and calico-printing.[1] In medicine it is extensively utilized in the preparation of ointments and plasters.

The oil-crushing of the province falls into two obvious divisions, the *kóhlú*[2] industry and the mill industry.

The trade of the *téli* or oil-presser has been on the decline ever since cheap kerosene oil was imported into the country.[3] The indigenous mill, however, still persists even in places like Gujranwala, where modern oil-crushing machinery of sorts has been set up. Delhi stands first in the province with 300 *kóhlús*, Ludhiana second with 175, Amritsar third with 150, and Multan fourth with 130. While, however, Delhi imports oil, Ludhiana exports it not only all over the Punjab, but to the United Provinces and even Bengal. In many places these bullock-mills are worked on the factory system, as for example in Ludhiana, where a Municipal Commissioner, an Arain by caste, owns as many as sixteen.

The *téli* either buys his oil-seeds on his own responsibility, as is generally the case in Amritsar, Hoshiarpur, Sialkot, Ludhiana, Hansi, Sirsa, etc., for cash or on credit—most frequently the latter—or he merely hires out his *kóhlú* and his labour to the shopkeeper, as in Gujranwala and in Bhiwani. In the latter case the wage is fixed in various ways. Often, as in Gujranwala, the oil-cake is kept in return for crushing the customer's seed. Payment may,

---

[1] Watt, *Indian Art at Delhi*, pp. 229-260.

[2] The *kóhlú* or *ghanni* is the indigenous wooden oil-press.

[3] In many places, however, the *téli* adds to his income by manufacturing soap.

however, be made in cash, the rate in the same town being from 9 to 10 annas per maund of seed crushed.

The *téli's* average earnings are said to be from 10 to 12 annas in Delhi, about 6 annas in Ludhiana, and from 6 to 8 annas a day in Multan and Sirsa. The *kóhlú* may be assumed to crush about two maunds of seed daily on an average, and to produce 28 seers of oil.

There are two modern methods of extracting oil : (1) by volatile solvents, and (2) by mechanical pressure.

The extraction of oil by chemical solvents is entirely unknown in the Punjab. The advantages of the benzine process, which is the one commonly used in Europe, are said to be : (1) unfailing yield of 98 to 99 % of the total oil-content of the seed (an oil-crushing mill will not obtain more than 90 %) ; (2) reduction of the cost of working ; and (3) complete sterilization of the meal. The weak point of the process is that benzine is rather a dangerous material to handle. Further, the cake, being practically devoid of oil, would not fetch much in this country, as it is valueless except for manure.

The extraction of oil by mechanical pressure can be effected by two kinds of machinery. The Anglo-American system, by which the seeds are steamed, ground, pressed and filtered, is universal in the Punjab. Beside this, there is the so-called *ghanni* plant, in which the seeds are gradually crushed in the *ghanni* without preliminary steaming.

An Anglo-American plant to crush five maunds of seed per day of ten hours can be set up for about Rs. 5,000, and a *ghanni* plant for Rs. 4,500. The cost of working would be nearly Rs. 10 a day. [1]

---

[1] A complete plant to treat 25 tons of ground seed would cost about Rs. 38,000 at Karachi. The approximate cost of working it would be about Rs. 40 daily for labour and chemicals.

The Lahore district is the centre of the factory industry of the Punjab. The Punjab Oil and Flour Mill at Lahore is one of the largest establishments of the kind in the province, its annual output being about 20,000 cwt. of castor, and 16,000 cwt. of *mahua*, rape and linseed oils. It imports great quantities of castor-seed from the United Provinces and crushes chiefly for the North-Western Railway. There is also a mill at Lalliani and another at Ichhra. Strange to say, there are no oil-mills now at Ludhiana or Multan, one which was started at the former place having failed through the inexperience of the promoters. There is an oil-mill at Delhi which was worked at a loss by its former owners, and is not paying now for the same reason—want of experience. This is also the case of the two oil-mills at Gujranwalla, and the one at Jullundur. There are mills also at Lyallpur and Sargodha, and three flourishing ones at Amritsar.[1]

One of the main reasons for the unsatisfactory position of many of these mills is the popular belief that the oil industry needs neither practical experience nor scientific knowledge and training. It is supposed to be a purely mechanical business which can be carried on by any fitter who knows how to run an engine. With a few notable exceptions, oil-mills have been set up by ignorant capitalists, who do not realize the necessity of employing expert oil-millers.

[1] There is a water-driven oil-press capable of crushing 25 maunds of seed in 12 hours at Tarsikka, in the Amritsar Tahsil. The power is derived from the Kasur branch of the canal, which runs only during 5 or 6 months in the year. The factory is not flourishing owing to its distance from the markets and the intermittent nature of the power supply.

Further, very few managers in the Punjab have given a thought to the question of utilizing their by-products by setting up subsidiary industries.

Oil-cake.

The greatest obstacle in the way of the industry, however, is the difficulty of disposing of mill oil-cake. The Punjabi cultivator is used to the product of the *kóhlú*, which, in his opinion, contains more oil, and is consequently more nourishing, and he will not buy mill-cake except at a much cheaper rate. He is quite wrong, of course; for, in the first place, it is not universally true that the *kóhlú* extracts less oil than the hydraulic press, and secondly, cattle cannot digest all the oil, even in the poorest mill-cake.

His prejudices in the matter are, however, too strong as yet to be easily overcome. It is suggested that the Agricultural Department should make detailed analyses of various grades of *kóhlú* and mill-cakes, and of the excrement of cattle fed on them, and publish the results in a popular form for the information of the public. Even educated people are entirely in the dark on this subject.

About 10,000 maunds of castor-cake are already being used, every year, for manure in the Lahore district, and the Agricultural Department is doing useful work in further popularizing it. Much, however, remains to be done, for quantities of castor-cake have to be burnt in Lahore because heavy freight-rates[1] prevent any considerable export to Poona or Calcutta, where it is in demand.

Another means of popularizing mill-cake is that discovered at Ludhiana, the chief centre of the oil-cake

---

[1] Castor-cake is only useful for manure, and yet ordinarily pays the same freight-charges as oil-cakes used for cattle-food.

trade of the Punjab. Mill-cakes shaped like *kóhlú* cake are brought there from Patna and Cawnpore, and sell readily. It ought not to be difficult for a well-equipped mill to set up machinery to remould its cake into the popular form. Ingredients calculated to give them a palatable flavour might be added.

Until a good local market for oil-cake is created, it is hopeless to expect a great oil-crushing industry to arise in the province. The export of oil-cakes and oil together will not be profitable, as, in addition to the risk of leakage on the way, there will be heavier charges to pay altogether by way of freight, brokerage, and clearance dues, than on the uncrushed oil-seeds.

The great problem of the export trade in oil is to find proper receptacles for transport. Kerosene tins are wasteful, and the use of anything more durable is out of the question, because of the heavy freight-charges on the returned empties.

The following solutions of the difficulty may be suggested :—

1. A cask-factory might be set up in connection with the oil-mill, if suitable wood can be found in the neighbourhood. If the industry is on a considerable scale, light steel drums might also be imported in the form of stampings, and made up on the spot.

2. Oil might be exported in receptacles which should also be used to import commodities such as caustic soda and bleaching powder.[1] The Punjab Oil and Flour Mills of Lahore import caustic soda for their soap-works in iron drums which they return filled with oil. Their

[1] The cost of bleaching powder f.o.b. in London is £4-2-6, and in Madras £10-9, per ton. This great difference is due to the necessity of packing it in drums in place of casks. If the drums were used backwards and forwards as suggested, it is obvious that a great saving would be effected in packing charges, as well as in freight on empties.

export trade in oil depends on the supply of empties at their disposal.

It is hardly necessary to add that this arrangement is only possible under special circumstances.

3. Soap manufacture is not difficult and ought to be introduced on a large scale in this country. Oil might be exported in the form of cheap but good soap, for which it might be possible to find markets in the Persian Gulf, and even in Europe.

4. There seems to be no reason why oil should not be transported in tank-wagons to Karachi and carried thence to Europe in tank-steamers, as proposed in the case of the soya-bean oil in Manchuria.

Cotton-oil. The Punjab annually raises over thirty lacs of maunds of cotton-seed. With the exception of a little over three lacs of net export, and about a lac and a quarter used for sowing, the whole of this stock is given to milch cattle.[1]

---

[1] Cotton-seed is largely consumed by cattle in the Cis-Sutlej tract, which produces a large crop itself and imports in addition from ½ to 1½ times as much from the U. P. The districts between the Sutlej and the Jhelum, on the other hand, use an amount equivalent to about 22% of their crop and export the rest to Karachi.

The following table gives the *net* imports by rail, in maunds, at the largest importing stations:—

	Budhlada.	Rohtak.	Ludhiana.
1906-07	98,469	78,655	100,381
1907-08	168,317	171,889	62,843
1908-09	90,995	120,945	58,506
	Barnala.	Phagwara.	Jullundur.
1906-07	55,639	185,544	160,901
1907-08	51,783	101,860	88,952
1908-09	40,245	135,442	111,374

(Barnala is in the Patiala State, between Bhatinda and Patiala, 41 miles from the former.)

The only large exporting station is Kasur, the *net* export figures for which are :—

1906-07	15,552
1907-08	127,509
1908-09	100,777

Cotton-seed yields 18% of its weight in a valuable oil, most of which is useless not only as cattle-food, but as manure in the excrement with which it is ejected. Weight for weight, therefore, cotton-cake is a more valuable food than the seed, as the greater proportion of the oil contained in the latter has no nutrient value whatever. It is calculated that the Punjabi cultivator thus throws away every year no less than sixty lacs of rupees.[1]

Well-refined cotton-oil forms the main constituent of what is consumed in Europe under the name of salad-oil,[2] while the lower grades are largely used in soap-making and as a lubricant and leather-dressing. The best cotton-oil would make an admirable substitute for *ghee*, with which it corresponds as nearly as possible in chemical composition.

	Ghee.	*Cotton Stearin.*[3]
Carbon	75·63	76·85
Hydrogen	11·87	12·36
Oxygen	12·50	10·79
	100	100

Treated with 35% of its weight of butter, cotton stearin will be as good as *ghee*, not only in flavour and appearance, but in chemical composition. Cotton-ghee will be cheaper than the very worst of the expensive stuff called *ghee* now on the market, which is

[1] Cotton-oil has never been used in India, perhaps because the husk and the lint would soak up most of the oil if pressed in the *kóhlú*.

[2] Margarine, the artificial butter so popular in Europe, is composed of cotton-oil and the fat of the cow or the pig.

[3] The portions of cotton-oil which remain solid or liquid at 32° F. are termed winter and summer oils, respectively. Winter oil is the stearin.

invariably adulterated, often, it may be noted, with undesirable substances.[1]

Cotton-cake is used in England to fatten cattle, the cake of Indian seed being preferred to the Egyptian, in spite of its husk and lint, because it is so much cheaper. The estimation in which Indian cotton-seed is held abroad is proved by the rise of the import from about 1,500 tons in 1907-08 to over 200,000 tons in 1908-09.[2]

The interest now taken in cotton-seed pressing by Indian capitalists is of very recent date, and the industry still offers a number of problems, which can only be solved by the experience of many years. A brief account of some of the factories already established in various parts of India will be of interest.

It might be mentioned in passing that the Punjab Oil and Flour Mills of Lahore have been crushing a certain amount of cotton-seed for over 15 years. The owners complain of the poor yield[3] and high cost of the local seed, and of the lack of a market for cotton-cake in the province.

---

[1] See Mr. Moreland's remarks to the Agricultural Conference at Allahabad on January 19, 1911—*Indian Trade Journal*, January 26, 1911, pp. 111-2.

[2] A new use for cotton-seed is the manufacture of cotton-seed flour, which, it is said, can be cooked into wholesome *chapâtis*.—*Indian Trade Journal*, December 8, 1910, p. 260.

[3] The management state that Punjab cotton-seed yields 18% of its weight in crude oil exclusive of the 4½% that remains in the cake. The total oil-content of the seed, therefore, is 22½% of its weight. The Premier Cotton-Oil Factory of Cawnpore, on the other hand, extracts from 13·25 to 14·25 % of the weight of the seed in oil, leaving 6·6% in the cake. The total oil-content of the seed is thus between 20 and 21 % of the weight of the seed. The refinery losses come to 9 % of the crude oil.

The Premier Cotton-Oil Factory of Cawnpore was set up in 1908 by the Government of the United Provinces, on a site belonging to Messrs. Begg, Sutherland and Co., at a cost of about Rs. 55,000. The arrangement with the firm is that they are to carry on the work at their own expense for the time being, any deficit that may occur being made good by the Government. The firm are also to provide the requisite scientific supervision of the establishment, including laboratory experiments, etc., and to keep such records as the Government may require. In return for these services they receive Rs. 500 per month from the Government. Cawnpore.

The factory is fitted with an Anglo-American plant specially designed for undecorticated seed, capable of crushing one ton of seed per hour. Attached to it is a refinery which can deal with three tons of crude oil in 24 hours.

The oil sells without difficulty in Cawnpore at about Rs. 13-8 per maund, and the price is improving. It is locally used for cooking, mixing with ghee and other oils, and, to a small extent, for soap-making. There is no market yet for a highly-refined oil, but a local demand appears to be springing up for the "foots" at a low price for the manufacture of common soap.

The chief difficulty lies in the disposal of the cake. It realized Re. 1-5 per maund when exported to Europe in 1909, but could not be sold locally to any extent, even at Re. 1-3. A large quantity is being distributed free, through private and Government agency, but it is anticipated that some years will pass before it secures the favour of the local consumer.

The average price given by the factory for the seed is Re. 1-12 per maund, and it is calculated that the undertaking will pay if Re. 1-5 is realized for all its cake.

Akola. Another factory is the one just set up at Akola, in which the Hon'ble Rao Bahadur N. R. N. Mudholkar is largely interested. No expense seems to have been spared on the machinery, which is said to be the best available in Germany or America, and is in charge of a German chemist, who has handled oil-seeds both in Germany and Manchuria. It is capable of crushing 50 tons of cotton-seed per day of 24 hours. The seed is carefully decorticated.

Bombay. Messrs. Tata and Co. are also setting up a cotton-oil mill near Bombay, under the supervision of an English expert. The machinery is all British, and is calculated to handle 200 tons of decorticated seed per week, working 24 hours per day.

The progress of the two rival systems, the German at Akola, and the British at Cawnpore and Bombay, will be watched with the keenest interest all over the country.[1]

The cotton-oil industry appears to offer an opening to capitalists in the Punjab. The seed is no doubt dear, but the soya-bean is cutting into the market in England, and this is bound to lower prices in India. Further, whereas in the case of the other oil-seeds

---

[1] The other cotton-oil factories are those at Baroda, working since 1909, with a capital of a lac, and at Broach, set up in 1908, with a capital of Rs. 70,000, and recently wound up because of mismanagement. The former neither delints nor decorticates seed, while the latter did both. Both factories found it difficult to dispose of the cake as well as the oil, and the Baroda factory is now finding it more profitable to crush other oil-seeds.

both the oil and the cake would have to be exported for an indefinite period, cotton-oil at least will probably find an immediate local market.

A cotton-oil refinery should be located near one of the great provincial markets for ghee, and connected with it there might be a dairy to produce the butter for mixing with the stearin.[1] There might also be, in the same enclosure, a soap-factory to use up the "foots," or residue of the refining process, and a glycerine factory to work the "lyes" of soap manufacture. The crushing of the seed, however, would probably have to be done separately in the cotton-producing areas, where, as in America, it could be combined with cotton-ginning. The crude oil would be railed in tank-wagons to the central refinery. Along with the oil would go, for use in the dairy, so much of the cake as was not disposed of locally.

Soap and glycerine are produced when oils or fats are boiled with caustic soda or caustic potash.[2] **Soap.**

Tallow, which gives a hard soap, is more largely used in Europe than any other fat,[3] but of late years

---

[1] It is calculated that a factory turning out one ton of cotton stearin daily would require a herd of a little over two thousand cows or a thousand buffaloes (Noel-Paton, *Indian Cotton-Seed*, p. 18). The dairy cattle would dispose of 20% of the oil-cake (*Indian Trade Journal*, March 4, 1909, p. 202), but they would require, in addition, a constant supply of green succulent food.

From the experience of the Sargodha oil-mill, it would appear that it is difficult to sell any kind of oil-cake in the Canal Colonies. The cultivators only give it to cattle when green fodder is not available, which is rarely the case.

[2] When soda-ash is used, it has to be converted into the caustic by boiling with quicklime. The consumption of caustic soda for refining oil and soap-making may be sufficient to warrant the manufacturer in making it himself from soda-ash.

[3] Hurst, *Soaps*, p. 118.

cotton-oil, a large proportion of which is not fit for table purposes, enters into the composition of most of the common household soaps. Rape, mustard, and sesame and, in some places, castor-oil and tallow, are all used by the Punjabi soap-maker for making common washing soap—the so-called "*dhobi* soap." Mahua oil, imported from the United Provinces, and cocoanut oil from Bombay are, however, said to yield the best results and are in demand for the better grades. Caustic soda is almost invariably used, except in Multan and Ludhiana, where a few old-fashioned workers still cling to *sajji*[1] and lime. Further, in some places, *e.g.*, Khushab, imported carbonate of soda is causticised with lime by the soap-maker himself. "*Dhobi* soap" is often weighted with soapstone (locally called *dudh pathri* or *palaon*), which is brought in large quantities from Jeypore, Jodhpur and Jubbulpore to Amritsar, the distributing centre.[2] The stone sells at about Re. 1 per maund.

The implements used by the local soap-maker are often very crude, consisting only of a few pans and knives, the whole factory with the stock-in-trade being generally worth less than Rs. 250. The better sort are said to have a plant worth from Rs. 100 to Rs. 500 and stock-in-trade of Rs. 2,000 to 5,000.

Toilet soap is produced by the factories at Lahore and Delhi, and by a few stray individuals in other towns. "*Dhobi* soap" is made in considerable quantities at Lahore, Amritsar and Delhi, and indeed in

---

[1] *Sajji* is crude carbonate of soda (see p. 141).

[2] About 4,000 maunds of this commodity is said to be annually imported to in Amritsar, of which 25% is used locally, and the rest exported to Pind Dadan Khan, Multan, Peshawar, Rawalpindi, Gujranwala, etc.

every town of any importance in the province, by all castes from Khattris to Telis. There are, for example, 25 factories in Multan, all except two owned by Hindus, and 20 in Pind Dadan Khan worked by Mohammadan Khojas. There are five Hindu soap-makers in Sialkot and an equal number of Telis in Gujranwala.

With the coming of better methods and chemicals, the industry is gradually passing from the hands of the poor and ignorant Teli to that of the Khattri or Khoja capitalist—chiefly the former. Competition in the manufacture of "*dhobi* soap" is very keen, and the profits are getting smaller day by day. Toilet soap, however, is imported in large and increasing quantities, the figures for Karachi harbour alone amounting to 26,000 maunds, valued at five lacs of rupees, in 1908-09. Its manufacture, even with imported caustic soda, might profitably be combined with the allied industry of oil-seed crushing, and offers a lucrative career to men with business capacity added to some scientific knowledge.[1]

Not many years ago Japan imported nearly all her soap. In 1907, however, she had some fifty factories, which not only satisfied local needs, but exported a good proportion of their output, which came to no less than 180 million tablets yearly. The exports to China, Korea, the Philippines, Asiatic Russia and British India, in 1906, amounted to over 12 million tablets, valued at 7½ lacs of rupees. Of the raw materials, cocoanut oil came from India, tallow from Australia

[1] A small soap plant would cost Rs. 5,000, and the stock-in-trade Rs. 5,000 more. It must be remembered that really first class toilet soap cannot be produced without efficient milling and pressing machinery.

and China, caustic soda[1] and perfumes from England, France, Germany and Switzerland.[2]

Given some enterprise and scientific knowledge, the Punjab ought to be able to do what Japan has found so little difficulty in achieving.

Candles. Candles are largely made in Europe from stearine extracted from tallow and wool-fat, materials available in the Punjab. The art, though known in India from time immemorial, is now lost in this province. It is worth resuscitating, however, for the imports of the commodity at Karachi port alone average about 2,000 maunds a year, valued at Rs. 60,000.[3]

Glycerine. Glycerine is obtained from the by-products of candle and soap factories, and has of late become valuable enough for candle-makers to adopt those processes which yield the largest amount of it. Enormous quantities[4] of glycerine run to waste in the spent lyes of soap-making. Indeed, a London firm of repute offers to guarantee to any soap factory producing, say, 5 maunds of soap per day, the recovery, in the shape of profits, of the cost of an up-to-date plant within a year.

---

[1] Japan now manufactures a portion at least of the caustic-soda consumed by her by the Le Blanc process (see Note on Alkalies, on p. 23 of the *Report of the Chemical Industries Committee*, Madras).

[2] *British and Colonial Druggist*, Vol. 51 (1907), p. 32.

[3] For an account of the manufacture of candles, see Thorpe, *Dict. Appl. Chem.*, Vol. I. Art. *Candles*; Spon, *Workshop Receipts*, Vol. I. Art. *Candles*, and Sadtler, *Ind. Org. Chem.*, pp. 66 *et seq.*

[4] Tallow and the oils used in soap-making contain glycerine in the proportion of 10 to 15%, all of which is usually wasted. With proper treatment most of this can be recovered from the soap lyes. The recovery of glycerine has now become an essential branch of soap manufacture and no firm which neglects it can hope to compete with European manufacturers.

Glycerine is chiefly used in India in medicine and pharmacy. In Europe it is in great and increasing demand also in the manufacture of explosives and the printing of woollen and worsted fabrics. It is invaluable as a lubricant for machinery, and for sizing cotton yarn.[1]

Pitch[2] is the residuum of the destructive distillation of various organic substances such as coal-tar and oils. We are here concerned only with the products of the latter class, of which the best known in commerce are the "stearin" or cotton-oil, wool-fat and bone-oil pitches. Pitch.

Crude cotton-oil refined with caustic soda gives a more or less viscid residue called "foots," which, after treatment with dilute sulphuric acid and distillation, is separated into stearin and pitch.

The uses of the former have been mentioned. The latter is extensively employed for the preparation of the special black varnishes used by coach-makers, and in the manufacture of tarpaulins and waterproof packing paper. Wool-pitch, prepared by an analogous process, serves similar purposes and is also used as a lubricant for heavy machinery under the name of "hot and cold neck grease."

Bones and other animal substances when submitted to dry distillation yield a substance called bone-oil, from which, on the process being continued, a firm hard pitch representing about 23% of the weight of the oil is recovered. Bone-pitch, if properly handled, can be made into a superb black varnish.[3]

---

1 On the subject generally, see Koller, *Waste Products*, pp. 214 *et seq.* Thorpe, *op. cit.*, Vol. II. Art. *Glycerine*, and Sadtler, *op. cit.* pp. 70 *et seq.*

2 See Thorpe, *op. cit.* Vol. III. Art. *Pitch.*

3 Livache and McIntosh, *Varnishes*, II. p. 37.

The manufacture of pitch in the Punjab is worth consideration, as the large local demand, chiefly for coal-tar pitch, is at present met by imports. A certain quantity, however, is now made by the Shalimar Paint Works of Calcutta.[1]

Linoleum.

Linoleum is made of solid or completely oxidised linseed oil, sawdust, colophony and powdered cork.[2] All these materials are available in the Punjab except powdered cork, for which the bark of the *chil* (*P. longifolia*) could be satisfactorily substituted. A cheap floor-covering like linoleum, at once cool and sanitary, is bound to create a good market for itself in a semi-tropical country.

Turkey-red oil.

Turkey-red oil is a preparation largely used for dressing tanned leather, and also as a mordant by calico-printers and dyers, especially in the Turkey-red and alizarine red industry. It is imported at present in considerable quantities, whereas it really ought to be exported. The usual base is castor oil, which is treated with concentrated sulphuric acid and then with sodium sulphate and ammonia, or salt and caustic soda.[3] The process is simple.

Rubber substitutes.

Linseed oil, as well as non-drying oils, such as rape oil, are extensively used in the manufacture of rubber substitutes[4] in Germany and other European countries.

---

[1] Coal-tar and pitch are by-products of coke and gas making. Dandot coal (see Appendix IV.) will not coke. It is worth inquiring whether it could profitably be worked for pitch and tar only.

[2] See Livache and McIntosh, *op. cit.* I. p. 57.

[3] Blount and Bloxam, *Chemistry for Engineers and Manufacturers* (1900) pp. 235-6. The caustic soda could be imported in drums to be used for exporting oil. See pp. 181-2. *supra*

[4] For an account of the manufacture, see Livache and McIntosh, *Varnishes, etc.*, Vol. I. Chapter V.

There are two varieties of imitation rubbers, (*a*) oxidised oil, and (*b*) vulcanised oil substitutes.

(*a*) *Oxidised oils.*—The process consists in boiling rape oil into a brown viscous mass, which is afterwards treated while hot with nitric acid until it assumes a thick plastic consistency. When cooled in the air it solidifies into a rather elastic substance with the appearance of rubber. Unlike rubber, however, it softens in hot water.

The material, though rarely used by itself, is a common adulterant of the real article. As it adheres perfectly to all fabrics without damaging them in any way, it is often used for making canvas and similar fabrics waterproof. It can similarly be applied to wood, stone and metals.

(*b*) *Vulcanised oils.*—Linseed, rape, or earthnut oil, treated with 25% of its weight of sulphur chloride, gives a hard, solid material, suitable for making printing-rolls, knife-handles, etc. If further treated with carbonate of lime it is converted into a white spongy mass, which, like oxidised oil, serves to adulterate natural rubber for all industrial purposes. It can be used by itself in the manufacture of water-proof cloth, water-pipes, and similar articles.

CHAPTER XIII.

SUGAR.

Sugar constitutes a cheap and highly nutritious article of diet in warm climates, and it is no wonder that the Punjab, yielding to the temptation of low prices, imports it in ever-increasing quantities. Its annual purchases amount to 175,000 tons, made up of 65,000 of refined and 80,000 of unrefined sugar, and 65,000 of *gur* or jaggery. The first is almost entirely foreign, while the last two come chiefly from the United Provinces.

This province, like the rest of India, but unlike other countries, has two distinct and independent markets for sugar and for *gur*, respectively, and of these the latter is undoubtedly the most important. The price of *gur*, which is the favourite sweetmeat of the rich and poor in India, in no way depends on the supply of foreign sugar, but fluctuates constantly in sympathy with the Indian crop.

Sugarcane cultivation. Sugarcane, the only source of sugar in this province, occupies only 1·2 per cent. of the total cultivated area,[1] but is nevertheless one of its most important and profitable crops. It is most largely grown in the submontane tract that extends between the Jumna and the Chenab, the averages for the more

[1] The average area under sugarcane in the period 1903-08 was 322,245 acres.

important districts during the period 1903-08 being as follows :—

	Area under sugarcane. Acres.	Percentage of total cultivation.
Gurdaspur	47,096	5·9
Hoshiarpur	21,295	3·9
Sialkot	31,160	3·6
Jullundur	25,445	3·1
Rohtak	19,404	2·1
Karnal	19,340	2·1

The Punjabi cultivator spares no pains on this crop and is quite ready to grow new varieties of cane when he sees that they are good. He has not yet learnt, however, the value of manures such as castor-cake,[1] nor in most districts discovered the advantage of cutting the cane as close to the ground as possible. He often forgets, besides, that the tops, which are as good for propagation as any other part, should be removed and preserved for planting, as is done in the United Provinces. The juice of the tops is usually more acid and less rich in sugar than the rest of the cane, and its presence in the boiling pan is apt to cause inversion.[2]

Experience has taught the cultivator that inversion is also caused by leaving the cut canes stacked for any The crushing.

[1] Oil-cakes (castor, rape and sesamum) are generally used in Behar and Bengal during the earthing of sugarcane. In Northern Gujrat (Bombay Presidency) a dressing of castor-cake is given to the fields prepared for the crop, and in the Deccan from 30 to 40 cartloads of cattle-dung, with about 100 lb. of castor or *karanj* (*Pongamia glabra*) cake per acre, form the chief sources of manure—see *Proceed. Bd. Agr. Ind.* (1907), *Papers on Sugar Cultivation, passim.* Large quantities of various manures, particularly castor-cake, are also used in the Godavery delta.

[2] Inversion is the process by which cane-sugar or sucrose is converted into glucose, a sugar less sweet and of simpler composition than sucrose. Glucose is also more soluble in water and holds its own weight of sucrose in solution. The bulk of the glucose, along with the sucrose it holds in solution, is lost with the molasses in sugar-making, as it will not crystallize.

length of time; and he, therefore, takes care, as a rule, to crush them as soon as possible. This operation is commonly performed in the fields where the bullocks are kept busy day and night during the season. The old wooden mill (*bélna*) was formerly in general use but it now survives only in a few of the most backward villages. Its place has been taken by the more efficient iron presses, the best known amongst which are the 2-roller mill which yields from 45 to 55% of juice, the 3-roller Nahan mill, which extracts from 55% to 65%, and lastly the "Babu" 4-roller which extracts as much as 68%. These figures, it may be noted, are correct for efficient machines only, and not for the worn-out article sometimes palmed off on the unsuspecting customer.[1] As a rule, the mills are taken on hire (the "Babu" mill can only be so taken), as the services of the manufacturer's itinerant "mistri" are thus secured. The village blacksmith is unable to keep them in repair.[2]

In Behar and the United Provinces the European planters use steam-crushers. Mr. Lehmann found in Mysore that about 26% of the juice was left in the megass by the best 3-roller bullock-mill, whereas a steam-driven one (6½ H.P.), with three rollers, 18 inches long by 12 inches diameter, left only 18·2%; or, in other words, saved one-third of what the other wasted.[3]

[1] For an account of the various mills, see Hadi, *Bullet. Agr. Dept., U.P.*, No. 19.

[2] Cf. *Assmt. Rep. of Delhi Dist., North* (1909), § 30.

[3] Lehmann, *Sugar Industry in Mysore*, in *Agr. Journ. Ind.* Vol. II. (1907), p. 57.

The yield of juice in the case of any given mill will vary with the percentage and quality of the fibre in the cane. The figures in the text are the result of extensive trials with certain common varieties of canes and are of no value except for comparing the relative efficiency of the different mills.

Other causes of loss are the insanitary condition of the vessels into which the juice flows, and also the delay in boiling which often occurs. The present system is to catch the liquid in a single large earthenware pot, strain it every two or three hours, and then pour it into the boiling-pan. Now the use of earthenware is objectionable as its pores harbour the bacteria of fermentation. Mr. Hadi suggests the substitution of the kerosene-tin, but, where the cultivator can afford it, brass and copper vessels are by far the best.[1] In any case the receptacles should be thoroughly and frequently cleaned. Further, two of these must be kept for each mill, so that when one is full another could take its place. The juice of the first could then be poured immediately into the boiling-pan and thus kept sufficiently hot to prevent fermentation.

Moreover, it has been found that the presence of even small pieces of cane causes considerable loss of sugar. For this reason a strainer, consisting of a perforated sheet of iron in a wooden frame, should always be placed over the vessels that receive the juice.[2]

Practical demonstrations of the advantages of improved methods of crushing cane are very necessary in the villages. The writer found, for example, a 2-roller and a 3-roller mill working in adjacent fields in Harchowál, where the men are fairly intelligent. No one could say positively, nor indeed had any one tried to find out, which of the two mills was the more efficient. On the writer's instructions, a maund of cane taken from the same stack was crushed in each

---

[1] Lehmann, *op. cit.*, p. 59.

[2] Hadi, *op. cit.*

mill, and the result of the experiment proved conclusively to the village worthies that the 2-roller wasted more every season than would have sufficed to buy the other several times over. The incident illustrates the apathy of the cultivator in such matters.

The manufacture of *gur*.

Gur is generally made by the cultivator himself by methods which are as primitive as they are wasteful. One boiling-pan is held sufficient, whereas three are used in the western districts of the United Provinces.[1] Reference has already been made to the tendency of the juice to ferment. Another danger is the presence of free acids in the juice, which, when not neutralised by lime, decompose sugar into glucose. Indeed, Mr. Lehmann found, after extensive trials in Mysore, that heavy losses due to fermentation were rarer than those caused by underliming, which is usually responsible for the disappearance of 13½% of the total amount of saccharine matter.[2]

Mr. Moreland proposes the adoption of the Hadi system in the manufacture of *gur*;[3] but it must be observed that the experiment was tried, and proved a failure, in Madras. It is doubtful whether it is any use expending time and money in improving the traditional methods; for within certain limits the inversion which takes place does not affect the value of the product. The invert sugar formed becomes a corporate part of the *gur*, and causes no loss in weight or in price so long

---

[1] Hadi, *Monog. on the Sugar Industry in the U. P.*, p. 67.

[2] Lehmann, *op. cit.*, p. 58. On the subject of liming, see also Clarke and Bannerjee in *Agr. Journ. Ind.* (1910), Vol. V. p. 38, where finely ground carbonate of lime is suggested.

[3] Moreland, *Sugar Industry in the U.P.*, in *Agr. Journ. Ind.* (1907) Vol. II. pp. 17 *et seq.* The Hadi process is described in the *U. P Agricultural Bulletin*, No. 19.

as the mass remains solid. It would seem, therefore, that the only thing the cultivator can do is to pay greater attention to the process of liming and to the removal of the scum and other impurities, thus producing an article of greater market value.

The methods of the *khánchi* (indigenous sugar-manufacturer) need not detain us, for, besides being unsavoury and grossly inefficient, they are of little more than historical interest.[1] The industry is dead except in a few villages of the Gurdaspur, Hoshiarpur and Ludhiana districts, and no improvements can ever recall it to life. Even the Hadi process, which has achieved popularity in the United Provinces, will not help, as it is unsuited to Punjab conditions.[2] It was tried at Malsian and Sri Govindpur by private individuals, and found unsatisfactory. The *khánchi*.

The only modern sugar factory in the province is the one at Sujanpur. It has two water-propelled mills capable of crushing 140 tons of cane daily, but, as it is located on the edge of the cane-area of the district, it can obtain only half that quantity.[3] The rest of the machinery is driven by steam (40 H.P.). The megass is used as fuel, but about 200 tons of coal, and 20,000 maunds of wood, are also consumed every year. **Sugar factories: Sujanpur.**

Besides a European managing-director, and a Parsi engineer, the staff includes from 300 to 400 coolies during the crushing and refining season, which lasts

---

[1] For an account of his methods, see *Proceed. Bd. Agr. Ind.* (1907), p. 102, and the *Hoshiarpur Dist. Gazetteer* (1904), pp. 104 *et seq.*

[2] *Rep. of the Punjab Dept. Agr.* (1909), App. V. p. 7.

[3] The Rosa Factory of Shahjehanpur, which has plant for crushing from 200 to 350 tons in 24 hours, also suffers from the shortage of sugarcane, and so does the Champaran Factory which could crush 300 tons per diem.

from four to five months (March to November). The majority of these are recruited from the Sialkot District, as the proximity of the head-works of the Bari-Doab Canal has made local labour very scarce.

The cane of the locality is the *káthá,* which is bought standing, and is cut and cleaned by the employees of the factory. No advances are made to the cultivators, but half the price is paid on purchase, and the balance when the cane has been removed and the area finally measured.[1] The management have made great efforts, by the offer of better prices, to induce the cultivator to improve his methods, and the results have so far been encouraging.

The following interesting statistics of the working of the factory have been furnished through the courtesy of the manager :—

Season.	*Cane-area bought.*	*Price per ghumao.*			*Total uncleaned cane.*	*Yield of juice.*	*Yield of sugar.*	*Yield of molasses.*
	Ghumaos.[2]	Rs.	a.	p.	Maunds.	Gallons.	Maunds.	Maunds.
1904-05	730	19	11	10	148,004	300,650	3,647	2,500
1905-06	212	20	9	6	33,648	61,950	1,068	1,025
1906-07	428	31	9	5	92,532	183,750	2,574	1,127
1907-08	408	28	0	8	83,616	180,775	1,649	1,162
1908-09	568	29	14	6	99,382	212,975	2,863	1,500
Average	469	25	15	7	91,436	188,020	2,360	1,463
	acres	Per acre			Per acre	Per acre	Per acre	Per acre
	390·54	£2	1	7	9·2 tons	481·4 gall	·24 tons	·137 tons

These figures do not indicate the yield of rum distilled from the molasses and the washings of the sugar-

[1] The system followed by the Rosa Factory is to buy the canes ready cleaned by weight, an ingenious arrangement having been adopted for weighing the carts. The factory also advances from sixty to seventy thousand rupees a year to the cultivators.

[2] 1 ghumao = $\frac{5}{6}$ of an acre. 8 gallons of cane-juice = 1 maund = ·089 ton.

cane, which is a good source of profit. It may be mentioned here that attached to the factory there is a workshop for making soda-water machines, as well as plant for generating carbonic acid gas from *gur* and molasses, which are bought for the purpose.

Almost all the sugar is consumed in the Amritsar and Gurdaspur Districts, where it is in great demand, especially for sweetmeats at marriage festivals. Customers have been known to leave hundreds of rupees with the manager for long periods in order to be sure of their supply.

The nominal capital of the factory is Rs. 1,60,000, on which it has paid a dividend of 10 % since 1904, when it commenced the manufacture of carbonic acid gas.[1] It had been a failure before. The causes of its present success may briefly be said to be : (*a*) utilisation of by-products and manufacture of carbonic acid gas, (*b*) efficient management, (*c*) scrupulous avoidance of the use of blood, bone-black and other impure substances,[2] and (*d*) the prevalent belief that the sugar, though slightly dearer, is sweeter than imported sugar.

Other factories.

Two years ago the Amritsar Distillery Co. set up a refinery in connection with their works, with the intention of feeding it with *ráb* from branch factories, and boiling the juice on the "Hadi" system at Chhina, Batala and Jaintipur on the Pathankot Rail-

---

[1] The figures are rather deceptive. The original capital in 1877 was Rs. 400,000. The company went into liquidation in 1886, when the factory was bought up for Rs. 60,000 by a private syndicate, which added new plant to it at a cost of Rs. 1,00,000. It is incorrect to say that the real assets of the company are worth Rs. 500,000, but they are doubtless more than Rs. 1,60,000.

[2] The bleaching is done with sulphurous acid generated by burning sulphur.

way. They are now removing the Jaintipur mill to Amritsar to crush *pounda* cane. The Harkishen Sugar-mill, recently erected by R. S. Ganesh Das, a sub-engineer, and another capitalist, at a cost of Rs. 50,000, manufactures sugar from *gur*, and is capable of producing two tons a day. It is stated that the factory is run at a loss, not quite a maund of sugar, selling for Rs. 11 a maund, having been made so far out of three maunds of *gur*, costing at least Rs. 12. The Punjab Sugar Manufacturing Co., Ld., registered on April 25, 1910, with a capital of Rs. 2,50,000, propose to set up their works at Batala at a considerable distance from the cane-fields.[1]

Prospects of the industry. The area under sugarcane in the Punjab in 1908-09 was 365,600 acres, and the estimated yield 265,600 tons of *gur*. The area in Java for the same period was 284,600 acres, which produced 1,217,390 tons of *sugar*[2] of all kinds. The average outturn of the Sujanpur Factory, which is as efficiently run as circumstances will allow, is ·24 tons of sugar per acre; that of the Tjomal Factory, representing the maximum yield attained in Java, is 6·4 tons[3], or more than twenty-six times as great.

---

[1] The "Pure Indian Sugar Factory" of Nabha has a "Hadi" plant, and was started in January 1910, in combination with two flour-mills with a capital of Rs. 24,000, of which the State has subscribed a portion. It is too early yet to pronounce upon its financial success.

[2] *Dip. and Cons. Rep. on the Trade of Java*, No. 4224, Ann. Ser. (cd. 4446-48). It must be noted, however, that the official estimate of the yield in the Punjab, appears to be somewhat below the mark.

[3] At the Tjomal Factory special attention is paid to the precise point of ripeness of the cane.

The cost of production in different districts of Java varies from Rs. 3-12 to Rs. 5 per maund of sugar. See Burkill and Weinberg, *Central Factory System*, in *Agr. Ledger* (1903) No. 9, p. 254. This very useful article should be consulted by all Indian manufacturers of sugar.

Figures such as these are enough to cause despair. The example of Formosa, however, where before the Japanese occupation the sugar manufacturer was in a like depressed condition, is so encouraging, that it ought to brace the people of the Punjab to renewed efforts in this industry. Before the Japanese occupation, the yield of sugarcane per acre in Formosa was 8·3 tons. The matter was taken in hand in 1902, and five years later the Chinese peasant, more conservative by far than the Punjabi, had been taught to improve the yield to 14·5 tons of a much superior variety. Before 1902, the Formosan mills were of stone, and yielded 45% of juice. The modern 11 roller now gives 78%.[1]

Turning again to Java we find that even now the native Javanese obtains only about 2½ tons of sugar per acre, whereas the Dutchman, with his superior methods, produces from 3 to 4½, and even 6 tons per acre.[2]

Lines of progress. What can Government do to assist the industry? This is a question for experts to answer in detail, but speaking generally, Government could help the sugar-manufacturer by helping in the improvement of the sugarcane, and in the establishment of central sugar factories.

The sugar-cane. The essentials of a good variety of cane are that, in addition to yielding the maximum amount of sugar per unit-area, it should (1) be hardy and disease-free, as, for example, the rose-bamboo has been discovered to be in Formosa, (2) ripen uniformly and at the required time,[3] (3) yield a pure juice, *i.e.*, juice with

---

[1] See the consular report cited above.

[2] See Burkill and Weinberg, *op. cit.* pp. 245 *et seq.*

[3] While it is essential that cane should ripen uniformly, it is also important that a factory should have a uniform supply of cane over as long a period as possible. This result could possibly be obtained by growing varieties ripening at different times.

the minimum of glucose and other impurities, and at the same time as concentrated as possible, so as to save fuel in the boiling process.

The best canes known to the Punjabi sugar manufacturer so far are the *káthá* and the *dhaulu*, hardy species which give good results with a modicum of labour and manuring. It has been pointed out, however, in a recent pamphlet, that the relative sucrose values of the *pounda*, a cane hitherto raised only small quantities for chewing, and of the *dhaulu*, are as 3·32 to 1, and that, under proper conditions, the outturn of the former could be made almost to equal the results obtained in Java.[1] This certainly sounds very hopeful, and doubtless the Agricultural Department will lose no time in verifying these statements, and will further inquire whether the *pounda* fulfils the first two conditions of a good cane, and does really cost less to raise, in proportion, than the others. Besides, the *kâthá*, the *dhaulu* and the *pounda*, could be improved by selection or hybridisation. The former method has been found successful in Java, but is only sparingly employed, as the varieties produced by hybridisation have given distinctly better results.[2]

Both Java and Formosa owe no small debt to the labours of the eminent scientists who have guided their research-stations. The Punjab too has awakened to the need of such institutions, and experimental farms will shortly be established in the sugarcane areas of Gurdaspur and Jullundur. It is not too

---

[1] Carter, *Sugar Manufacture in the Punjab* (C. & M. G. Press, Lahore, pp. 12-14.)

[2] Mr. Howard's Note in *Proceed. Bd. Agr. Ind.* (1907), p. 95; J. C. Willis, *Agriculture in the Tropics*, p. 58.

much to hope that the Panipat *tahsil* will soon be equally favoured. As soon as the stage of experiment is passed, the Agricultural Department will no doubt make every effort to popularise the improved varieties by giving lectures and demonstrations.[1]

There would appear to be room for two large central factories in the province, handling say 50,000 tons of cane each per season, one at Harchowál in the Gurdaspur District, and the other possibly in the Sialkot or Jullundur District, or in the Panipat *tahsil* of Karnal.[2] Of these places the first, suggested by Sir Louis Dane, is fourteen miles from Batala by road,[3] and is surrounded by a tract which raises more Central factories.

---

[1] Most of the canes now grown in the Godavery Delta are the offspring of the foreign varieties introduced by the Madras Department of Agriculture. They are less liable to disease than those they have replaced and yield a richer and purer juice.

[2] The selection of the site must depend on the supply of raw material, proximity to markets, and facilities of transport.

The figures in maunds for the traffic in *gur* and unrefined sugar at the following stations will be useful. The exports are almost entirely of *gur* and the imports of unrefined sugar.

	1906-07.		1907-08.		1908-09.	
	Inward.	Outward.	Inward.	Outward.	Inward.	Outward.
Batala	26,213	196,002	29,390	181,778	22,104	158,463
Lyallpur	26,870	18,295	24,893	38,439	26,057	50,568
Gojra	25,877	42,646	16,466	81.419	20,549	86,126.

The E. I. Ry. has supplied the following figures for *gur* alone in maunds) :—

	1907.		1908.		1909.	
	Inward.	Outward.	Inward	Outward.	Inward.	Outward.
Sonepat	272	70,451	408	67,048	163	40,609
Samalkha	27	123,562	109	77,665	109	98,572
Panipat	408	105,650	299	51,695	1,306	109,055

[3] The two places could conveniently be connected by mono-rail. The materials for one 14 miles long would cost Rs. 20,000.

sugarcane than any other like area in the province.[1] It has the further advantage of an ample supply of water-power.[2] His Honour's idea is to unite the cane-growers with the moneyed men of the neighbourhood in an enterprise which would combine the best elements of capitalism and co-operation, and at the same time secure the advantages of a large plantation in a land of small holdings.[3] The cultivators who have learnt the benefits of such enterprises through their own co-operative societies, have accepted the proposal with alacrity, and have already offered to subscribe one lac of rupees. It would be well if the Gurdaspur District Board were also invited to join as a shareholder.

State-aid.

It may be observed in this connection that the sugar industries of Java, Formosa and Mauritius would never have attained to their present level of efficiency had they not been liberally helped by their respective Governments.[4] It was the Dutch Government which in 1830 laid the foundation of the central sugar-factory system in Java, by advancing loans to the pioneers, and compelling the Javanese peasant by law to grow cane for their benefit.[5] Japan too has

---

[1] About 6,600 acres of sugarcane with an estimated yield of 170,000 maunds of *gur* are grown within a ten-mile radius of Harchowál.

[2] From 350 to 550 H.P. is available from the Upper Bari-Doab Canal at full supply.

[3] Many Indian factories experience difficulty in buying cane at fair rates. A few have been ruined by combinations among ignorant cultivators, who, forgetful of their own real interest, insisted on exorbitant prices. Were the growers themselves part-owners of the factory, this danger would be minimised.

It may be mentioned here that beet-sugar is often manufactured in Central Europe on co-operative lines.

[4] See the *International Sugar Journal* of May, 1911, for the first of a series of articles on the industry in India. The writer details the marvellous results of state-aid to the beet and cane-sugar industries all the world over.

[5] Burkill and Weinberg, *Agric. Ledger* (1903), No. 12, p. 258. The drastic regulation about planting has long since been relaxed.

helped the cane-grower, as well as the sugar-manufacturer in Formosa by subsidies both in cash and kind. The Formosan Sugar Bureau gave the cultivator a quantity of castor-cake, free of cost, for every unit-area planted with cane-slips supplied by itself. To some sugar factories it gave, for five years, an annual bonus equal to 6% of the paid-up capital, while to others it advanced loans to the extent of 20% of their total assets. In one case, a factory was allowed to borrow all its machinery, free of cost, for five years.[1] Finally, the Government of Mauritius has recently made its sugar-planters a loan which has enabled them to follow the example of the Javanese factories, and cover their estates with a network of light railways.[2]

Date-sugar. There are two local varieties of the date-palm—the *Phœnix dactylifera*, which yields large bunches of excellent dates, and the *Phœnix sylvestris*, the wild variety, which produces a small worthless fruit, relished only by the birds. The former chiefly thrives in the plains stretching to the south-west of Jhang; the habitat of the latter is the Salt Range, the Sewalik tract, and parts of the Eastern Punjab.[3]

The *Phœnix sylvestris* yields, when tapped, a liquid which can be made into a very palatable *gur* or sugar

---

[1] See the Consular Report on the Sugar Industry of Formosa, cited above, *passim*.

[2] *The "Times" Engineering Supt.*, Feb. 11, 1910. Their example might be followed with advantage by some of the Indian factories which have to deal with the sugar crop over large stretches of country. Portable tramways in Java and Mauritius have not only diminished the cost of transport, but reduced to a minimum the loss occasioned by the factories not being able to deal with the whole of the cane-crop at the time of its greatest richness.

[3] Cf. Stewart, *Punjab Plants*, pp. 243 *et seq.*, and the *Multan Dist. Gazetteer* (1902), p. 228.

by exactly the same process as cane-juice goes through. Date *gur* is manufactured to a large extent in the northern half of Jessore, as well as in other districts of Northern Bengal, where nearly every substantial cultivator engages in the industry, which holds, in some places, a position second only to agriculture.[1]

An ordinary date-palm in the South-Eastern Punjab bears a rupee's worth of fruit every year. A single tree in Bengal, on the other hand, yields 240 seers of juice, which gives 30 seers of *gur*, meaning a net annual profit of three rupees.[2]

Some sixty years ago Mr. Edgeworth, then Commissioner of Multan, "got men from Jessore who were acquainted with the method of extracting sugar from the juice of *P. sylvestris* there. They remained at Multan for some time experimenting; and, although they seem to have been hostile to the success of the scheme, and said there was less saccharine matter in the juice of this than of the other species, it seems to have been shown that the fruit of a female tree is much more valuable than its sugar was likely to be, and the male tree has but little juice."[3] The experiment can hardly be considered final even as regards *P. dactylifera*, while the now unused groves of the wild variety seem to offer a field for a new village industry.

---

[1] See *Quar. Journ. Dept. Agr., Bengal*, Jan. 1908, pp. 161 *et seq.*; *Indian Forester*, Vol. XVIII., Dec. 1892, p. 75.

[2] See Mr. A. P. Ghose's note on this industry in App. III. to the Report of the Madras Industrial Conference (1908). He gives figures to show that it would pay to plant the tree for the sugar.

[3] Stewart, *op. cit.* p. 245.

CHAPTER XIV.

WOODWORK.

The worker in wood might naturally be expected to flourish best where his raw material is most plentiful; and if the census figures are true, his craft is best represented in the submontane districts of Hoshiarpur and Sialkot, which have an abundance of timber within their own borders, and again in Karnal, Lahore, Amritsar, Jullundur and Gujranwalla, which are within easy reach of their sources of supply. On the other hand, the industry languishes on the treeless plains of Hissar and Mianwali, Ludhiana and Multan. This rule, however, is not a very sure guide, for Kangra, Gurdaspur and Rawalpindi, in spite of their timber, are not specially distinguished for their wood-industry, while the Jhang district is noted for the skill, if not the number, of the artisans who have won for the carving of Chiniot a fame that has travelled far beyond the Sutlej.

Besides the timber cut and sold by private persons, District Boards, and other bodies in the province, about 3 million cubic feet are annually sold by the Forest Department and 5 millions are imported, chiefly from Kashmir, by private agency.

The raw material.

Among the woods most in demand may be mentioned the *kikar* (*Acacia arabica*) and the *phuláhi* (*A. modesta*), which are used for posts, beams and rafters, cart-wheels, axles and Persian wheels, and agricultural implements generally in every district; the *shisham* (*Dalbergia Sissoo*), a very hard wood highly valued for all purposes requiring strength and elasticity, *e.g.*, for house-building, furniture, toys, sporting requisites, etc.; the *siris* (*Albizzia Lebbek*), a handsome and fairly durable wood, much resembling walnut-wood in appearance, and in request for furniture and agricultural implements; the *tun* (*Cedrela Toona*), a soft and easily-worked timber for furniture and carriages; the *deodar* (*Cedrus Deodara*), a moderately hard, oily, but very durable wood, for railway sleepers, house-building, rough furniture, and general carpentry;[1] the *biár* (*Pinus excelsa*), a moderately hard wood of good quality for house-building; and finally the *chíl* (*P. longifolia*), inferior to the last-named, but still in considerable demand on the plains for house-building, and in Gujrat in particular, for cheap furniture and packing-cases.

The artisans. The carpenter is one of the five necessary menials of every village in the Punjab, and renders important aid to the dominant industry of agriculture. There is no need, however, to linger over the simple round of his tasks, and we will leave him to shape the plough, and make the cart, and build the home of his rustic patrons, and proceed to the more highly developed activities of his brother in the town. His numbers in a few representative districts, however, are worth indicating.

Sialkot	7,469	Karnal	4,271	Rawalpindi	1,656
Amritsar	6,033	Gurdaspur	3,594	Hissar	1,181
Hoshiarpur	5,552	Jullundur	2,998	Ludhiana	1,061
Lahore	4,839	Kangra	1,750	Mianwali	1,001
Gujranwala	4,636	Gujrat	1,730	Multan	763

[1] *Deodar* is not really suitable for indoor work as its oily surface collects dirt.

The wood-work of the towns falls into several divisions which are fairly well marked, in spite of the fact that they overlap to some extent. Of these the trade of the journeyman-carpenter who engages in house-building, and prepares doors and windows, beams, posts, and rafters, is the most important, but is beyond the scope of this inquiry. The various other branches will be reviewed in their order.

The Jullundur district must now be considered, without question, the foremost centre of artistic carpentry in the province. Its artisans, like those of Amritsar and Hoshiarpur, find lucrative employment in Simla and other stations in the hills, and supply a fair proportion of the skilled labour on the North Indian railways from Baluchistan to Bengal. In Jullundur city itself there are about 50 joiners and 30 carvers, cabinet-makers, and brass and ivory inlayers, all of them (whether Hindus, Mohammadans or Sikhs) Tarkháns by caste. They work separately, each man in his own workshop, and gain from a rupee to Re. 1-2-0 each per diem. Artistic work.

Carved and inlaid trays, picture-frames, tables, and numerous other articles, cheap, well-joined and well-finished, are made and exported all over the country. The wood most esteemed is the *shisham* imported from Hoshiarpur and costing from Re. 1-8-0 to as much as Rs. 3-0-0 per cubic foot. The ivory for inlaying usually consists of bracelet-turners' waste and the brittle inner portions of the tusk, and costs eight annas or a little more a seer. Camel-bone, which looks like ivory, is occasionally substituted, but soon betrays itself by decaying and losing its gloss. Box-wood or *chikri* (*Buxus sempervirens*) which resembles inferior ivory in colour and grain, and costs only two annas a seer, occasionally serves the same purpose.

Hoshiarpur. Hoshiarpur city owes its reputation for carving and inlaying to the efforts of Mr. W. Coldstream, I.C.S., who first turned the skill of the local artificers from boxes and pen-cases to articles for the use of Europeans. Nearly 100 joiners and 20 artistic workers are to be found in the city itself, and 40 carvers and inlayers in Bassi Ghulam Hussain, 2½ miles off. A good proportion of the local work is done for shopkeepers, who give cash advances to the artisans.

The local productions are often ingenious, but, except when a model is given to be copied, are of absurd design and adorned with trivial and inconsequent patterns. Of late years the workmanship has deteriorated.

Chiniot. Chiniot is well known as the home of the Mohammadan style of carving, as distinguished from Jullundur, which is the centre of the Sikh school. Here "is wrought an inlay of brass in *shisham* wood, bearing a general resemblance to that of Hoshiarpur, but much bolder, freer and better in design. This is applied to desks, glove-boxes, screens, etc., but is obviously capable of more varied and extensive application."[1] The local workers, about 140 in number, are all Mohammadans of various castes and ply their trade, singly, or in small factories under a master-carpenter. Wages are said to range between Re. 1-0-0 and Re. 1-8-0 a day. The *shisham* wood used for artistic work is procured either from the surrounding villages or from Wazirabad. It costs from Re. 1-8 to Rs. 2 per cubic foot.

[1] Mr. Kipling's note in the *Jhang Dist. Gazetteer.*

Other centres.

Wood-carving of a somewhat rough though not unpleasing kind is done at Bhera, where one occasionally finds good specimens of carved entrances and window-frames. Richly worked doorways are also affected by many of the hill-folk of the Kahuta *tahsil* (Rawalpindi) but they have no artistic excellence.[1]

The wood-carving industry is flourishing on the whole, but is capable of considerable expansion if more business-like methods are adopted by the artisans. A possible line of future development is the manufacture of carved and inlaid panels, which could conveniently be sent to Europe to be worked up there by the cabinet-maker.

Furniture.

Plain furniture of European pattern is made in almost every cantonment and large city in the province. In Lahore, for example, there are a dozen workshops large and small, in Multan five, and in other stations in proportion.

Gujrāt.

Gujrāt City, however, has earned a special fame for its goods, which, though plain and admittedly copies, are yet appreciated in every affluent Anglo-Indian home for their good joinery and finish. There are three large and eight small factories, of which the largest employs thirty carpenters, and six miscellaneous artisans such as polishers, etc. All the persons engaged in the industry, from the proprietors downwards, are Tarkhans by caste, and, with a single exception, uneducated men. An ordinary carpenter earns about Rs. 30 per mensem. Most of the firms work with borrowed capital.

---

[1] No wood-carving is done at Ratya (Hissar district). The Punjab monograph on woodwork needs revision on this point.

Good timber, *shisham*, *phuláhi*, and *kikar*, is locally available, but besides these teak is imported from Karachi and *deodar*, *chil* and *biár* from the Jhelum and Wazirabad depôts.

Kartárpur.

Kartárpur has an equal reputation for cheap and well-joined office furniture, such as chairs, tables and cupboards.[1] It has about 100 carpenters, who work in 25 shops, but, in addition to these, a large number of artisans come in for the day from the surrounding villages. Though the factory system is the rule here also, a fair proportion of the work is done on contract by individual workmen. Wages are said to be about 12 annas a day.

Eight thousand rupees' worth of furniture, on an average, is exported annually in every direction, about half of this being sent out by a Brahmin ex-station-master of the name of Salwan, who has built up a lucrative business by his energy and enterprise. He says he gets a return of ten per cent. on his capital.

Wood is cheap because of the proximity of the Beas depôt, and costs Re. 1 per cubic foot for *shisham*, and from Re. 1-8 to Rs. 2 for *tun* and *deodar*. The cane-work is done by a few Bhanjars, a very low caste, who charge a rupee for doing the seat and back of a chair. The cane is of second quality, imported *via* Calcutta, and costs Rs. 4 a maund in Kartárpur.

Bamboo work.

Bamboo furniture is made in most large cantonments by wandering Hindustánis, who make very fair copies of designs in illustrated catalogues. There is a fairly large and settled colony of these men in Ambala, where

---

[1] When the writer was at Hoshiarpur he found it cheaper to order furniture from Kartárpur, 18 miles by cart-road, than to have it made locally.

they have 15 or 16 small factories or workshops. Cane is imported from Calcutta and Bareilly, and bamboo from Kalka and Najibabad.

The manufacture of wickerwork articles offers an opening to a capitalist who will collect good specimens of foreign workmanship, especially of the folding kind, and get them copied by his men. The official in particular, who is liable to constant transfers, would prefer cheap, strong and portable wickerwork to cumbersome articles of wood, which lose their finish in a few moves.

The *kharádi* or turner is found in every village, for he is the original cabinet-maker of the land. It is he who makes the stools, and settees, and bed legs, and boxes, that constitute the traditional furniture of a Punjábi's household and the gaudy wooden toys that are the delight of his children. The turner's art is, as might be expected, primitive in the villages, but develops with the taste of his customers in the towns. Turnery.

Delhi, with 450 turners, is the largest centre and is followed by Amritsar with 100. There are about 80, most of them Mohammadans, in Hoshiarpur, and the same number in Bassi Ghulam Hussain. The peculiarity of Hoshiarpur work is that the lines of a pattern are often scratched in one colour and then filled in with another. The general effect is rather lurid, owing to the use of a tin-foil ground, over which lac-mixed with aniline dyes is laid. Pákpatan, in Montgomery, has a provincial reputation for wares of a solid surface and design. Sáhiwál, in Shahpur, is also well known, but its work, though marked by great freedom in design, is crude, ill-finished and badly coloured.

The turner mostly uses the wood of the *shisham* and

the *phuláhi*, but the soft and resinless *ubkán* (*Populus euphratica*) is preferred in the Multan division. The timber of the *khair* (*Acacia Catechu*), the *kangu* (*Flacourtia Ramontchi*) and the *kau* (*Olea ferruginea*), are also used in several districts. In buying articles of *shisham* care should be taken to select those made of the red heart-wood, which worms never touch, and to avoid the white sap-wood, which they relish.

Walking-sticks.

Walking-sticks are made at Wazirabad, Hoshiarpur and other places, generally of bamboo or *kau*, the wood being frequently lacquered or inlaid. At Nizamabad there is also a considerable trade in Malacca canes with silver or horn handles. The industry is capable of development in the hands of enterprising men. They could utilize a great many trees in the Punjab which would yield a much handsomer article than the stock style of cane offered to every passenger at Wazirabad station.[1] If the sticks are neatly finished, they will command a good market in the larger cities.

Combs.

Combs are largely used in the province, particularly by the Sikhs. There are 120 artisans in Amritsar, 60 in Delhi, 50 in Lahore and 90 in Nurpur (Shahpur), in addition to a large number scattered all over the country. The only instruments required are a saw, a lathe and a cold chisel, with which a skilful workman can turn out from 20 to 30 combs a day, and earn from 4 to 8 annas.[2] The wood used is that of the *chikri*, the *garna*

---

[1] See Troup, *Indian Woods and their Uses* (*Ind. For. Mem.*) 1909, p. 50, for a long list of suitable woods. Before any varieties are used in large quantities, samples should be sent to the dealers for trial. The manufacture of walking sticks is described in Spon, *Workshop Receipts*, Vol. IV.

[2] For an account of hand machinery for combs see note 4 on page 123 *supra*. For machinery for making penholders, see *ibid.* note 5.

(*Carissa spinarum*), the *haldu* (*Adina cordifolia*), the *kiláwá* (*Wrightia tomentosa*), the *kau*, the *kangu*,[1] and the *shisham*.

Carts and carriages.

The country-cart with a *shisham* body and *kikar* wheels is made everywhere. At Lahore, for example, there are 25 factories, while the villages round about Gujrat City export cart-wheels in large numbers to the Attock district. There is also an expanding industry in carriages of European style, and a number of factories make vehicles such as *tumtums*, cabriolets and victorias, in Lahore, Ambala, Jullundur and other important places. Parts of carriages, as well as timber, are generally imported from England by the best manufacturers, but *teak* and *tun* are also used.

Boats.

The builder of boats was important before the railways killed river-navigation, and his trade with it. Kalabagh, on the Indus, once a noted centre, now produces only half a dozen boats per annum, and so does Isa Khel a little further down. Five or six artificers each at Jhugian and Jalálpúr in the Pind Dádan Khan sub-division and a few more in the Jhelum, Wazirabad and Amritsar *tahsils* are all that survive of the industry in the rest of the Punjab.

Suggestions.

The Punjabi artisan is skilful and ingenious, but he is a poor joiner. The strength of him is sometimes wasted into the fineness of a web, but a Ruskin could scarce complain that it is daily racked into the exactness of a line. He has, in fact, much to learn in the way of improved methods. Even such a cheap and simple contrivance as the fret—saw[2] is not known save

---

[1] For other woods, see Troup, *op. cit.* p. 25.

[2] A fretsaw on an iron stand, with treadle-motion can be had for Rs. 15 in Calcutta.

in Jullundur, and in a single workshop in Hoshiarpur: the untravelled artificers of Chiniot have not even heard of it. Moreover, even in the places where it has been introduced, the tool is not fully utilized. The "mistri" only perforates panels with it preparatory to carving, though it could very well be made to do the work of a frame-saw, and cut joints much more accurately and neatly than is now done.

Further small circular saws, mounted on foot-driven lathes,[1] such as are common in Germany, would be admirable for work with soft woods like *deodar* and *chil*, and would do away with the boy-assistant, who spoils as much as he finishes.[2]

2. There is no organisation at all for introducing improved tools and machinery among the artisans. This ought really to be one of the functions of the industrial schools, which should not only teach the use of such appliances to their pupils, but also serve as demonstration stations for all carpenters. Some central school should keep a good collection of these, and make loans, from time to time, to the district schools. Such an institution might also maintain with advantage a show-room, where all the less known timbers of the province could be exhibited by the Forest Department, along with articles made from them.

3. The existing official scheme of industrial education, more particularly in carpentry, is unsatisfactory. It comprises too much drawing, too much carving, too much reading and writing, and too little plain

---

[1] Such a saw need not cost more than Rs. 50.

[2] See also p. 169.

carpentry, to turn out good workmen.[1] Industrial schools should aim not merely at teaching, a handicraft, but also at preparing their pupils mentally, morally and physically, for steady and strenuous manual labour for eight hours in the day. Carpentry in itself is not a difficult art to learn. It is often acquired by amateurs, but they do not thereby become fit persons to be employed as journeymen carpenters. It is absolutely futile to expect a boy who has played with a few tools for a couple of hours, and then scribbled on paper the rest of the day, to take kindly to a workman's arduous life. His training has left him fitter to wield the pencil than the hammer, and he will prefer to drag on existence as an inefficient draftsman in a P. W. D. office.[2] As suggested in the Introduction, the present system needs to be overhauled by practical experts familiar with the crafts and local conditions of Northern India, and also having experience in industries and industrial schools in the more advanced European countries.

4. There are too few schools of carpentry in the province : one at least of the right sort should exist in

---

[1] While the Punjab industrial schools devote only two hours on an average, daily, to practical work, the Saharanpur C. M. S. Industrial School devotes five or six, with better results.

[2] It should be borne in mind that these remarks are directed against *industrial* and not against *technical* schools, to which quite different principles apply. The former aim at turning out skilled "hands," and perhaps foremen, and only so much study should be allowed in them as will enable a workman to make the best use of his hands. The latter are meant to be training grounds for the commissioned officers of industry, who must, in addition to some business training, have a better general education than the rank and file of artisans. In connection with every technical school there should be a higher elementary school in which general education is associated with manual training.

every district, for there is a great dearth of good joiners everywhere. As has been mentioned before, all artisans engaged in decaying industries, as, for example, the Kashmiri weavers of Sialkot, are most anxious to start their sons in fresh walks of life where they may have better success than in the old ones, and it is time to set to work to satisfy this desire.

Carpentry is, in a way, the mother of all industrial arts, and a good carpenter will master any other craft just as easily as a good cricketer learns a new game of ball. Even if the schools send forth more carpenters into the world than are needed, that will be no loss, for the surplus will be welcomed by the mills and factories, that are now crying aloud in vain for intelligent and steady labour.[1] Let this country for once, take a leaf from the industrial history of the German nation, among whom "there appears to be a consensus of opinion that schools for wood-workers have proved a great blessing to the people: for, besides bolstering up the industries of the country, they add greatly to the artistic pleasure and development of the people themselves."[2]

---

[1] A school of carpentry need not cost more than Rs. 250 to start, with a recurring annual expenditure of Rs. 800 (exclusive of scholarships). Such schools are already flourishing at Muzaffargarh, Jhang, Chiniot, Hissar, and other places. They should be paid for both by the District Boards and the Municipalities, for carpenters are equally necessary to agriculturists and townsmen. The first thing to do is to select a place where the people want a school of this kind. Inquiries should be made, and a list prepared of such children of school-going age in the neighbourhood as are willing to enrol themselves. A certain number of scholarships in the form of free board and lodging should also be offered to boys from outstations, and both the artisan and non-artisan classes encouraged to join.

[2] *Jour. Soc. Arts*, Vol. LIII. July 21, 1905, p. 915.

5. Finally, an urgent need of the province is a separate inspector of industrial schools, who should be charged not only with the supervision of existing institutions, but also with the duty of giving advice or encouragement to local authorities in the setting up of new schools. His office might at the start be combined with that of director of the "Railway" technical school at Lahore until there is sufficient work for him in his proper sphere. Under the present rules, the Principal of the Mayo School of Art is burdened with this task, for which he has little time, and often little inclination. Specialists in art do not necessarily know anything about industries. Few, if any, artists, for example, who exhibit at the Royal Academy, frame their own pictures, or make their own shoes. The existing arrangement owes whatever success it has had in the past to the ability, versatility and enthusiasm of the eminent men who have presided over the Mayo School of Art.

CHAPTER XV.

MISCELLANEOUS WOOD INDUSTRIES.

This chapter covers a few sections that could not conveniently be grouped in the preceding one. In addition to saw-mills it treats of the manufacture of toys, sporting requisites, casks, matches and pencils, *i.e.*, industries involving the use not only of wood but also of other raw materials.

Saw-mills. A steam saw-mill is attached to the harmonium works of Shankar Dass and Co., of Lahore, and a much larger one has been just set up in the same place under the name of the Premier Saw Mills in connection with a furniture factory, but mainly with the object of doing job-work for the public. There are also two in Amritsar, one with a steam-engine, in the municipal workshops, and the other, driven by electric power, in the canal establishment. A furniture firm in Gujrat has a steam-saw which will cut from 125 to 150 square feet of *shisham* per hour. The two biggest contractors in Rawalpindi also have one each, and so has Ganda Singh Uberoi, the well-known maker of sporting requisites in Sialkot. A band-saw worked by electricity, with a motor stand-by has just been purchased by a tinsel maker in Delhi. Lastly, a timber contractor is setting up machinery at Phillour, near the forest depôt, with the object of supplying fir planks, ready tongued and grooved, to the markets of the province.

The Lahore mills charge the public from Re. 1-8 to Rs. 3 per hundred square feet of soft timber, while the Gujrat furniture firm is content with Re. 1-4 for *deodar,* Re. 1-8 for *chil,* and Rs. 2 for *shisham.* The charges for hand-sawing, on the other hand, are very heavy in some places, as the following table will show.[1]

100 sq. ft. of	Sargodha. Rs.	Jhelum. Rs.	Wazirabad. Rs.	Delhi. Rs.	Lahore. Rs.	Ambala. Rs.
Deodar	3-0	2-4	4-0	2-8	2-0	3-2
Shisham	6-0	5-0	6-0	—	3-6	6-4
Kikar	7-0	6-0	6-0	—	3-6	6-4

With the exception of Delhi and Lahore, none of these places possesses a steam-saw.[2]

Saw-mills are of two kinds : the one squares tree-trunks into logs, and the other cuts up the logs into scantlings and deals. The former should be located within a convenient distance of the forest from which the trunks are to be brought, while the latter may be set up, if possible along with a planing mill, in any town where, roughly speaking, 30,000 maunds of

---

1. A pair of ordinary hand-sawyers will saw in a day :—

From 60 to 80 sq. ft. of deodār.
„ 48 „ 60 „ „ shísham.
„ 32 „ 35 „ „ kikar.

2 It will be useful to give the railway traffic figures for unwrought timber at some of the chief stations. The figures do not, of course, include material carried by road or river. It would be a matter for further inquiry what proportion of the timber is received or sent ready sawn.

Stations.	*Inward.* 1906-07.	1907-08.	1908-09.	*Outward.* 1906-07.	1907-08.	1908-09.
Delhi	203,533	210,865	274,515	66,048	45,043	52,336
Ambala	50,934	30,472	32,980	5,192	8,950	7,106
Lahore	111,741	95,377	45,652	7,620	7,278	8,345
Jhelum	10,104	13,847	8,178	251,162	254,059	171,133
Rawalpindi	46,297	38,587	51,260	10,562	12,020	25,009
Lyallpur	49,242	53,386	47,354	1,539	8,480	1,914
Gojra	16,045	28,229	44,099	2,044	3,241	945
Toba Tek Singh	7,203	27,353	36,361	148	49	641
Sargodha	30,362	24,554	32,113	1,647	592	1,761

timber is available annually for sawing. Water power is very suitable for this industry, and where this can be had, 16,000 maunds of wood every year would suffice to make a large saw-mill profitable. Moreover, small engines of two to four H.P., fitted to burn wood-waste, can now be had quite cheap,[1] and makers of boxes, furniture, etc., will save labour, and do more uniform work, if they set them up to turn their saws.

Sporting requisites. The increasing love of field sports in India has given rise to an important industry. Requisites for games are made at Lahore, Rawalpindi, Amritsar, and other places, but Sialkot has achieved a fame which is not confined to the Indian Empire. There are a great many factories in the last-named city, that of Messrs. Ganda Singh Uberoi and Co., being the largest. This one fitted with all the latest appliances, and employs on an average a hundred men and boys under European foremen.[2] The second largest firm is that of Jhanda Singh Uberoi and Co., who have initiated the novel though excellent system of apprenticing boys of all castes at a starting salary of Rs. 4 per month, the parents giving security in each case that if the apprentice leaves service before five years they will refund all moneys received by him.

The Sialkot manufacturers would warmly welcome a school of carpentry, as the sole obstacle in the way of their indefinite expansion is want of skilled labour.

[1] A 4 B.H.P. oil-engine would cost about Rs. 1,200, the working expenses for six hours, with oil at Rs. 2-12 per 4 gallons, coming to Rs. 35 to 40 a month.

[2] From the papers of this firm it appears that they send a regular supply of tennis and badminton rackets to one of the best-known English makers, and have instructions to despatch weekly as many cricket balls as they can supply. For an unknown reason the Sialkot firm is not to stamp any names on these goods.

From the polo field and the hockey ground the transition is easy to the gambols of the nursery, where the Indian child grows in the happy companionship of what Dr. Coomaraswamy would call symbolical representations of men and animals. Rude dolls and toys of wood, mostly turned and lacquered, or inlaid, are made everywhere, particularly in Delhi, Amritsar, Jullundur and Lahore, where there is a constant demand. The taste for more finished articles is, however, growing,[1] and efforts should be made to satisfy it locally. Toys.

In Germany [2] and Japan, where enormous quantities of cheap and attractive toys are made for export, the industry is mainly practised by peasant families in their homes, while in America large factories do the work of human hands with automatic machines. The raw material costs very little. Given a handful of waste wood, a few bits of leather, a little wool or hair, some paint, and a modicum of skill, the resulting sheep or bear will be the joy of any nursery in the world. The Indian workman does not lack the requisite deftness, and, with proper guidance, he ought to rival the German or Japanese artificer. The Mayo School of Art at Lahore might engage a Japanese instructor in toy-making, and classes might also be started at Delhi and Amritsar, which are great centres for such minor industries. A museum of suitable toys, with models of

---

[1] India imported toys to the value of Rs. 31,32,102, from countries outside the British Empire, in 1908-09.

[2] Germany exports toys to the value of over 2½ millions sterling every year. Over 50,000 persons are engaged in the industry, chiefly in Nürnberg and Sonneberg. In the former town toy-making is a factory industry, and in the latter a household one.—*Jour. Soc. Arts*, Dec. 18, 1903, pp. 111-2.

tools and processes, would cost little, and do much good, if set up in connection with these classes.

Casks.

Casks are made to hold liquids such as paint, or dry goods like colophony, cement, soda or fruit. *Quercus dilatata* and *Q. incana* have been found fairly suitable for beer casks, while the following might be tried for dry goods. It may be noted that a cask-factory need only have waste timber of the length of the staves and head boards :—

1.	Abies Pindrow [1] Picea Morinda [2]	Cement and colophony.
2.	Populus euphratica, [3]	Fruit and possibly cement.
3.	Quercus Spp.	More durable dry-goods casks.

There is hardly any opening yet for cask-making in this province, but there will be one if Portland cement is ever manufactured in large quantities. Rupees 15,000 would suffice for a factory (including a 17½ H.P. engine) turning out from 40 to 50 oil-barrels per day of ten hours.

Matches.

The manufacture of matches has a great future in India, and if the factories set up from time to time in various provinces have failed, it is chiefly because they were built on unsuitable sites, without the advice of experts, and often without adequate capital.

The dominant factor in this industry is, of course, the supply of wood, which must be available at the works at three to five annas a cubic foot for the coloured, and seven annas, at the most, for the white varieties. For an outturn of 700 gross of filled boxes a day 66,000 cubic feet of wood would be required annually.

---

[1] *Abies Pindrow*, Eng. silver fir, vern. *Pandrau*, *tós*.

[2] *Picea Morinda*, Eng. Himalayan spruce, vern. *rai*, *rau*.

[3] *Populus euphratica*, vern. *ubhán*, *bahán*.

A small factory with a capital of Rs. 8,000 has just been started at Solon, on the Kalka-Simla Railway. It is fitted with Japanese hand-machines, and is said to be well suited for its wood supplies. *Chil* (*P. longifolia*) will be used for splints, and *semal* (*Bombax malabaricum*) for boxes.

A model match-factory will shortly be set up in the Bareilly district of the United Provinces by a limited company with a capital of three lacs of rupees. Among its promoters is Herr Roller, a German manufacturer of match-machinery.

One of the sites suggested by Mr. Troup for match-manufacture on a large scale in the Punjab is Ghazi Ghat on the Indus, where an annual supply of 35,000 c.ft. of *Populus euphratica* is now available, and 100,000 c.ft. could be had 20 years hence. The cost at Ghazi Ghat would be from 8 to 15 rupees per 100 cubic feet solid.

Jagadhri is perhaps the best place for utilising Himalayan coniferous woods (*Pinus excelsa, P. longifolia,* and *Picea Morinda*), obtainable in large quantities from the Jaunsar Forest Division of the United Provinces.

Mr. Troup suggests plantations, in waste areas, of *Bombax malabaricum, Ailanthus excelsa* and *Populus euphratica*, to serve as feeders for match-factories. A plantation of 500 acres of *Bombax malabaricum* would yield, at the present rates, an annual revenue of at least Rs. 7 per acre.[1]

Pencils, too, are consumed in large and increasing quantities, and could, perhaps, be manufactured here at a profit. An establishment of the size of the Small Industries Co. of Calcutta, capable of turning out from Pencils.

[1] On the subject generally see Mr. Troup's recent monograph on match-making (*Ind. For. mem.*).

150 to 200 gross a day, would require a supply of about 75 to 100 c.ft. of wood. Timber of good quality yields three gross per cubic foot, but, if full of knots and cracks, it will only produce two. To enable the pencils to be sold at Re. 1-4 per gross, with a margin of profit, the wood must be delivered at the factory at Re. 1-2 per cubic foot. It may be mentioned that German pencils sell wholesale at Delhi at from Re. 1 to Rs. 3 per gross, according to quality.

The following Punjab woods are suitable for pencils :—

1. *Deodar* (*Cedrus Deodara*), the best for the purpose, is available in sufficient quantities at Shahdara, Wazirabad, Jhelum and Jagadhri, but it costs a rupee per cubic foot and its price is rising.

2. *Chil* (*Pinus excelsa*) is another fair pencil-wood. It can be had in abundance at Jhelum, Wazirabad and Jagadhri, at about 12 annas per cubic foot, but its price is sure to rise four or five years hence.

3. *Rhododendron arboreum* has also been suggested, but it is so scattered that its cost is uncertain. Moreover, a good part of its timber would be wasted on account of the knots. It is even doubtful if sufficient quantities would be available for more than a few years.

4. *Picea Morinda* and *Abies Pindrow* may possibly answer the purpose. They can be had in unlimited quantities at 8 annas a cubic foot, at any place where the railway crosses the Punjab rivers. The timber is poor, and is not used except by the cultivators of the Canal Colonies, on whom it is palmed off as "white deodar."

The other materials used by the pencil manufacturer are Ceylonese graphite,[1] China clay, varnish, turpentine and wax.

[1] *See* Holland and Fermor, *Rev. Min. Prod. Ind.* in *Rec. Geol. Surv. Ind.*, Vol. XXXIX. (1910), p. 97.

CHAPTER XVI.

Iron and Steel.

An inexhaustible supply of iron ores of the very best quality is found in Kangra,[1] in some of the Hill-states,[2] and in the Narnaul district of the Patiala State.[3] Attempts to exploit the deposits in British territory have failed through lack of fuel, labour, and communications, and the indigenous iron-smelting industry is nearing extinction at Bashahar[4] and

---

[1] In the valley of the river Ul. See *Kangra Dist. Gazetteer* (1904), p. 170.

[2] Iron is no longer smelted in Kot Khai (Simla district), as the Forest Department has stopped the supplies of free fuel. There are a few ore-bodies of poor quality in the Suket, Jubbul and Sirmoor States.

[3] Iron ore, magnetite with haematite of exceptionally good quality (57·42 per cent. of iron in average sample), is found in the low ridge between Chhapri (7 miles south of Narnaul) and Jaunpur. Formerly it was in much request in the neighbourhood, and was exported to Jaipur and Alwar. (P. N. Bose, *Geology and Mineral Resources of Narnaul* in *Rec. Geol. Surv. Ind.*, Vol. XXXIII.) Mr. Bose recommends the construction of a railway from Narnaul to Attri for exploiting these ores.

[4] The iron mines in the Rohru *tahsil* of the Bashahar State still provide metal for local agricultural requirements, but there is no hope for the industry, as the charcoal used for smelting is prepared by a most wasteful process. If the villagers will make charcoal of large trees in modern kilns of the Jaunsar pattern, the end may be delayed. At one time iron to the value of Rs. 4,000 to 5,000 a year used to be smelted here and sold in the neighbouring states and at Simla. The State appears to be rich in minerals, and a regular mineralogical survey might yield valuable results.

Mandi,[1] where alone it survives, through similar causes. The imported material is now so cheap that, except in a few inaccessible places, it no longer pays to work the ores by the primitive native methods.[2] The possibility of extracting iron from the Punjab ores by electricity, according to the methods now being tried in Sweden and Norway, deserves to be seriously studied by experts.[3]

The 64,000 maunds of unwrought iron that comes every year into the Punjab finds its way direct to the foundries in the chief cities of the province, and also, through the medium of the shopkeeper, to the workshops of the town and the village blacksmith. These artisans, however, largely use old scrap-iron, rails, etc., periodical auctions of which take place at Lahore and other centres. The ordinary material costs them from Re. 1-8 to Rs. 7 per maund, but the steel most prized for cutlery is that of old files, at Rs. 10 per maund.[4]

---

[1] The ore-bodies of the Saraj Waziri of the Mandi State are almost inexhaustible, but are only slightly worked.—*Mandi State Gazetteer* (1904), p. 50.

[2] On the iron resources of the province generally, see Baden-Powell, *Punjab Products* (1868), pp. 1-9; Ball, *Econ. Geol. Ind.*, pp. 504-6; and Watt *Dict. Econ. Prod. Ind.*, Vol. IV. pp. 510 *et seq.*

The ore deposits of the Kirana Hills (Shahpur) are meagre and inaccessible.

[3] *Cf. Ind. Tr. Journ.*, March 30, 1911, p. 400. For power near Simla, see note 1, p. 89. For power at Delhi the notes under Aluminium in Chapter XVIII. should be consulted.

[4] The following table, showing the inward and outward traffic of wrought iron for 1908-09 at selected stations on the N.-W. Railway, is of interest:—

Stations.	*Outward.*	*Inward.*
Amballa	11,812	41,440
Ludhiana	3,403	18,747
Jullundur	4,354	56,050
Gujranwala	24,308	34,961
Wazirabad	1,363	2,747
Jhelum	10,309	46,924
Multan	5,887	27,880
Batala	7,595	19,508
Lyallpur	3,994	25,689

There are a fair number of iron foundries in the province, though, curiously enough, only a small one exists at Jullundur, which is the centre of an important *gur* yielding district. There are as many as seven at Batala that make good flour and sugarcane mills, lathes, etc., and export them all over the province. A three-roller sugarcane mill costs from Rs. 28 to 31, and a flour mill, seven maunds in weight, Rs. 37. Some of the foundries hire out their sugarcane presses for the season and send round itinerant mechanics to look after them—a system which might be adopted with advantage by dealers in other agricultural machinery.

The iron-ware usually made in the Punjab includes :—

(1) Ordinary agricultural implements, such as ploughshares and scythes.

(2) Common hardware, such as door chains and hinges, nails, frying-pans and charcoal stoves (*angíthís*).

(3) Cutlery, plain and ornamental.

(4) Locks.

(5) Safes.

(6) Trunks and boxes.

(7) A few other miscellaneous articles.

The first class, though the most important to the cultivator, includes the simplest and rudest articles, payment for which is generally regulated by traditional rules, and consists of a certain proportion of the crop doled out at harvest time. The exact profits of the village blacksmith defy determination.

The manufacture of common hardware is mainly the province of the town blacksmith though his country brother not seldom engages in it also during his spare moments. Chains, axe-heads, etc., are made in every district for home consumption and at many large centres, such as Jullundur, Batala, Gujranwalla, Sialkot and Multan, for export. Only the cheapest grade of iron is used for these articles.

The chief industry of Jullundur is lock-making, which will be treated later. Jullundur's manufacture of hardware is not important. At Batala there are a hundred families of *lohárs*, many of whom seek employment abroad, and a certain proportion are engaged in the seven foundries, while the rest do ordinary work. Sialkot owes its fame for iron-ware chiefly to the two villages of Kotli Lohárán (Eastern and Western), a few miles off. In the eastern village there are 200 families of blacksmiths, but most of the adults are in service as regimental smiths, railway employees, etc., at Rs. 30 per mensem and more. Only physical unfitness or the force of domestic circumstances keeps these men from seeking employment outside their village. There are 30 workshops altogether, where stirrups, bits, etc., are made for various regiments all over India, orders being received through relations employed in the said regiments. "Koft" or damascened ware is prepared in half a dozen shops for sale to Europeans as curios.[1]

The outside demand for blacksmiths from this village is greater than the supply, and a school of iron-work would probably succeed here and draw other castes into a profitable and expanding industry. A

1 These and three shops in Gujrat complete the tale of damasceners in the Punjab. The latter do a cheap and rough kind of work for the local public and are flourishing, which is more than can be said of the master-workers of Kotli. The art is really out of date. It is curious but not beautiful.

co-operative society would probably fail, as the people are very factious and quarrelsome.

The situation in the western village is similar. There are from 200 to 300 households, but only from 25 to 30 workshops.

Cutlery is the speciality of Nizamabad, a village two miles from Wazirabad, and to a much smaller extent of Sialkot and Bhera. The census of 1901 enumerated 46 "knife and tool makers" in Lahore and 30 in Amritsar. Cutlery.

In Nizamabad there are about 125 families of blacksmiths, many of whom have taken service abroad. There are about 25 workshops, giving employment to 100 men, amongst whom, besides the hereditary craftsmen, one finds a few Juláhás, Móchis and Barwálás. The cutlery is generally inferior, being made of iron costing Rs. 5-8-0 per maund, but for the best kinds old files at Rs. 10 per maund are used. Some of it is sent to Kotli-Loharan in Sialkot to be damascened, as that craft is not practised in the locality.

Besides knives, some of the artisans make walking-sticks and others tube wells, which they undertake to set up near Nizamabad for Rs. 30, taking on themselves the risk of not striking on water.

The industry of Nizamabad is flourishing, there being a large export both of cutlery and walking-sticks to Bombay, Calcutta and other places in India. The workmen earn from ten annas to a rupee daily. Some of them have got together a little capital and set up factories with a number of workmen under them, while amongst the rank and file a co-operative society would seem to have a chance of success.

A very promising venture is the Punjab Cutlery and

Sporting Works at Wazirabad, started by three educated young men with brains, capital and energy, who are making an effort to turn out the best quality of goods with the aid of all available labour-saving appliances. Their exhibits at the Lahore Exhibition were excellent, and they were awarded a silver medal at the Franco-British Exhibition in London for their cutlery, which was all sold on the spot.

At Bhera there are 20 workshops for cheap cutlery, which is exported to Peshawar, Multan, etc. Besides these, three or four families make knives and walking-sticks with fancy stone handles for sale to Europeans in the hills, and have thereby earned for the Bhera industry a somewhat fictitious importance in Simla-written literature.

The firm of Shivdeo Singh Uberoi and Co. of Sialkot is one of the two or three in India making surgical instruments. Their manufactures have been certified to be of great excellence by many distinguished medical officers and are exported all over India and Burma, chiefly to private practitioners. The best Sheffield steel at Rs. 40 per maund is used for the blades. They complain that with the exception of commissions for repairs they get scant patronage from Government departments.[1]

Locks.

Two kinds of locks are made in the Punjab. The first is the local variety with a screw-key, and the other an imitation of the English lever lock. Both are generally heavy and rudely made, but their popularity is increasing with the rise of wealth among the agricultural classes, who, like the small shopkeepers of

---

1 It appears from the Consular Report for 1908 that there is a good demand for cheap cutlery in Java, now chiefly met by Germany.

the towns, prefer them to the cheap but unsubstantial German article. Even in out-of-the-way places like Jhang, Rupar and Hansi one often comes across rustic geniuses who almost rival Chubb.

Imported sheeting costing from Rs. 5 to Rs. 7 per maund is used for the outside, but very inferior material serves where it can be hidden from the eye. The chief centre of lock-making is Jullundur, where there are 150 artisans who make padlocks of both kinds. The locks when ready are given by the smith to the polisher, who takes two annas in the rupee for his trouble. An ordinary artificer will make about ten big locks a day and earn 12 annas. No improved tools or appliances are used, the cutting, bending, etc., being all done by hand.

The trade is in the hands of the Khoja shopkeepers who export the manufactures of Jullundur to Rawalpindi, Peshawar, Ludhiana, Multan and Sukkur. They generally supply the raw material and pay piece-wages, but where the lohar uses his own material, they buy his locks at Rs. 4 to Rs. 12 a hundred.

The local workers in iron and wood, as well as the masons, are all Mohammedans and form one community, any one of the three crafts being open to every member of it. The locksmith of Jullundur is more dependent on outside help than the carpenter and, unlike the latter, will take apprentices from other castes. A large number of the workers in iron were formerly in the brasslock trade, but gave it up because it ceased to pay. Jullundur seems to be a suitable place both for a co-operative society and for a school for iron-work. It would also appear to be a favourable centre for a large foundry and workshop for sugar-mills and agricultural implements generally, as well as for a workshop with modern machinery for making locks.

There are over a score of locksmiths in Sialkot City who make rough locks of galvanised iron for export to the Canal Colonies and other places in the Punjab. An equal number are engaged in this industry in Kotli Loharan (West), a few miles off. Three-lever locks ($2\frac{1}{2}$ inches) cost Rs. 6 a dozen.

Safes.

Of the 40 iron workshops in Gujranwala, 24 make safes and strong-boxes. These are entirely made by hand and their finish and quality leave much to be desired, but they are exported to every place in the Punjab. They cost from Rs. 10 to Rs. 16 a maund, the iron used being purchased locally at Rs. 6 a maund. A rather more elaborate article with panels of figured brass and handles of the same material is produced in Jagadhri, which is also a noted centre of brass manufacture. Ferozepur has half a dozen artisans who are modest enough to admit that their safes are not so good as those of Gujranwala, and are for local consumption only. These are made of iron sheeting costing Rs. 5 a maund, and sell at Rs. 7 to Rs. 7-8 a maund. They are often weighted with iron filings to give them a false appearance of solidity. All safe-makers make their own locks.

Trunks and boxes.

Steel trunks and boxes are made in Delhi, Amritsar, Lahore and Multan, and most of all in Sialkot, but they are also produced in small quantities in several other places, such as Wazirabad and Ludhiana. They are growing in popularity with all classes, as they protect clothes against the ravages of rats and white-ants, and only cost three or four rupees each.

Trunks are made in Sialkot in 25 factories and also by

ordinary blacksmiths in their slack time. Multan owes its fame for boxes to Messrs. Allibhoy Vallijee, whose dispatch-boxes are known all over India.[1] They use imported tinned sheets and locks, and have a factory well equipped with modern machinery. The proprietors are themselves practical tinsmiths.

Miscellaneous.

Among miscellaneous industries may be mentioned the manufacture of scientific apparatus by the Punjab Institute of Science Workshop in Lahore, of guns and swords by stray workmen in Gujranwala, Nizamabad and other places, and of gramophones by a poor *lohár* in Gujrat.[2] Nibs are made in the same place by another *lohár* who has fitted up a small factory with neat hand-machines, which, by his own account, he made himself.[3] One of the *koftgars* of this town (which seems to be fertile in mechanical talent) makes fountain-pens of nickel, which are unfortunately useless owing to neglect, through ignorance, of certain elementary details.[4]

Umbrellas.

India annually imports ready-made umbrellas to the value of about nineteen lacs, mostly from England, but there is a considerable industry in Bombay and Calcutta in their manufacture from imported "furni-

---

1 They are not sold in the Chandni Chowk at Delhi, where cheap imported boxes seem to be more popular.

2 His name is Mohammad Hasan and he calls the machine he has invented the "Swadeshi Hasanophone."

3 The manufacture of nibs as well as of penholders seems to offer an opening for energetic men with a little capital. The processes are not difficult, and a set of hand-machines for steel nibs can be had for about £250, and for penholders for £90 C. I. F., Karachi. For penholders the waste of iron, brass and wood workshops could be utilised.

The manufacture of steel nibs is described in the *Indian Trade Journal*, Sept. 8, 1910, p. 258.

4 For an account of the manufacture of fountain and stylographic pens, see the three Cantor Lectures, published in the *Jour. of the Soc. of Arts*, London, of Oct. 20, 1905, and subsequent numbers.

ture "[1] and locally-made cloth. The industry is one which ought to pay at centres like Delhi, Lahore and Amritsar, as umbrellas are gaining in popularity everywhere.

Enamelled ware.

As a consequence of the increasing price of copper, enamelled ware is making headway amongst the Mohammedan section of the population. There is hardly any village of importance where a few pieces are not displayed for sale by the local *bisáti* or pedlar. The Hindus have not, so far, taken kindly to it, as they suspect that the composition of the enamel, which is a trade secret, includes impure substances. It may be mentioned, however, that though bone-ash can be used to produce opacity, it is in no way an essential ingredient, and is, as a matter of fact, usually replaced by a metal oxide.

India annually imports the ware to the value of about 18½ lacs of rupees. Over 92 per cent. of this comes from foreign countries, chiefly Austria and Germany, where the industry has attained vast proportions. In Germany alone there are over 70 factories, employing 22,000 men and women, and with an estimated output of four and a half crores of rupees per annum. Iron-enamelling is a very easy process throughout, and requires simple materials and apparatus, the essentials being a thin coat of suitable enamel evenly distributed over the surface of the metal, and a clear fire for melting or fusing it. Muffle furnaces, though sometimes an advantage, are by no means necessary.

Indeed, large enamelled iron plates (such as signboards, etc.) are commonly fired over a clear coke fire in England and on the Continent. The metal-work

---

1 This is the trade name for the separate parts of an umbrella. An unsuccessful attempt was made at Poona to produce these and undersell the imported articles. The Khatau Mills and the Kaisar-i-Hind Mills of Bombay make cloth suitable for covering umbrellas.

also, is largely done by hand, vessels like cups, saucers, spoons, etc., being all made of single pieces of iron sheeting by cutting and punching machines.[1]

The capital required is small compared with the outturn and profit, and the raw material of which enamel is made is so plentiful here that India, with her comparatively cheap labour, has a very good chance of building up, under good business management, an industry that will not only put a stop to all imports but curtail her annual bill for the more expensive metals. The great essential of the industry is to procure an enamel adapted to the metal employed, and if a constant supply of sheet-iron of uniform texture is procurable, there should be little difficulty in forming the mixture suitable for it. If, however, a great variety of sheet irons must be dealt with, the difficulties are proportionately enhanced.

The following simple formulæ for white enamel may be cited, not for use in a factory, but in order to indicate roughly the nature and relative importance of the materials chiefly used. They will be useful for commencing experiments, other ingredients being added to give colour, opacity, etc., as required :—[2]

Flint-glass . .	130	Sand . . .	48
Carbonate of soda	20½	Red lead[3] . .	30
Boracic acid .	12	Carbonate of soda[4]	30
		Boracic acid[5] .	10
Total	162½	Total	118

[1] Enamelling will not pay without the metal-stamping and cutting industry.

[2] See Thorpe, *Dict. Appl. Chem.* Art. *Enamel.* It must be noted that compounds of antimony are poisonous and their use in enamels is not allowed in Austria and Germany. Compounds of lead are similarly forbidden, but the writer is informed by one who ought to know that there is no danger in red lead.

Borax might be substituted for boracic acid and the carbonate of soda should perhaps be reduced to one-half the amount mentioned.

[3] See p. 146. [4] See p. 141. [5] See p. 144.

The Imperial Enamel and Iron Works of Batala, owned jointly by an Englishman and some *lohárs*, is one of the very few of its kind in India. The enameller to the firm is an illiterate *lohár* who learnt the art from a man who had passed through the Victoria Technical Institute at Bombay.[1] The work produced by the Company, so far as one can see, is excellent and the prices are 25 per cent. below those demanded for similar work done anywhere else. The firm state that all the materials used for the enamel abound in the neighbourhood.[2]

The Punjab Enamelling Works of Amritsar was started in September 1910 by Messrs. Mahendar Singh Bros., and is in charge of an ex-pupil of the Victoria Jubilee Technical Institute. The factory restricts itself for the present to the enamelling of sheet iron by manual labour.

Suggestions. The iron industry of the province is handicapped by scarcity of fuel as well as of raw material, but its general progress must be along the lines indicated in the chapter on Wood-work.[3] The prosperity of Indian agriculture is closely connected with the efficiency of the blacksmith, and one of the reasons why improved machinery cannot be introduced into the Punjab villages is the difficulty of getting it properly repaired.[4]

---

[1] The class for enamelling on iron was closed in December 1909.

[2] An excellent book on the subject is "Enamels and Enamelling" by Paul Randaw, London, 1900. This gives clear explanations and directions, besides receipts, but of course a few practical experiments will teach more than any book.

[3] See pp. 217 *et seq.*

[4] The village lohar cannot look after even a two-roller sugar-mill. See p. 196.

The Railway and Canal workshops, as well as some of the private foundries, have done much to raise the general level of skill. But this is not enough. Schools of iron-work should be started along with those of carpentry at every important centre and, amongst other things, the pupils should be made familiar with better tools and appliances for cutting, punching, etc., and also be taught to set up and repair simple agricultural machinery.

CHAPTER XVII.

COPPER AND BRASS.

Copper is found along the outer Himalayas, and was formerly smelted in large quantities in various places in Kulu. Its ores are also widely distributed in the Narnaul district of the Patiala State, especially in the southern half, where they were extensively worked in the past.[1] Copper pyrites occur in the Simla Hill States and in Kulu,[2] and also at Dariba, in the Bikaner State.[3]

Brass is an alloy of copper and zinc, usually in the proportion of 4 to 3 or 2 to 1. It is not made in large quantities in the Punjab, except at Panipat and

---

[1] Especially near a village called Mokata or Motaka.

There is no sign of rich ore anywhere, but Mr. Bose was able to extract 15 seers of copper from 2 maunds of a sample of ore by a rough smelting (*Geol. and Mineral Resources of the Narnaul District*, by P. N. Bose, B.Sc., F.G.S., in the *Rec. Geol. Surv. Ind.*, Vol. XXXIII. (1906), p. 57.

[2] Ball, *Econ. Geol. Ind.*, pp. 266-67.

[3] Not at Bidasar as incorrectly stated in the *Imperial Gazetteer*, Vol. VIII. p. 211. The Bikaner Mineral Department states that the Dariba mine was worked successfully many years ago, but had to be closed down as it was flooded. The Durbar is now making arrangements with a well-known firm to pump out the water and work the deposits.

Jagadhri, and probably one or two other places, being usually imported in sheet.[1] *Bharat* is a cheaper alloy of copper and zinc with an occasional admixture of lead, while *phúl*[2] is made of copper and tin in the proportion of 7 to 2.

The net annual imports of unwrought copper into the province amount to about 14,000 maunds, and of unwrought brass to 21,000 maunds, all *via* Bombay and Karachi. In addition to this, however, a great quantity of old metal is broken up and re-made into pots and pans.

The present price of copper sheeting at Delhi is Rs. 42-8 and of brass Rs. 35 per maund, but the rates fluctuate greatly and naturally increase with the railway freight as one goes northwards. Old brass can be purchased in any bazaar for Rs. 25 and old copper for about Rs. 32 a maund. *Bharat* sells at about Rs. 25 and *phúl* at Rs. 50 per maund.

The orthodox Hindu, especially in the town, will not cook his meals except in utensils of brass or *phúl*. He finds earthenware too expensive, as he cannot use itmore than once, and he has to reject copper because it poisons food, save when covered with tin—to him an impure metal. The Mohammadan, on the

---

[1] India imports unwrought brass and copper, chiefly from Great Britain and Germany, and to a certain extent from other European countries, the Persian Gulf, Straits Settlements, etc. The imports of copper from Japan have recently been growing in importance.

Zinc comes from Great Britain and Germany, and tin chiefly from the Straits Settlements. Lead has been imported chiefly from the Persian Gulf during recent years.

[2] *Bharat* is also called *kansa* in Rewart and *kút* in Ludhiana. *Phul* is also known as *kansi*. Copper and brass are *tamba* and *pital*, respectively. Lead is *sisa* or *sikka*, zinc is *jast* and tin is *kalai*, *rang* or *tin*.

other hand, very rarely uses brass, but invests in copper when he can afford it. In the villages he is as often as not content with an earthenware cooking-pot.

The census tables show that practically the whole of the brass, copper and bell-metal industry of the province is to be found east of the meridian which passes through the town of Jhelum, while to the west, where the population is predominantly Mohammadan, it is insignificant in extent. The largest number of brass and copper smiths in any district in the western half is found in the Multan district, where it only comes to 140, *i.e.*, two per ten thousand of the total population, whereas in Delhi the proportion is 31 per ten thousand. Moreover, all the great centres are situated on or near the trunk railroads. Formerly every group of villages had its own workers in brass and copper, but with improved means of communication the artisan's commercial instincts have made him gravitate towards the main arteries of provincial traffic. Of the 2,172 workers in the Delhi district, 1,894 were recorded in Delhi itself, and Amritsar and Lahore account for 337 and 71 respectively, out of the district totals of 428 and 108.

The craft is one of the very few in the country that have no grievance against the foreign manufacturer. True, the province annually imports about 7,000 and 8,500 maunds more of brass and copperware, respectively, than it exports. This, however, consists in hand-made articles chiefly from the United Provinces, preferred for their superior art and finish. There are hardly any imports of foreign brass ware. This satisfactory position is due to the specialised character of the goods turned out, and also to the fact that in addition to hammering out a pot or a plate the local manufacturer is prepared to pay a fair price for it when it is no longer of use. The only dark cloud on the horizon is the continued rise in the price of the raw material, amounting to about 25 per cent. in the last few years, which has given an opening to imported enamelled ware amongst the Mohammadans and the lower orders of the Hindus.

Division of Labour.

A minute division of labour is the rule in the industry, especially in the Delhi division, a single vessel often passing through the hands of as many as six operators. The workers realize that this arrangement not only leads to greater efficiency and manual dexterity on their part, but effects a great saving of time. Further, a sharp line of division persists in every district of the province between the makers and sellers of this ware—the Thatheras and Kaseras. The great majority of the persons engaged in the industry are Hindus, the Kaseras claiming to be a section of the higher castes, Banyas and Khattris— a claim which is generally admitted—while the Thatheras are a class by themselves, having been recruited in many places from Lohars, Ahirs and others. As may be expected, the trade is entirely in the hands of the Kasera, who brings capital and knowledge to the industry, whereas the artisan has only his labour. The shopkeeper knows the markets and it is his raw material that the artisan works up in accordance with the designs dictated by him. The artisan's remuneration is calculated on the maundage of the finished articles, and he is also allowed a certain proportion, usually one-ninth of the weight in the case of brass, for wastage. The shopkeeper takes the risks and the profits of the industry.

The relations between the capitalist and the artisan vary in different places. They are distinctly unfriendly at Rewari and Multan, where the Kasera is denounced as a blood-sucker, but are said to be amicable at Sialkot and Jagadhri. Everywhere, however, the Thathera is bound hand and foot to the Kasera with the chains of debt. He is a sort of town-serf, unable to move to the best labour-market, and his immobility is no doubt the cause of the great dissimilarity in the wages of labour at the various centres. It must be noted, however, that the Thathera, being a Hindu, is a better man of business than, say, the Mohammadan blacksmith, and is therefore better qualified to assert his economic position. He has not permitted the rise in the price of the raw material to prejudice his wages, which are nowhere very low. The burden has fallen partly on the shoulders of the shopkeeper and partly on those of the consumer.

Owing to the method of payment by piece-work, the Thathera's daily wage is rather difficult to calculate, but the following table is believed to be fairly accurate :—

	Rs. A.		Rs. A.		Rs. A.		Rs. A.
Jagadhri	—		1 0	Amritsar	—		1 0
Lahore	2 0	to	3 0	Jhang	1 4	to	1 8
Gujranwala	0 12	to	1 2	Multan	0 8	to	0 14

A few representative prices of the finished article may be given for the benefit of the general reader. The rates vary greatly according to the state of the market as well as the finish of the articles. *Gharras* (*kalsas*)[1] of hammered brass sell at Rs. 42 per maund in Gujranwalla, Rs. 50 in Multan and Rs. 52-8 in Rewari, while the same vessels cast are Rs. 50, 55 and 60,

[1] Large narrow-mouthed vessels for carrying water.

respectively. Plain copper ware varies from Rs. 55 to Rs. 70 per maund in Multan, and *phul* drinking-cups from Rs. 70 to Rs. 90.

We will now review the industry briefly under its chief centres. Taking first the district totals, we find that the Delhi district heads the list with 2,172 workers, followed by Sialkot with 1,185; Amritsar is third with 428, and Gujranwala fourth with 294. **Chief Centres.**

Amongst the manufacturing centres the city of Delhi stands pre-eminent not only on account of the number of its artificers (in 1901 there were 1,894), but also of the artistic finish of its products.

"Most of the smiths from other places admit that they are not so skilful with the hammer and stake (*sandan*) as those at Delhi. In shaping a circular vessel of changing diameter they find it necessary to solder pieces on; while a good Delhi copper-smith shapes the whole without joint from one piece. Nests (*ganj*) of cooking pots (*degchis*) with cleanly-defined edges fitting closely into each other, are the usual articles made, and they are often admirable specimens of plain hammer work. Brass[1] articles are tastefully ornamented with foliage in low relief. There is a considerable production too of small fantastic toys in brass, roughly made but often ingenious. The merry-go-round seen at fairs furnishes one model, and railway trains, *raths*, grotesque figures and toy vessels of all sorts are also made. The best Hindu sacrificial brass wares come from Benares, Muttra and Brindaban, but many are now made at Delhi."[2] In addition to these may be mentioned the

[1] As well as copper.

[2] Mr. Lockwood Kipling's note in the *Delhi Gazetteer* (1883-84), pp. 128-29.

manufacture of cheap brass lamps and fittings of very fair workmanship, which find a market on every side.[1]

Rewari, 30 miles by rail from Delhi, is an important centre with 100 to 125 Kaseras and 24 Mohammadan makers of *phul* ware, who make, in addition to ordinary pots and pans, a few articles such as *hukkas*, lamps, etc., of some artistic merit. The artisans appear to be intelligent and enterprising and not very greatly in debt ; and they have some literate men amongst them. As has already been mentioned, they resent their economic dependence on the shopkeepers. It is believed that with due support they would gladly form themselves into a co-operative society.

Travelling northwards by the E. I. Railway, the inquirer arrives at Panipat, where there are 50 workshops owned by Thatheras, who make ordinary vessels of hammered brass. There are five or six establishments, however, where articles of a more ambitious design are cast of brass alloyed with a proportion of zinc and lead and then turned. Besides these, must be mentioned some Mohammedan copper-smiths who turn out ordinary kitchen utensils.

Panipat ware finds a market all over the Punjab[2] and as far south as Khandwa and Indore.

Jagadhri has about 80 shops, with 300 brass-smiths who have a reputation for artistic ware such as branching lamps and also for locks and bells. Brass is made

---

[1] The figures for the trade of Delhi in wrought brass and copper goods in 1908-09 are as follows :—

Copper	Imports	1,474 maunds	*Brass*	Imports	2,213 maunds
	Exports	1,224 do.		Exports	3,826 do.

[2] The writer was told at Gujranwala that Panipat brassware was not known there.

in the locality, the alloy consisting of 32 parts of copper to 11 of zinc. The annual export of the ware is estimated at Rs. 60,000. Jagadhri is also the entrepôt of the Punjab trade in borax,[1] a material almost universally used as a flux in brass founding.[2]

There are only seven thatheras in Jullundur, but a number of Mohammadans of the Lohar caste are engaged in making brass locks. The work involves less labour but is also less paying than the manufacture of iron locks, and is therefore done only by the weaker and less enterprising members of the community. The brass is cast and the articles polished and finished on the premises. An average workman will make about 20 small locks a day which he sells at, say, Rs. 6-4 per hundred. He finds work, however, only during fifteen days in the month and his average daily wage is not more than six annas.[3]

Close on 250 persons are engaged in the industry at Amritsar and 250 at Jandiala, 11 miles off, both of which export brass ware in considerable quantities in every direction. Only plain ware is made at Jandiala, but at Amritsar there are two styles of work, one of the ordinary kind and the other in imitation of the tinned and chased ware of Kashmir. The latter is the speciality of Kashmiri workmen, who turn it out for the use of their caste-fellows. They make, amongst other things, copper salvers ornamented with alternate circles of tinned and plain surface. A certain number of samovars for making hot water, an imitation no

[1] See p. 144. In former days iron and copper used to be brought from the hills, but this trade has long ceased.

[2] See p. 236.

[3] His economic position is the same as that of the maker of iron locks. See p. 285

doubt of those of Kashmir and Central Asia, are also made.

Other Centres.

There are 40 artisans in Jagraon and from 60 to 70 each in Lahore, Gujranwala and Daska. The process of centralisation does not seem to have gone far in the Sialkot district, for its headquarters does not boast of many workers in brass and copper and has to import utensils from outside to meet its wants. Pind Dadan Khan not only caters for the Jhelum and Shahpur districts, but also exports to Rawalpindi, the North-West Frontier province and Sind. It has twenty workshops with 100 workers in *phul*, and in addition to these 60 who work in brass. Multan has half-a-dozen workers in copper, 18 in brass and 5 in *phul*, all Hindus except the copper-smiths.

Factories.

A factory for turning brass vessels with a capital of Rs. 40,000 was started some years ago in Amritsar but failed, as the public would not buy its goods. The Ganesh Flour Mills Co., Ld., of Delhi, have attached to their factory a workshop for brass and aluminium vessels which does not seem to thrive. One of the reasons is that it is in charge of the milling expert, who has neither the time nor the knowledge to look after it properly. Another reason is the peculiar organisation of the brass trade in Upper India. The dealers, who form a close ring, cannot set aside the Thatheras who are in their debt and who can only repay capital or interest if their manufactures sell. Besides, the former no doubt get, or think they get, better terms from the individual artisan than they would from such a factory. Skilful pushing by good commercial travellers is indispensable if any enterprise of this kind is to succeed.

A specially promising field for co-operative societies is offered by the brass industry. The elimination from it of a certain number of superfluous middlemen, whose brains and energy will be useful in other directions, will be almost as great an economic gain as the moral and material elevation of the workers themselves. The artisans, as has been noticed before, possess some business capacity and are in most cases already used to being governed by a "panch" or a committee of elders. The difficulty about the taking of interest does not arise in their case. Suggestions.

The brass-work of this province, even that of Delhi, does not come up to the standard of Jaipur, Burma or Southern India in finish or design. A school of art brass-ware at Delhi would do much good to the industry by introducing higher standards of art, Further, brass tarnishes very quickly in the Indian climate. It will be for the school not only to teach better work, but to introduce proper methods of lacquering with transparent as well as coloured varnish that will enable the metal to withstand the action of the atmosphere.[1] The art of enamelling on brass and copper, which is well known in Kashmir, could be taught with advantage by the Mayo School of Art.

In Germany a great deal of brass work is done in the worker's home with the aid of simple machinery. The Lahore technical school, as well as the proposed school at Delhi, should have a collection of all such appliances, amongst which may be mentioned :

1. A wheel and axle arrangement to make the brass-turner's lathe go one way continuously. At present the

---

[1] For an account of the art of lacquering on brass see Spon, *Workshop Receipts*, Vol. I. Art. *Lacquering*.

coolie, who turns it backwards and forwards with a strap, wastes about half his efforts. The big wheel could be left flat for a leather belt, or grooved like a V to take a rope.

A rude machine of this kind has actually been set up in Multan by a man who turns Thatheras' vessels and cleans old ones for customers for a small fee.

2. Hand machinery for shearing straight pieces and cutting circular or oval shapes.

3. Hand-presses for shaping flat pieces into various forms[1] and for the manufacture of buttons.[2]

4. Lathes for shaping brass and copper vessels instead of hammering them—a process not yet practised in the Punjab.

---

[1] As suggested by Mr. Chatterjee on p. 125 of his *Industries of the United Provinces*.

[2] A complete set of hand machines for making iron, brass and zinc buttons, with a set of tools for producing trouser-buttons also, can be had from Taylor and Challen of Birmingham for about £75, c. i. f Karachi.

CHAPTER XVIII.

THE PRECIOUS METALS, ALUMINIUM, ETC.

About £300,000 worth of gold in addition to an enormous quantity of silver, is annually imported into the Punjab,[1] almost all to be converted into ornaments. There is no surer proof of the general prosperity of the Punjabi, especially in the Canal Colonies, than the large sums he is investing in the precious metals.

The ornaments worn by women in this province are often very handsome, but they are always of a simple and massive character. Sometimes, indeed, they are hardly more than mere ingots of gold and silver. With the exception of watchguards, rings and studs, jewellery of European fashion, in which art counts for more than the metal, is nowhere gaining favour.

The industry in gold and silver, which it may be mentioned is invariably practised by the same person, is dominated by the *sráf*. It is he who supplies the precious metals to the workshops, as well as to the

---

1 Gold is collected in insignificant quantities from the sands of many of the Punjab rivers.

The galena of Kulu, which is only slightly argentiferous, contains from 13 to 89 oz. of silver per ton of lead. Nothing definite, however, is known about the extent of these ore-bodies. Native silver is rare in nature and has certainly not yet been discovered in this province. The statement in the Kangra District Gazetteer (1899) Vol. II. p. 10 about "veins of silver" needs revision.

general public. Orders are often given through him, and sometimes he employs the artisans and makes himself responsible for their work. To these functions he frequently joins those of a banker, and waxes rich with the profits of money-lending and pawnbroking.

The *Sunárs*, or goldsmiths, are uniformly spread all over the province. They are found in almost every village, where they practise all the branches of their craft. In the larger towns, however, and especially in Delhi, the industry is very much subdivided.

The goldsmith is generally a Hindu in the eastern districts of the province and in the Salt Range tract, while to the west he is often a Mohammadan. He is generally poor, as the handling of the precious metals no more makes him rich than the carrying of appetising dishes satisfies the hunger of a table-boy. Popular opinion, however, ascribes his poverty to his misdeeds; for, as a type, he is neither liked nor trusted.

The ornament-maker's charges vary in different places and for different things. The simplest articles of silver may only cost a pice per tólá to make, but the ordinary rate is from half an anna to two annas, while for the best workmanship of Delhi, Lahore or Multan it may be as much as four annas. The charge for fashioning gold into very simple ornaments need not be more than one anna per tólá, but for average work it is four annas, and the best may go up to Rs. 3 per tólá. Gold jewellery of European fashion costs anything between Rs. 4 and Rs. 100 per tólá in Delhi. An ordinary goldsmith probably earns from Rs. 20 to Rs. 30 a month, but the best Delhi artists are said to make as much as three rupees a day.

---

[1] 80 tólás = a seer = 2 lb. 6 oz. (Troy).

In special cases, individuals order ornaments from the better-known centres ; but it may safely be asserted that there is no trade of any importance in ornaments except in Gujranwala and Delhi and perhaps a few other towns. The artisans of Gujranwala have a considerable reputation for fair dealing in the districts north of Lahore and in the Canal Colonies, and are said to export as much as 1,000 tolas of gold and 4,000 of silver ornaments every month. The usual practice is to make purchases through one of the dozen local *sráfs* who give a guarantee for fineness.

Delhi is the largest centre in Northern India for all kinds of articles made of the precious metals. Its jewellers have agents in Bombay and Calcutta, where they supply a good deal of the jewellery of European fashion increasingly affected by Indian ladies in those parts. The Delhi industry has, however, much declined, curiously enough, since the date of Lord Curzon's Durbar. The export in former days is said to have amounted to about eight lacs of rupees per annum, of which five went to the Native States, and three to European tourists and others. The Indian chiefs have now transferred their custom elsewhere, and the Chandni Chowk has to be content with orders for a paltry 2½ lacs every year. **Delhi.**

There are fifty artisans in Delhi who can copy most of the trinkets one sees in a Bond Street shopwindow with tolerable success, while there are over a thousand who make ordinary country jewellery.[1] To these

[1] Cfr. Bernier: "Among other things, the Indians make such beautiful gold ornaments that it may be doubted if the exquisite workmanship of those articles can be exceeded by any European goldsmith." *Travels* 1658-67 (Constable 1891) p. 254.

must be added twenty workshops where *howdahs* and similar bulky articles of silver are still prepared for the Indian princes. Finally, there is a host of polishers, engravers, setters of stones, stringers of pearls, and others.

The use of silver vessels of all kinds has increased amongst the wealthier classes of the Indian population with the fall in the price of the metal. Rose-sprinklers, trays, betel-leaf boxes, etc., made of it, have always been in vogue, but an increasing number of people now also affect silver drinking-cups and other utensils, and decorate their rooms with similar articles of ornament.

The silversmiths of Delhi can make this ware cheaply and well in any required style of art, and do the work entirely by hand, from start to finish. The price of the finished article depends on the fineness of the metal used, and the art and labour expended on it, but it may be said to vary between 14 annas and Re. 1-4 a tólá. In Amritsar there are 15 workshops for plain silver vessels. A drinking-cup can be made for an anna per tólá, and a rose-sprinkler at 2½ annas, in addition, of course, to the price of the metal.

Little art is expended on Amritsar ware, which makes rather a poor show by the side of the imported Kashmir articles of the same type. The only other place in the Punjab where this particular industry exists is Lahore, which has a few workshops.

There is an unlimited market in Europe and America for good handmade articles, provided they are well finished. The Indian silversmith, however, must realise that the practice of extensively alloying the metal, which has unfortunately become prevalent in some places, has done much to lessen the popularity of his goods. It is very desirable, in the interests of the craft itself, that a system of hall-marking silver, on the lines suggested for the tinsel industry[1] should be adopted in the province.

An attempt to introduce machinery into the industry on a large scale is likely to lead to disaster; some of the preliminary operations, however, such as the flattening of silver sheets, could be more efficiently done by mechanical means. Stamping implements could be introduced for articles made in a single piece, such as trays; but all those that have to be joined by solder are far better done by hand. A hand-beaten silver bowl will easily outlast two spun or stamped ones.

The goldsmith's craft is well worth the attention of outsiders. It is not very difficult to acquire, and is certainly not so laborious as iron-work. Though European fashions are not coming into vogue, one notices a distinct development in popular standards of taste which the illiterate *sunâr* is not able to satisfy. A class of educated goldsmiths, able to conceive and execute original designs in harmony with the old, is now wanted. The goldsmiths' class in the Madras School of Art is very popular. If jewellery is added to the curriculum of the Mayo School at Lahore it will draw to industrial pursuits many youths whom the rougher trades of the blacksmith or the carpenter have so far repelled.

The precious metals are largely used to decorate the holiday attire of the people of India in the form of wire and a hundred-and-one varieties of tinsel.[2] The Tinsel.

[1] See p. 259.

[2] For an account of the gold and silver tinsel industry of the province, and especially of Delhi, the reader is referred to Mr. Burdon's excellent monograph on the subject.

manufacture of these has held an important position amongst the artistic crafts of India since the earliest times and given employment to a large number of men, women and children who might otherwise have been a burden on the community. In Delhi, for example, which has always been one of the chief centres of this industry as well as of the allied art of embroidering on silk and velvet,[1] no less than a hundred thousand souls were estimated to be engaged in its various branches not very long ago.

The last few years, however, have witnessed a rapid and general decline, due mainly to the large imports of all grades of wire and tinsel, good, bad and indifferent, from France, Germany and Russia, indistinguishable in appearance from the local article, and much cheaper. The manufacture of *salmá, sitárá* [2] and similar articles is dying. Though gold and silver wire is still produced in Delhi it forms a very small proportion of what is used in the still thriving gold-lace and *kalábatún*[3] industries. Most of the material is imported.

The bulwark of the industry was the system of municipal hall-marking which prevailed in Lahore till 1890 and in Delhi till less than a decade ago, and which practically guaranteed to the public the purity of the metal used. It is impossible to overestimate

---

[1] The most noted embroiderers of Delhi are Ali Jan, who makes gold-embroidered robes, curtains, etc., for the Indian princes, and Manak Chand Kishen Chand, who specialises in European dress-pieces.

[2] *Salmá* is a thin close curl of round or flattened wire like the tendrils of a creeper. *Sitárá* is the ordinary round sequin.

[3] *Kalábatún* or *tilla* is silk thread wound round with very thin gold or silver wire. *Gótá-kinári* is the generic term applied to all gold and silver lace. The *gótá-báf* is the weaver of the lace.

the value of such a guarantee. The wearing of false tinsel is as repugnant to the Indian mind as the use of false jewellery is to the upper classes in Europe. The best customers of the industry are the wealthier classes, who would rather pay a little more and be sure of what they get than run the risk of their embroideries tarnishing after a few years. Garments worked with gold and silver are not flung away in India with the change of every fashion, but are often handed down as heirlooms from generation to generation.

Outside Delhi the industry is still carried on at Amritsar, Jullundur, Lahore and Multan, where the conditions are practically the same as in the Imperial City. The following table gives approximate statistics :—

Kandla-Kashi.[1]	Tár-Kashi.[2]	Dabkái.[3]	Gótá-báfi.
		In Delhi.	
20 workshops with altogether 125 artisans, mostly Hindus.	90 workshops with a thousand artisans, mostly Mohammadans.	60 workshops with a thousand workers, Mohammadans of different castes.	120 factories and thousands of *parda* women.
		In Amritsar.	
16 workshops each with 4 to 8 Hindu artisans.	12 workshops with 2 to 8 men each, of all castes.	20 workshops with 4 to 10 men each of all castes, Hindus as well as Mohammadans.	16 to 17 workshops in addition to a large number of Mohammadan women.

[1] The term *kandla* includes all gold or silver wire not below the thickness of ten to twelve yards per tola, and the man who draws it is called a *kandla-kash*.

[2] The *tár-kash* draws the *kandla* into still finer wires (*tár*), of which 800 to 1,000 yards go to the tola.

[3] This wire is flattened by the *dabkaya* by hand or with a hand-machine.

Kandla-Kashi.	Tár-Kashi.	Dabkái.	Gótá-báfi
In Lahore.			
4 workshops each with Khattri artisans.	100 workers, mostly Mohammadans.	50 artisans all Mohammadans.	Chiefly Mohammadan women.
In Jullundur.			
7 workshops each with 3 artisans.	37 workshops, all Mohammadans.	Do.	Mohammadan men and women who work in their homes.
In Multan.			
6 workshops with 25 artisans of all castes.	6 workshops with 14 artisans, all Mohammadans.	60 to 70 workers, Hindus as well as Mohammadans.	Not done at all.

The daily wage varies between the two annas usually earned by the *parda* woman who weaves gold lace to the eight or twelve annas of the *kandla-kash*.

Factories. Two steam factories for the manufacture of *kandla, tár*, etc., were established in Delhi in 1898 and 1900, respectively, both of which came to grief through the incompetence of the men in charge. Of these the Lametta Company had a capital of Rs. 75,000 and used machines made in Delhi in accordance with its "expert's" designs. All the machinery of the other factory was German and cost Rs. 50,000.

A third factory, that of Kanjimul Nathumal, has a capital of Rs. 10,000 and is worked by electric power. It is doing well under the management of the proprietor himself, who was trained in Bombay. For the present *kalabâtun* only is made from imported lametta. The machinery was partly imported and partly made in Delhi itself.

Practical suggestions.

Among the measures that could be adopted to restore the tinsel industry to its former prestige and prosperity may be mentioned the system of public hall-marking. The local wire-drawers, as opposed to the more short-sighted artisans of Lahore, will welcome any such arrangement provided they are not required to pay more than the bare cost of the establishment; and provided the metal used is tested for a 2 per cent. alloy and its purity duly certified.

The following labour-saving appliances, which are already in use in other parts of India, might be introduced among the workers :—

1. English drawbench for drawing wire.

2. Machine for flattening gold wire 1,600 feet per tola, to be had for Rs. 50.

3. *Kalabatun* winding machine with 26 reels, to be had for Rs. 130.

4. Machine for weaving gold-lace like those used in Bangalore and elsewhere. One Akbar Ali of Ludhiana has patented one such. Another inventor from Kahnuwan (Gurdaspur district) exhibited an ingenious contrivance for the same purpose at the Lahore Exhibition in 1909-10.

5. The electric processes followed at Lyons in France.

Enamel work.

No enamelling worth mentioning is done in any town in the province except by eight workshops in Delhi, seven in Jhang-Maghiana, six in Kulu, twenty in Kangra and fifteen in Multan.[1] The Delhi enamellers work on gold, and often equal, if they do

---

[1] Bahawalpur, it may be mentioned, still has a reputation for this art which no longer exists in Lahore. For an account of Indian enamel work, see Watt, *Indian Art at Delhi*, pp. 21 *et seq.*

not surpass, their fellow-craftsmen of Jeypore, while those of Multan, Jhang and Kangra can only handle silver and produce very second-rate effects. They export, however, a large quantity of cheap articles of jewellery, such as brooches, scarf-pins and studs, all over India and even to Europe.

The reason why Multan enamel-work is so inferior is that the artisans alloy the silver with copper and nickel to the extent of 20 per cent., thus lowering its melting point below that of good "hard" enamels.[1] All the finest colours are "hard" and can only be set on pure silver, which alone will withstand the heat required to melt them. The best old work was entirely done on pure silver and there need be no difficulty whatever in reproducing quite accurately, any of the classic greens and blues, provided unalloyed metal is used.

The enamellers of Multan and, for the matter of that, elsewhere, will largely increase the popularity of their wares if, in addition to the above remarks, they will bear the following in mind.

1. Extreme care must be exercised to keep everything connected with the work very clean, as dirt of any kind affects the purity of the colour.

2. Red and yellow should never be applied to silver, though, like any other colour, they can be set on gold.

3. Opaque colours are only suitable for bronze and copper. On silver transparent colours only should be used.

---

[1] A "hard" colour is one that will melt only at a high temperature.

4. In no case is it permissible to use opaque and transparent colours together. The two qualities do not harmonise, and will not give good artistic effects.

5. In cheap European work patterns are sometimes stamped preparatory to enamelling. This is not advisable, as enamel does not adhere to the surface of the metal so treated as well as to the surface produced by the graver or other hand-tool. Cheap stamped jewellery continually loses its enamel coating and causes much disappointment.[1]

Lapidaries.

There is a small colony of lapidaries in Delhi (a relic of the Moghul Imperial Court), who work on rubies, sapphires, turquoises and emeralds. Quantities of these stones, particularly emeralds of the cheaper kind, are sent to them by London jewellers, through firms in Calcutta, to be cut and polished, and above all to have their surface-flaws excised. It appears that with their simple implements the Delhi artists do the work as well as their fellow-craftsmen in Europe, and charge much less, but only three cutters (*katayyas*), all Hindus, and 100 polishers (*bēgsis*), all Mohammadans, are now left. There was a time when a first-rate cutter or polisher earned Rs. 200 per mensem. But times are bad, and the former has now to be satisfied with Rs. 10 to Rs. 15, and the latter with Rs. 30 to 50.

---

[1] A great deal has been written on enamelling in recent years in various magazines, but unfortunately no very good books are available. About the only one worth having is Cunynghame's *Art Enamelling on Metals*, London (1901), and that too gives more attention to Limoges (or painted) enamels than to the *champlevé* enamels produced in the Punjab.

Aluminium. Aluminous laterites, though not occurring in the Punjab, are found in large quantities in other parts of India. If it pays the British Aluminium Co. to transport French and Italian bauxites to Ireland for the extraction of alumina, and then to send the alumina[1] to Scotland for electrolysis, it might also pay Indian capitalists to extract alumina on the spot from the highly aluminous[2] and easily quarried laterites of the Central Provinces or Bhopal and rail it for further treatment to Jagadhri[3] in the Punjab, where a constant supply of cheap electrical energy could perhaps

---

[1] Besides being the immediate source of the metal, alumina or aluminium oxide (Al_2O_3) is used in dyeing, and as a base for the manufacture of aluminic salts, such as aluminic sulphate and aluminium ferric, which are used in dyeing. It also yields alum (see p. 135.)

It is understood that the secret process for the manufacture of synthetic rubies and sapphires, which are turned out in large quantities at Idar on the Nahe (Germany), and at Boulogne, consists in the fusion of pure aluminium oxide by means of the oxy-hydrogen blowpipe, the colour being imparted by the addition of chromic compounds in the case of rubies, and of some salt of cobalt for sapphires. (*Ind. Trade Journal*, September 15, 1910, p. 278.)

[2] "The laterites from Balaghat compare very favourably with the bauxites placed on the British market . . . . The percentage of silica is low . . . a feature of great advantage in the extraction of alumina by Bayer's process." Prof. Dunstan's Report in *Rec. Geol. Surv. Ind.* Vol. XXXVII. (1908-09), pp. 216-17.

On the aluminium resources of India, see also *Rec. Geol. Surv. Ind.*, Vol. XXXII. (1905), pp. 175 *et seq.* and Vol. XXXIX. (1910), pp. 210 *et seq.* For information on aluminium in general see J. W. Richards' *Aluminium*, published by the *Aluminium World*, New York.

The bauxite deposits at Madh in the Bikaner State, the nearest to the Punjab, appear to be of poor quality.

[3] Jagadhri is 557 miles from Bhopal and 623 miles from Jubbulpore.

be made available from the Jumna and the Tons rivers.[1]

The brass and copper now used in India all come from abroad. If Indian aluminium ever becomes cheaper than these metals, we may expect an industrial revolution vaster and more beneficial in its results than even that predicted to follow the manufacture of cheap sulphuric acid.

As in the Bombay and Madras Presidencies, aluminium ware is gaining popular favour in the eastern districts of the Punjab, though it has not yet made headway in the west except in a few places. It is much in evidence in the bazaars of Amritsar, where it is displacing not only enamelled ware, but also the white utensils of Moradabad. In Gujranwala there are 40 shops belonging to dealers in brass-ware, of whom no less than 20 also sell aluminium vessels, to the extent altogether of Rs. 7,000 to 8,000 per annum. The retail prices quoted are Rs. 4-8 per seer for tumblers and Rs. 3 per seer for *dekchis*. At Bhera a

---

[1] At Kalsi, about 20 miles from Dehra Dun railway station, a constant supply of 40,000 to 50,000 H. P. is said to be available from the Jumna and Tons rivers. Major-General Beresford-Lovett, R.E., C.B., C.S.I., M.I.E.E., prepared a scheme some time back to develop a maximum of 19,500 kilowatts of electrical energy from this supply for distribution within a 150-mile radius. He estimated the cost of energy per kilowatt-hour in quantities not less than 750 kilowatts (12 hours a day) at 4¼ pies at Jagadhri or Saharanpur and 5½ pies at Delhi. If only 75 kilowatts are supplied the cost per unit would be about 25% more. Another scheme is to utilise the two falls of 17 feet altogether at Salempur on the Ganges Canal about 10 miles from Roorkee; from this about 720 kilowatts would be availabe at 4·23 pies per kilowatt-hour all the year round. For an account of the extent to which water power is used by the aluminium factories of the world, see *Indian Trade Journal*, April 18, 1907, p. 185.

shopkeeper displays some aluminium drinking-cups (*katórás*), which he says people are beginning to like.

The Mohammadans have of course no prejudice against the metal, and the vast majority of even orthodox Hindus place it on the same level as brass. Some educated Hindus go a step further, and appreciating its attractive appearance, and the fact that it needs no tinning, elevate it to the rank of gold and silver, which can be rendered ceremonially pure by simply washing with water, as distinguished from brass, which must be scoured with earth or wood-ashes.[1]

Aluminium would gain more rapidly on its rivals if the manufacturers saw their way to set up local agencies to do repairs and to buy up the old metal. A copper vessel with a hole in it can be made good again or sold to the nearest copper-smith for a substantial portion of its cost price, whereas a leaking aluminium *dekchi* has practically to be thrown away. The Indian Aluminium Co. of Madras state that they sell their ware at about Re. 1-8 a pound and are prepared to buy it back when discarded at eight annas. But they are too far off. Manufacturers will do well to offer the best prices they can without actually losing on the transaction.

It ought to pay to make aluminium ware in the Punjab from imported sheet-metal, because (*a*) the

[1] Aluminium ware should be cleaned with smooth sand or fine gravel. Wood ash is also excellent, but gives a dull appearance to the pots. If a bright finish is desired wood ash should be followed with fine sand or Brooke's soap on a hard nail brush. The pots should then be well washed with water and put out in the sun to dry. If this method is adopted, the more they are used the brighter they will become.

freight and duty on sheet is less than on the finished article, (*b*) the skilled labour required is locally available, (*c*) such labour is cheaper than in Europe, and (*d*) local tastes and fashions can be much better studied by the local manufacturer.

The Ganesh Flour Mills of Delhi have set up machinery for turning aluminium vessels,[1] from German sheet-metal. This department appears to have suffered through lack of push and advertisement, as it is little known in Delhi itself.

German silver. German silver, 50 per cent. of which, it may be noted, comes from the United Kingdom, appears to be gaining favour amongst the poorest classes. The distributing centres for the raw metal are Delhi and Amritsar, and the industry is carried on by stray artisans in Delhi, Lahore, Jullundur and a few other cities. The articles usually made are bangles, rings and similar plain ornaments, which are cast, polished and then gilt by the same person.

The metal, old or new, costs about fourteen annas to one rupee a seer. The charcoal used comes to four annas per seer of metal prepared, and the polishing and gilding to the same amount. The cost price is thus Re. 1-8 per seer. As the finished article is disposed of at the rate of Re. 1-12 to Rs. 2 a seer, the smith, who on an average handles three seers a day, makes a profit of Re. 1 to Re. 1-8. The industry requires less skill and labour than lock-making, and the profits appear to be greater.

Antimony. Antimony ores occur in the Shigri glacier in Lahaul at an elevation of 13,500 feet. A mining lease to

[1] The machinery also turns brass vessels.

work these was granted in 1904 to Colonel Rennick, who, in spite of difficulties of labour, communication and supplies, was able to ship 15 tons of stibnite (antimony sulphide) to England in the following year. He calculates that his deposits are capable of yielding from 200 to 400 maunds annually. Galena and blende are also found in the same locality.[1]

The chief use of antimony is in type-founding, but its compounds are much in demand in medicine, paint-making[2] and the manufacture of red india-rubber.

---

[1] See Holland and Fermer's quinquennial review in Vol. XXXIX. (1910) of the *Rec. Geol. Surv. Ind.*, p. 214.

[2] See Thorpe, *Dict. Appl. Chem.*, Vol. I. Art. *Antimony*.

CHAPTER XIX.

POTTERY.

Pottery is an important and evenly distributed craft, which affords a livelihood to 240,000 souls, of whom a third are workers. All potters, whether Hindus or Mohammadans, are Kumhars by caste. The Mohammadans predominate in the western districts, while the Hindus are in a majority in the Delhi Division. In Kangra all potters belong to the latter community.

The potter's services are indispensable to the domestic life of every section of the people, but for kitchen utensils in particular the Mohammadans are his chief patrons. The Brahminical scriptures enjoin that an earthen vessel once used for food must be thrown away, whereas brass and copper can be rendered ceremonially pure by cleansing with ashes or earth. Hence the Hindus and Sikhs, with the exception of the Jats of Ferozepur and some other districts, have always preferred metal to earthenware for cooking, eating, and drinking. Even the Mohammedans, it must be noted, are now taking more and more to imported porcelain or enamelled ironware, which they find cheaper and otherwise more satisfactory.

The potter's craft is not very lucrative (he rarely earns more than four to six annas a day), as is proved by his readiness to leave it whenever he has the chance. He thrives best as a village menial or *kamín* in all those villages where irrigation is carried on by means of the Persian-wheel with its long rows of pots. His prosperity varies, in fact, with the system of irrigation in vogue. Thus in Dera Ghazi Khan the increase in the number of wells has improved his position, while in canal-irrigated tracts much of his work is gone, and he has to content himself with the less profitable system of cash payment for services rendered.

Fortunately for himself, the village potter by no means confines his activities to the making of pots. During the rains he adds to his income by weaving, plastering, sewing sacks, making saltpetre, and, above all, working as an agriculturist or farm-labourer. His work necessitates his keeping several donkeys, which he also uses to carry his village patrons' grain to the market for sale. Further, after he has supplied the needs of the villagers, he sells his wares to outsiders, and the town potter, who has only the subsidiary occupation of brick-making to fall back on, is unable to compete with the subsidised goods of his village brother at the weekly fairs held in many of the larger towns.[1]

The clay. There is hardly any village where clay suitable for the manufacture of rough unglazed vessels is not locally available. The potter generally digs up what he wants, free of all cost, from the common land, but in Kangra and Karnal he has to pay for his clay as he has no hereditary position as a menial in the village economy of these districts. Of course, even in the other districts, if he chooses to use lands in the individual possession of a villager, he has to give a *quid pro quo*, in cash or in kind, to the extent of a rupee or two per annum.

[1] *E.g.*, Hoshiarpur.

Each district usually has two or three varieties of clay, in different shades of grey and red. Yellow clay is common in the Karnal district, where it is used for all kinds of utensils except those meant for cooking, but it is not found anywhere else except occasionally in the Jhang district, and near the Salt Range in the Shahpur district. Terracotta clays of fine texture, yielding wares of good colour on being fired, are found in the Jullundur, Multan, Rohtak and Gujranwala districts. Most of them, however, are fusible at a comparatively low temperature, and are unsuitable for the manufacture of stoneware,[1] but they could be made into superior red facing-bricks, ornamental tiles and other fancy terracotta wares.[2]

China-clay is a white, almost pure, silicate of aluminium with mere traces of mineral impurities. The only variety known to occur in the province is the material called *khariá*, which is abundant in the Kasimpore and Rangpuri villages, about ten miles from Delhi. It enters to a small extent (as will be seen later) into the manufacture of "Delhi pottery," and is largely employed locally for whitewashing houses.

---

[1] Stoneware is dense, refractory and opaque. The finer qualities resist the action of acids and extreme changes of temperature. It is made of "ball clay" mixed with powdered flint or sand. "Ball clay" is a variety of English clay commonly found in Devonshire or Dorsetshire. It is of a grey colour and contains a small proportion of iron, but moderate or large amount of organic matter.

[2] The statement in Ball, *Econ. Geol. Ind.* (p. 566) to the effect that "as yet no material suitable for terracotta has been obtained in the Punjab," is now out of date. (See the Report of the Imperial Institute on a large series of Indian pottery clays, dated 15th May 1908, and published by the Reporter on Economic Products, Calcutta.) The places where good clays are found can easily be discovered by local inquiry.

Further, it is used all over the province for the manufacture of *kothalis* or goldsmiths' crucibles, as a coating on the wooden slates of boys in indigenous schools, and in some places, *e.g.*, Gujranwala, for the manufacture of putty. In Delhi city it costs from six to seven annas a maund, but its price is higher in Amritsar, whence it is distributed to the towns of the Punjab proper.

The clay is of a uniform pale buff colour. It contains some gritty matter, chiefly felspar, and a considerable amount of potash-mica (muscovite) in both fine and coarse plates. If it can be washed free of these impurities it might serve for the manufacture of terracotta as well as greyish white domestic wares. The addition of other materials, such as gypsum, might improve its colour.

Fire-clay.

Fire-clay resists very high temperatures without fusing or fissuring, and is therefore of importance to the glass-manufacturer, who uses it both for crucibles and furnaces. It usually occurs under coal-seams, but there are no deposits known at Dandot or elsewhere in the Punjab. The variety found in Jubbulpore, however, though in no way equal to the German, is suitable for all purposes except, perhaps, the crowns of furnaces.[1]

Very little accurate information is available as to the occurrence and composition of the clays, marls, quartzes, and other pottery and glass-making materials,

[1] Steatite or soapstone forms, in admixture with fire-clay, bricks of a specially refractory kind. (Mallet, *Materials for Pottery in Jubbulpore* in *Rec. Geol. Surv. Ind.*, Vol. XXII. p. 144.) Good steatite is found in the marble rocks of Jubbulpore, in the Orcha and Beawar States (C. I. Agency), and in some villages of the Jeypore State (Rajputana).

which abound in this province.[1] A careful inquiry into these is very necessary in the interests of the pottery industry, as well as of a prospective glass industry on modern lines. Preliminary information and specimens of all the best-known local varieties should be collected through the district officers and a detailed scientific survey should then be made by an officer of the Geological Department in consultation with a ceramic expert.[2]

Pottery. Pottery means any article made of clay, or of a plastic mixture of clay and other substances (such as quartz, gypsum, etc.), hardened by the application of fire. It includes such very different-looking things as roofing-tiles and Sèvres china.

The coarse pottery of the country is too well known to need description. The village potter makes it for local consumption (for there is very little trade in this commodity) in every town or village of the country on his *rám chák* or wheel, as he has done for thousands of years, and as the Egyptians of a still elder time did, long before India became Aryan. The potter is now, as always, a slave to tradition, and the lapse of untold ages has failed to alter his hard-set forms and methods.

[1] The Bikaner State has a series of valuable clays at Madh, Kotri and Surpura, suitable for making excellent cooking and domestic wares like those of Leicestershire, cream and buff-glazed tiles, terracotta, faience, Jolly-ware such as jampots, and salt-glazed drainpipes, bricks and sanitary ware generally. The only Bikaner clay, however, that approaches the kaolin used for earthenware in England is too aplastic and coarse in grain to be used for the same purpose. It may be noted that good white quartz suitable for pottery occurs in veins at Dariba and in the hills near Gopalpura and Dungras.

[2] *Cf.* p. 148. Some experimental work in the manufacture of tiles and ornamental pottery is being carried out in the J. J. Arts School, Bombay. The expert is in a position to test clays and to give advice regarding them.

He is indeed quite unsophisticated as regards "improved furnaces and ovens," and is equally innocent of all technical knowledge of his inherited handicraft. Better methods of baking and of preparing clay would doubtless "save the large loss that always takes place in his kiln," and enable him to turn out a superior article—for the durability and value of any kind of pottery depends on the way in which it has been fired. But he is very poor, and has not the means to follow expert advice, even if he had the least desire to do so.

A review will now be taken of the few forms of the craft to be seen in the province, other than what might be called "crude pottery."

Bricks and tiles.

Bricks are made by hand in the neighbourhood of every large centre where they are wanted. Ordinarily the clay used is what can be had on the spot, as the cost of transport bars any effort to bring better material from any distance. But the inferiority of Indian fired bricks as regards strength and durability is more often caused by the method of manufacture than by the material employed. One of the main shortcomings of the process, the use of bad moulds, could be overcome by the employment of machinery, but an even greater obstacle is at once encountered, namely, the cost of transport.

The introduction of glazed bricks into the plinths of buildings is a question that deserves the careful study of the Public Works Department, as it will do much to prevent the destructive saline efflorescence or "scumming" which threatens the existence of every new public building in the province.[1] Very good floor-tiles,

[1] If ordinary bricks were burnt at a temperature high enough to cause the soluble salts in the brick-clay to combine with the other materials in it, there would be no "scumming."

capable of resisting damp and wear, could be made of the terracotta clays mentioned above.

Kágazi (lit. paper-like) pottery is remarkable for its thinness, and is made by *kuzgars* (makers of this ware as distinguished from ordinary *kumhárs*) at Basti Sheikh in Jullundur, and also at Jhajjar, Panipat and a few other places.[1] Clay of good texture is used, and is prepared with very great care. The articles generally made are *suráhís* (water-jugs), and *katórás* (drinking-cups). Special wares.

In addition to *kágazi* ware, the potters of Jhajjar make black utensils of exceptional hardness, ornamented with scratched patterns in amalgam. Small quantities of both varieties are exported to Delhi.

A glaze (as distinguished from an enamel, which is opaque and semi-vitrified) is a transparent vitreous coating applied to any kind of earthenware to render it impervious to liquids, or to serve as a means of decoration. In this province it usually consists of a composition of lead, borax and crude glass, often coloured with mineral dyes. Glazed vessels are increasing in popularity amongst the poorer Mohammedans as they stand the kitchen fire better and thus come cheaper in the end. Glazed ware.

The best-known centre for the manufacture of this ware in the Punjab is Gujranwala, where there are about twelve families who make cooking-pots and lattices. The industry has spread from here to Gujrat, where five families are now engaged in it, and also to Sialkot, where there are four. The Sialkot artisans are somewhat ambitious, and, in addition to the usual pots and jars, make artistic tiles, lattice-work, tea-sets, etc.

---

[1] *Kágazi* ware is no longer made in Tanda (Hoshiarpur).

All three towns carry on a flourishing export trade in glazed ware to Lahore and the Canal Colonies. Rawalpindi has four families of Bágri *kumhárs* who immigrated from the Alwar State a generation ago and learnt the art of making glazed flower-pots and "conservancy *gamlás*" from "a man from Hyderabad (Sind)." Ordinary glazed vessels are made at Pasrur, and cups, vases, and similar articles at Lahore. A single individual makes them also at Amritsar but modestly owns that he cannot equal the artists of Gujranwala. At Batala three men turn out ordinary ink-pots with a kind of varnish, while at Panipat *kuzgars* make tea-sets and other fancy glazed articles for sale at fairs.

Enamelled pottery.

The enamelled pottery of the Punjab, like that of Sind, is "a sumptuary, not a village art," and was brought by the Moghuls from China by way of Persia. With the exception, however, of a single old artist in Jullundur, who has decided to take his art with him to the grave, Multan is the only place where it survives. Attempts to introduce it into Amritsar failed.

The Multan industry is a relic of the time when enamelled tiles of light and dark blue colour, with geometrical patterns and pious Arab inscriptions, were fashionable on tombs and mosques. In its origin it was entirely subsidiary to architecture, but now various kinds of vases, tea-sets and other fancy articles are made for Europeans. They are first prepared by ordinary potters and then painted and glazed by the *sanáuris*, as the workers are called. Formerly the painting was done by the *kamângars*,[1] the *sanáuris*

---

[1] The *kamângars* were originally the makers of painted bows (*kamán*) and arrows. Their original trade is now of no importance and they have taken to painting on wood generally.

confining themselves to enamelling; but the latter have themselves now learnt to wield the brush and the style. There is a good export trade in this ware, which is popular as a curiosity, and yet its actual use amongst the people does not extend beyond Multan city, where the Mohammedans use bowls made of it for curry, and the Hindus for fruit and cardamoms.

The industry is prosperous, but capable of much greater development if only the artisans showed a little more intelligence and enterprise. Both better materials and better designs are wanted. Multan enamel-work is especially suitable for the internal decoration of buildings, and it is to be hoped that it will not always be ignored by the Public Works Department of this province.

The enamel is made with limestone and soda, the best colours used being dark blue from cobalt, and a very fine turquoise from copper. Violet, brown, green and other colours have recently been introduced but with less success.[1]

The number of toy-makers is larger than of the Toys. persons engaged in the manufacture of glazed or enamelled pottery, although the industry is only carried on to meet the irregular demand at local fairs and festivals. The artisans, who are all Hindus, are most numerous in Lahore, Delhi and Ambala, but are found in all towns of any importance. The toys are generally glazed or coloured, and consist of very rude and often grotesque figures of gods, men and animals.

The importation of German toys is increasing in the

[1] For a good account of the Multan industry from an artistic point of view, see Mr. Lockwood Kipling's note, revised by Mr. Percy Brown, in the *Multan Gazetteer*, p. 246.

country,[1] and an effort might be made[2] to improve the work of the Punjab artists by a judicious distribution of plaster-of-Paris models as wlel as by the establishment of small museums in suitable localities. The admirable perfection to which Lal Chand of Rupar has carried the art of clay-modelling, as well as the achievements of the Lucknow artists, would lead one to hope that the industry has a future in the province.

China-ware.

What is known as "Delhi pottery" is probably the only China-ware made in the Punjab. Its "fine texture of glaze, a rough duck-egg-like coating," owes its fame to the enthusiasm of the late Mr. Lockwood Kipling, who exhibited it at the London Exhibition of 1870. Its commercial importance is *nil* at present, as only a solitary individual, a Hindu *kumhár*, Ram Parshád by name, makes tiles, vases and similar objects for sale to passing globe-trotters. Its possibilities, however, are very great. The materials used are Kasimpore kaolin, Tughlakábád quartz,[3] and gum, in the proportion of 40 : 4 : 1. The kaolin is freed from grit by passing it through a piece of coarse *khadar* cloth, and the quartz is powdered. After mixing, the mass is moulded, coloured, and then baked in a rude furnace.

The whole process is wrong and the ignorance and lack of enterprise of the potter combine to turn out an inferior curio, where a European ceramic expert would probably, as suggested above, produce useful domestic and other wares. In the first place the presence of

---

[1] See pp. 224-226.

[2] That which was made some years ago was a failure, but circum stances have changed since then.

[3] Kasimpore is three miles from Palan station, and Tughlakabad eleven, in the same direction.

quartz makes "Delhi pottery" porous, so a certain amount of felspar[1] is essential to improve its texture. The gum, too, increases the porosity of the vessels and is useless for any purpose except that of saving the potter the trouble of grinding and mixing the materials properly.

A kind of white ware is made by a potter in Gujranwala with a mixture of Kasimpore *kharia* and soapstone, of which the latter is brought, according to his account, from a place in the Kashmir State. The vessels are turned very thin and require a great expenditure of time and labour.

Factories. The only modern pottery-works that ever existed in the Punjab are those set up at Haranpur in 1894, and closed in the following year. It is said that the clay found not far from the site proved to be excellent, and that very good samples of ornamental glazed tiles as well as salt-glazed sanitary ware were turned out. Dandot coal was used for fuel. The undertaking failed only on account of the mismanagement of those on the spot, and the inability of the promoters to find a man in whom they had sufficient confidence to justify their spending more money.

Before concluding this chapter, it will not be out of place to remind the reader that as the value of the finer kinds of pottery is much higher than that of the raw material, it is by no means usual in Europe for the works to be near the clay-deposits.[2] A very large

---

[1] Felspar is an essential constituent of both gneiss and granite, and is found throughout the whole Himalayan area. Deposits probably occur near Kasimpore.

[2] It would appear that in the United States, out of the total cost of the manufacture of pottery, 90% is cost of labour, and the remaining 10% is cost of materials, power plant, depreciation, etc.

quantity of clay is exported, for example, from the south-east coast of England, not only to other parts of the country but also to France and Germany. What with the kaolin deposits of Kasimpore and Bikaner, and the terracotta clays found in various districts, there would appear to be an opening for the manufacture of acid-proof jars,[1] and sanitary and domestic wares, on modern lines, at several places in the province.

---

[1] The Lahore sulphuric acid factories use about 1,500 and the Delhi ones 2,500 jars a year.

CHAPTER XX.

GLASS.

Glass is mainly the product of the fusion of about two parts of silica or sand, and one part of an alkali[1], its quality being finally determined by the metallic oxides that also enter into its composition. The industry has been known in India from the earliest times, but, like many others, it is now decaying under the pressure of modern conditions.

Glass-making, as it now exists in the Punjab, is divisible into two well-defined categories : the indigenous household industry, and the modern factory industry. Both will now be discussed in their order.

The distribution of the indigenous industry will appear from the subjoined table. The reader will

---

[1] Sodium sulphate (p. 140 *supra.*) has never been tried in India, the alkali generally used being sodium carbonate or bicarbonate, which are the cheapest to import.

Attempts made in Europe to use soda in the still cheaper form of common salt have so far failed, as the action of silica on salt requires a very high temperature which volatilizes salt. "It would no doubt be possible to cause the reaction to take place at a lower temperature by introducing water vapour ; this, however, has not been attempted on a large scale." (Thorpe, *Dict. Appl. Chem.*, Vol. II. Art. *Glass*, p. 226.)

36

bear in mind, however, that where a craft is so rapidly hastening to its end, the figures of to-day will not be correct a year hence.

District.	Number of Furnaces.	Number of Artisans.	Centres of Manufacture.
Gurgaon .	6	32	Sohna (Gurgaon *tah*), Raipur and Pingor (Palwal).
Rohtak. .	3	24	Daola (Jhajjar).
Karnal. .	26	108	Thanesar, Ladwa, Nawarsi, Mahra and Ghalour (Thanesar); Bārna, Bindrāna, Siāna Saidān and Gumthala Garhu (Gula), Rajaund, Kaithal, Pharal, Hābri (Kaithal); Pānipat, Karnal.
Amballa .	2	16	Raipore, Sadhaura (Naraingarh).
Hoshiarpur .	7	26	Pindoga (Una); Jaijon, Sahba, Kathgarh (Garhshankar); Dasuya.
Kangra .	6	30	Indpur and Sohlda (Nurpur); Nadaun (Hamirpur).
Lahore. .	4	4	Lahore City.
Jhelum. .	6	36	Sultanpur (Jhelum).
Sialkot. .	8	44	Sialkot city; Sankhatra (Zafarwal).
Rawalpindi .	7	27	Shah Allahditta (Rawalpindi), Dhok Maniar, Dhakhli, Bagham (Gujar Khan).
Attock. .	10	38	Chohi Garhalah, Bagh Nilab (Attock); Jabi (Fatehjang).
Multan. .	7	40	Multan City.
Muzaffargarh	7	10	Basira, Kinjar and Khangarh (Muzaffargarh); Alipur, Shahr Sultan and Khairpūr Sādāt (Alipur).
Dera Ghazi Khan.	5	21	Dera Ghazi Khan, Rajanpur.

For the sake of clearness the subject[1] must further be subdivided into the manufacture of :—

(*a*) Crude glass.
(*b*) Bottles, bowls, etc.
(*c*) *Kumkumás* (large globes silvered within, which are broken up, the pieces being used as spangles on *phulkáris*).[2]
(*d*) Bangles.

Crude glass.

Home-made glass no longer competes with the product of the modern factories because of the dearness of fuel. The only places where its manufacture survives are Indpur (Kangra), Sahba and Kathgarh (Hoshiarpur), Sohna (Gurgaon), Dera Ghazi Khan, and, above all, Panipat. With the exception of the last-named place, where the *kumkuma* blowers make a special variety for themselves, the output of the furnaces is dwindling every year and will soon be *nil.* Factory-glass comes chiefly from Ambala and Ferozabad and costs from Rs. 3-10 to 4-8 a maund.

Glassware.

Small bottles, chiefly for the use of perfumers, are made at the furnaces in Sialkot City, and inferior kinds of chimneys, bowls, etc., by the four blowers in Lahore. There are three furnaces with eight blowers altogether in Gumthala Garhu and a few more at Bindrāna, Bārna and Siāna Saidān (Karnal District), where glass retorts, locally employed in the manufacture of sal-ammoniac are prepared.[3] The manufacture of

---

[1] For an account of the indigenous glass industry see *Monog. on the Pottery and Glass Industries of the Punjab* (1892), pp. 23 *et seq.* and an article by Mr. B. M. Mookerjee in the *Indian Trade Journal*, March 23, 1909, p. 280.

[2] See p. 41 for an account of *phulkáris*.

[3] See p. 137. 25,000 of these retorts are annually made at Gumthala Garhu. Inferior Ferozabad *kanch* costing Rs. 2-4 a maund is used. The cost price of a retort, including the blower's fee of three pies, amounts to 1½ annas.

glassware at Dasuya, once considerable, may be considered extinct for all practical purposes.

Kumkumas. Panipat is noted for a small *kumkuma* industry, which owes its continued prosperity, in spite of foreign competition, to the strong conservatism of the Jat peasant-women of Sind and the Punjab, who patronise it. There are three factories, each of which employs three blowers and half-a-dozen coolies, and works during eight months in the year. The making of the glass takes a fortnight each time, and this is followed by the blowing of the globes, which lasts for twenty days. A Panipat blower gets piece-wages and is said to earn one rupee a day when working. The spangles sell at from Rs. 14 to 16 a maund.

Bangles. Bangles are now the only important product of the indigenous glass industry. They are roughly made, and sell wholesale at from eight annas to three rupees a thousand. The *Maniár*, who alone knows how to slip these fragile ornaments over the hand, hawks them about among the poorer village-women, who lack the means to buy the handsomer and better finished Austrian article preferred by their sisters in the towns.

It may be mentioned here that in the Delhi Division glass bangles must be worn by every married woman, be she Hindu or Mohammadan, the only exceptions being certain castes among whom custom substitutes lac or ivory. In the eastern districts of the Punjab proper, their use is universal, though in no way obligatory, with all classes. Westwards, however, the place of glass is taken more and more by ivory, so that in Multan the former is only seen on the wrists of the poorest women-folk.

Although bangle-making is in some ways a household industry, it is really conducted on the factory system, a capitalist owning the furnace and supplying the fuel and raw material. The amount sunk in one of these establishments, however, is small—in Multan it is only about Rs. 60 or 70. The workers get piece-wages and earn from 4 to 8 annas a day, but many of them are partially agriculturists and at certain seasons leave the furnaces to work in the fields. In the Delhi Division, as in Hoshiarpur, the craft is monopolised by the *Maniár*, the hereditary bangle-maker of Hindustán, but in Jhelum it is practised by Patháns, and in Multan and other places by men of every tribe. The artisans are all Mohammadans save in the Gurgaon and Rohtak districts, where they are Hindus.

The indigenous glass furnaces are more defective than even those of Ferozabad, and are worked in a very unscientific manner. Their faults and the remedies proposed may be summarised as follows :—

1. The furnaces are so badly made at present that they will not outlast two or three meltings. As they cost from Rs. 10 to Rs. 50 to reconstruct, it would be more economical in the end to have a solidly built structure once for all.

2. The question of fuel now dominates the industry. Since coal is generally cheaper on the Delhi side than wood, it is necessary to contrive a furnace capable of burning both wood and coal. The present arrangement is for wood only.

3. A better regulation of the air-passages would enable the temperature of the furnace to be raised or lowered as required and would thus economise fuel. At present excessive heat is used for the Chinese and

coloured glasses which do not want it, and an insufficient amount for other varieties, which accounts for their being so often full of specks and bubbles.

4. Several kinds of glass of different melting points are often heated in the same furnace. It would obviously be more economical to melt only one kind at a time.

5. The present practice is to heat the furnace for a period and then leave it idle. The frequent change of temperature both shortens its life and diminishes its efficiency for the time being by causing it to crack. The furnaces should be worked continuously by a system of shifts, such as is actually in vogue in Nagina and Saharanpur.[1]

6. All glass objects must be annealed or cooled slowly, in order to prevent them from becoming brittle or even flying in pieces when they cool. There should be properly constructed ovens for this operation in connection with all furnaces, to save the loss now caused by frequent breakages.

Prospects of the cottage industry. Although the existing furnaces are bound to disappear, the manufacture of glass articles, as a household industry, appears to have a future in this province, and deserves encouragement. The big factories might be subsidised by Government to set up model furnaces near their works for the instruction of selected workmen, who could also be taught the use of the tools and presses that give such excellent finish to Austrian bangles. The manufacture of glass beads, pearls and mosaic, could also be introduced. These are made in various places in Italy, such as Morano near Venice, with a glass resembling that of the Indian bangle-

[1] Chatterjee, *Industries of the United Provinces*, p. 156.

maker and with simple implements which are easy to handle after a little practice. The Italian furnace, too, is by no means "modern," as the word is usually understood, but would, nevertheless, serve as an excellent model for this country.

Table glass-blowing.

Another hand-industry suited, in its simpler forms at least, to present conditions in the Punjab, is table glass blowing, which has attained considerable importance, in Central Europe as a household craft in some parts, and one for small factories in others. It includes the manufacture of a great variety of objects, requiring much of practice, but only a small amount of intelligence and capital to produce—from thermometers to test-tubes. The industry would consume a large amount of glass-tubing, the manufacture of which would afford a fresh outlet to the large establishments which will now claim the reader's attention.[1]

Modern factories.

There are two modern factories in the Punjab—the Upper India Glass Works at Ambala, and the recently started Panipat Glass Works. The former is efficiently managed, and, in spite of the many difficulties that must confront a pioneer industry, has paid fairly well since 1904, when it came into the hands of the present proprietors. It has two furnaces[1] heated by the regenerative coal-gas system, and employs a staff of about 60 persons, including a chemist and an Austrian furnace-man. The original idea was to specialise in glass-blowing, but this had to be given up for want of skilled labour. The management are, however, by no means despondent, and

[1] One of these furnaces will produce from 75 to 80 maunds of crude glass in 24 hours and the other from 112 to 128 in 30 hours.

fortified by the generous and well-directed help of Sir Louis Dane's Government, will try again.[1]

For the present, the factory only produces crude glass to the extent of 25,000 to 30,000 maunds a year for the use of the indigenous furnaces. It may be mentioned that Ambala and Ferozabad glass has driven the Belgian material out of the markets of Northern India, where it was formerly supreme.

Panipat Glass Works.

The new glass factory at Panipat is a much smaller venture than the preceding, and has a capital of only Rs. 10,000. It has a single furnace, directly fired, and capable of producing from 40 to 50 maunds of crude glass in 24 hours. The proprietors have already commenced with the manufacture of phials and hope gradually to direct their energies into other channels. They propose to train men of the lowest classes, such as chamárs and sweepers, as glass-blowers if apprentices of a higher standing do not come forward, but have no intention of employing the hereditary craftsmen, who hold sullenly aloof. The factory gets both quartz-sand and limestone from Dehra Dun at a cost of 12 annas and 7 annas a maund respectively, delivered at Panipat.

The promoters of the modern glass works set up in Northern India from time to time have had to contend with many difficulties, arising chiefly from bad management, want of sufficient working capital, and inexperience of the effect of the Indian climate on the

[1] The grant is of Rs 5,000 to 7,900 a year, for five years, and is conditional on the employment of a practical chemist and blower, and the training of five to ten apprentices at a time. It has been stipulated that three of these apprentices shall have a University qualification in science.

The Madras Government also has accepted the beneficent policy of encouraging infant industries by well-regulated subsidies. The Madras Glass Works Co., Ld., have been given the right to collect half the wood used by them for two years, subject to a maximum of 7,200 tons, free of all royalty, from the Government forests.

furnaces; but the greatest obstacle in their way has been the lack of skilled blowers. Foreign workmen, Austrian as well as Japanese, were tried and found wanting: the *Maniár* proved no less a failure on account of his inordinate vanity and conservatism.

One remedy for this lies in training up a new class of workman altogether, under expert instruction. It ought not to be difficult to find recruits for a trade in which any person with physical strength and a little education can learn enough in a couple of years to earn Rs. 100 a month or more.[1] That an adequate number of Punjabi youths suited to the work will come forward to take advantage of the facilities afforded to them by Government, is proved by the fact that the Ambala factory once received 500 applications in reply to an advertisement for two educated apprentices.

Further, there is a large field in India for the use of glass-blowing machines which do the work of a blower equally well and much more rapidly. It is only by adopting such machines that success could be hoped for in competition with imported glassware.

The question of a local supply of alkali has already been considered.[2] Another great difficulty is the one already considered in the chapter on Pottery, namely, the absence of information on the Punjab sands and quartzes suitable for glass-making, which need careful investigation.[3] An inquiry into *reh*[4] soils has also

---

[1] The Austrian glass-blowers, ordinary men of the working class, earn Rs. 250 a month and more in this country.

[2] See pp. 141 *et seq*.

[3] See p. 272. A pure quartz stone, apparently very suitable for glass-making, is found at Tughlakabad (note 3 on p. 278).

A white variety of quartz-sand with 99·14 per cent. of silica, equal to that of Fontainebleau, can be delivered at Palana Station (Bikaner State), at Rs. 12 a ton. Inferior kinds, which are also abundant in the State, can be had for less.

[4] See p. 140.

been suggested, but the advantage of this is more doubtful. The composition of these soils is so variable that it would need constant analyses to determine their alkali content.

Glass-works will only yield a profit if they confine themselves to producing a strictly limited variety of articles, which means that they must command a large market. The existing enterprises are greatly handicapped by the rates on glass, which are comparatively heavy between inland centres, and thus serve as a bounty to the imported article. The Ambala and Panipat factories ought surely to be given special quotations, such as are usually accorded to similar industries elsewhere.

APPENDIX I.

The Kashmir Silk Industry.

By W. S. Talbot, I.C.S., Settlement Commissioner, Kashmir State.

Sericulture has long been practised in Kashmir, but until recently on unscientific methods, resulting in disease and failure. Some 13 years ago the industry was established on modern lines, under a European sericulturist, and has already reached large dimensions. In the last year (1909-10) all previous records were exceeded. Over 36,000 maunds of cocoons were produced by 26,234 rearers, while the filatures at Srinagar, employing on an average about 4,000 hands, reeled about 30,000 maunds of cocoons: their extension is under consideration. Electrical power is used in the factory to a considerable extent and its use is likely to be much extended in the near future.

Sericulture has also been introduced in the Jammu Province, but is at present in its infancy. Prospects, however, are good, and a small filature is about to be established at Jammu to supersede the experimental filature already at work.

A silk-weaving factory was opened at Srinagar some years ago under European management, but a considerable additional expenditure on power-looms and other plant is required in order to make it a financial success, and as the Kashmir Darbar does not wish to incur the further expenditure needed, the industry will probably be made over to private enterprise. The cloth made has been mainly a light taffeta, which compares very favourably in regard to evenness with Japanese cloth of similar quality, and sells at about the same price: twills and suitings have also been made to some extent, but the outturn of these with the present plant is very limited.

The raw silk produced in the Kashmir filatures is almost entirely disposed of in the European market, where it has obtained a secure footing. The Indian market demands a coarser and cheaper silk.

APPENDIX II.

The Preparation of Loofahs for the Market.

Contributed by the Imperial Institute, London.

The loofah of commerce is prepared from the fruits of *Luffa aegyptiaca*, and consists of the network of fibres existing in the interior of the fruit.

The fruits should be allowed to remain on the vines until they have acquired a yellowish tint, but not until they have begun to assume a brown colour, as this indicates that the outer skin of the gourd is undergoing decay, which will cause the fibrous structure within to become discoloured.

The fruits should be cut from the vine with about two inches of stem attached, for convenience in hanging. They should be hung in an airy, draughty shed for two or three days, and the outer skin will then be found to be fairly soft and pliant; this stage of the preparation is assisted by cutting off the tip of the gourd at the lower end, leaving a small hole through which the contained moisture may drip.

The loofahs may next be removed by running the finger down the skin of the fruit on one side, splitting it open, and turning out the loofah, which is at once thrown into a washing vat containing lime-water (5 lbs. of slaked lime to 50 gallons of water). The loofahs are stirred about in the lime-water for a few minutes and are then removed to a draughty shed to dry. Care should be taken to shake the lime-water out of each loofah before drying.

If the loofahs are dried too quickly they are apt to become brittle and crack; they must not, however, remain damp too long, or they become mouldy, though the lime prevents this to a large extent and is, indeed, used in order to protect them from fungoid growths.

When the loofahs are dry the seeds may be easily shaken out of them by hand, and when this has been done they are ready for the market.

Loofahs are imported to the United Kingdom from Japan and realize from 10*s.* to 12*s.* 6*d.* per 100 of the following average sizes :—

About	25	measuring	16 to 18	inches.
,,	30	,,	14 to 16	,,
,,	30	,,	12 to 14	,,
,,	15	,,	10 to 12	,,

The loofahs are press-packed into bales containing from 2,000 to 2,500 each, according to length.

APPENDIX III.

Industrial Alcohol in the Punjab.

By A. M. Stow, I.C.S., Senior Secretary to the Financial Commissioners, Punjab.

Industrial alcohol includes both rectified and denatured spirit.

The use of alcohol, whether pure or denatured, in the industries of the province awaits development. It is in demand at present chiefly by furniture and clock-makers, and manufacturers of soap, varnish and perfumes, while a considerable and increasing quantity is required for use as fuel in stoves. The manufacture of explosives, in which large quantities of pure alcohol are consumed in Europe, is never likely to be extensive in this province, but its use in engines, which is not yet established even in Germany, where a cheap potato spirit is produced, may become of importance in the near future.

At present even the small demand for industrial alcohol cannot be met locally. Under the Excise Act alcohol can only be produced in a licensed distillery, and the distilleries of the province are almost entirely concerned with the production of potable spirits. The only distilling bases at present permitted in this province are sugar and the *mahua* flower. *Mahua* is hardly ever used as a base, as the tree is rarely found in the Punjab,[1] and the cost of sugar bases, in the form

[1] See note 1, p. 175.

of *gur* or molasses, does not conduce to the manufacture of cheap alcohol in large quantities. The demand for rectified spirit, that is to say, for pure spirit of high strength (50° above proof) is therefore principally met by import from the Rosa distillery in the United Provinces owned by Messrs. Carew & Co. who possess certain advantages over the Punjab distilleries in the shape of cheap labour, proximity to coal-fields and special freights, and the fact that their distilling business is merely a branch of their extensive sugar factory. The market for denatured spirit (*i.e.*, spirit rendered unfit for drinking by an admixture of light caoutchicine and mineral pyridine bases) is principally served by imports from Java, where the spirit is manufactured at an exceedingly small cost from the refuse of the large sugar factories of that island.

Before the province can hope to be self-supporting in the matter of industrial alcohol, a cheap distilling base must be discovered. The conditions under which sugar is produced in the Punjab do not admit of the waste products being fully utilized, and until the central factory system, as worked in Java and elsewhere, can be introduced either in large *zamindári* estates, or by the aid of co-operative efforts, it is idle to hope for improvement in this direction.[1] It is possible, however, that some results might be obtained by distilling from timber refuse or from the large quantity of fruit which is to be found in Kangra and other hill tracts. Experiments in this direction as regards the raw material available and the type of stills required are under consideration.[2]

The duty on rectified spirits is Rs. 9-6 per Imperial gallon of the strength of London proof, and on methy-

---

[1] See p. 205.

[2] Those interested in the industry should read *United States Dept. of Agric. Bulletin No. 29, Industrial Alcohol: Sources and Manufactures.*

lated spirit 5% *ad valorem*. It might be possible, by special concessions in the matter of duty, to assist certain trades to obtain their industrial alcohol locally at low rates.

The following statistics show the retail sales of rectified and denatured spirit in the province for the last two years :—

Year.	Punjab distilleries.	Import from other provinces.	Import from foreign countries.	Total
Rectified—				
1908-09	177	402	...	...
1909-10	16	82	...	...
Methylated—				
1908-09	4,801	4,706	5,543	15,050
1909-10	4,363	2,496	7,198	14,057

APPENDIX IV.

THE DANDOT COLLIERY.

The chief colliery of the Punjab is at Dandot in the Salt Range. There is only one seam varying in thickness from 6 inches to 39 inches (average 30 inches), and forming a basin under the nummulitic limestone. Both the Dandot colliery and the one at Pidh have been worked since 1884 for the North-Western Railway, which has now decided to close down both, as they have shown a loss during the last few years. The output has declined from 81,218 tons in 1899 to 27,946 tons in 1909.

Dandot coal is about 60 per cent. of the value of that of Jherria, and the cost of producing it was Rs. 9-12-7 per ton in 1909. Steam-coal is sold at Rs. 8 per ton to the North-Western Railway, and slack-coal at Rs. 6 to Government departments for brick-burning, and at Rs. 3-8 to the Haranpur factory for making briquettes.

The reduction of freight on Bengal coal has vitally affected the position of Dandot by contracting the circle within which its product could be used with profit. The question now before Dandot, as well as the Punjab coal-fields generally, is the provision of nearer markets, and the manufacture and sale of all available by-products of the industry. Lime-burning[1]

[1] There are inexhaustible deposits of excellent limestone all over the collieries. An average sample tested for the writer by the Geological Department was found to be "an exceedingly pure limestone (containing only about ½ per cent. of insoluble residue and from ½ to 1 per cent. of magnesium carbonate), that would give, on burning, lime of the very highest quality."

might be a profitable method of using both coal and shale, while the manufacture of alum from the shale might be developed into another source of revenue.[1] With shale at Rs. 2 per ton the cost of lime-burning is about Rs. 6 per ton of burnt lime, which sells readily at Dandot Station at Rs. 11 per ton. This gives a profit of Rs. 5 per ton. The shale, which is a waste product at present, is turned out in small quantities along with the coal and really costs nothing when coal is being mined in the first instance.

The possibility of exploiting the gypsum which occurs at the foot of the hill, and that of manufacturing pitch and tar from the coal, also deserve careful attention before the colliery is closed down.

If Government proved to the public the value of the mineral resources of Dandot, there would be no difficulty in finding private persons to take over the whole business.

The Haranpur Briquette Factory.

The North-Western Railway Briquette Factory is located at Haranpur, 14 miles from Dandot Railway Station. It was started in 1898 with a 40 H.P. engine, and turns out briquettes weighing altogether 22 tons per diem. Dandot slack-coal bought at Rs. 3-8 per ton is pressed with 8 to 10% of its weight of English pitch, which costs Rs. 46-9 per ton at Kiamari. The briquettes cost Rs. 10-2-11 per ton, the cost being made up as follows:—

Dandot slack coal . . .	Rs. 3-4-7
Pitch	Rs. 5-9-3
Manufacture . . .	Rs. 1-5-1

The relative calorific values of Bengal coal which costs the Railway Rs. 14-1-4 per ton at Haranpur, and Dandot briquettes, are 1·10 : 1·56.

[1] See pp. 134-135 *supra*.

APPENDIX V.

Petroleum in the Punjab.

The Geological Department will shortly make a careful survey of the highly promising oil-deposits of the Attock, Mianwali and Rawalpindi districts. The most notable outcrops are the ten springs at Jaba (Mianwali district), which produce about 600 gallons per annum of a thick dark-green sulphuretted liquid. Oil is also found at Ratta Hottar (Rawalpindi district), Fatehjhang, and a few other places. The Garrison Engineer of Rawalpindi Cantonment has used the Jaba product for a great many years to produce gas for lighting, but with this exception the existing springs have no commercial value.

In 1888 a concession was obtained by a Canadian named Noble and others to exploit the petroleum resources of the province, but nothing came of it, though Government undertook to give substantial help towards the cost of the borings. A prospecting license covering 26½ square miles in the Mianwali district, including the Jaba springs, has now been granted to Messrs. Bagram and Co. of Calcutta.

INDEX

OF PLACES IN THE BRITISH PUNJAB

TABULATED ACCORDING TO DISTRICTS